The Chivalric
Folk Tradition in Sicily

The Chivalric Folk Tradition in Sicily

A History of Storytelling, Puppetry, Painted Carts and Other Arts

MARCELLA CROCE

Forewords by Michael Buonanno *and* Christopher Kleinhenz

McFarland & Company, Inc., Publishers
Jefferson, North Carolina

All the photographs were taken by the author unless otherwise specified.

LIBRARY OF CONGRESS CATALOGUING-IN-PUBLICATION DATA

Croce, Marcella, 1949–
The chivalric folk tradition in Sicily : a history of storytelling, puppetry, painted carts and other arts / Marcella Croce ; forewords by Michael Buonanno and Christopher Kleinhenz.
p. cm.
Includes bibliographical references and index.

ISBN 978-0-7864-9415-6 (softcover : acid free paper) ♾
ISBN 978-1-4766-1731-2 (ebook)

Partially revised text based on the author's dissertation (doctoral) and translated into English.
1. Folklore—Italy—Sicily. 2. Knights and knighthood—Italy—Sicily—Folklore. 3. Puppet plays—Italy—Sicily—History and criticism. 4. Puppet theater—Italy—Sicily—History. 5. Folk art—Italy—Sicily. 6. Carriages and carts—Italy—Sicily. 7. Decoration and ornamentation—Italy—Sicily. I. Title.

GR177.S5C75 2014
398.209458—dc23 2014037035

BRITISH LIBRARY CATALOGUING DATA ARE AVAILABLE

On the cover: The female warrior Bradamante, Palermitan puppet of the Franco Cuticchio theater (photograph by Andrea Matranga)

Printed in the United States of America

McFarland & Company, Inc., Publishers
Box 611, Jefferson, North Carolina 28640
www.mcfarlandpub.com

Italy without Sicily does not leave any image in the soul. In Sicily can be found the key to everything.

—*Johann Wolfgang von Goethe,*
Italienische Reise *(Travels in Italy), 1816*

Table of Contents

Acknowledgments

Meeting Professor Christopher Kleinhenz and having him as my academic advisor in the years I was a graduate student at the University of Wisconsin–Madison was a privilege. He suggested I research the fascinating chivalric tradition in Sicily which is the subject of this book, and directed the research for my Ph.D. dissertation which is its first and most important nucleus.

Professor Michael Campo, former professor of Italian literature at Trinity College in Connecticut, was enthusiastic about this book when it was published in Italian, and he translated some passages which he authorized me to include in the English edition.

I thank my Italian publisher Dario Flaccovio from Palermo for allowing me to translate into English two of my books (*Pupi Carretti Contastorie* and *Pupari*) which form the basis of this book.

I am grateful to Alan Krysan, president of the Finney Co., for graciously agreeing and giving permission to reuse parts of another book of mine, *History on the Road: The Painted Carts of Sicily*, co-authored with Moira Harris, published in 2004 by Pogo Press, a small publishing company based in Minneapolis, Minnesota, and later absorbed by Finney Co.

I am also grateful to Michael Buonanno, professor of English and anthropology at the State College of Florida in Manatee–Sarasota, for his idea to translate this book and for introducing me to McFarland.

I would like to thank Giralamo Cuticchio and his family of puppeteers for sharing with me their memories and knowledge, and I am very glad I was able to meet the artisans who authored the puppet shows and the carts. The list is long and I will mention them all, even if unfortunately many of them are not living anymore: the painter Giuseppe Ducato, the sculptor Giovanni Raja, the iron worker Carmelo Saccaro, the horse trappings makers Michele Ajello and Rosario La Piana, the storyteller Gaetano Lo Monaco Celano, and the blind storyteller Fortunato Giordano.

I would also like to thank the personnel of the International Puppet Museum in Palermo where I did most of the research for my Ph.D. dissertation, and who have recently renewed their permission for the publication of the photographs taken in the museum. The personnel of the Pitrè Museum in Palermo have also been very helpful for the same reason.

Meeting Professor Antonio Pasqualino before his untimely death in 1995 was both informative and inspiring for my work. He was the founder of the International Puppet Museum and author of some of the most important works written on Sicilian puppets.

Foreword

by Michael Buonanno

When I traveled to Palermo in the winter of 1987 to embark on my dissertation research on the Carolingian Cycle in the oral tradition in Sicily, I really had little to go on beyond my understanding that the major source for that tradition still extant at Palermo was the city's famed marionette theater. I had met one puppeteer in the U.S., a certain Mr. Macrì—I no longer recall his first name—whose family practiced the marionette tradition characteristic of the city of Acireale (a bit different from the Palermitan tradition). Otherwise, I was approaching the subject somewhat haphazardly: seeing puppet plays when and where I could and talking to people here and there about their thoughts on the theater's productions.

Luckily, I chanced to meet Marcella Croce one day at the Giuseppe Pitrè Ethnographic Museum in Palermo and when I explained that I was most interested in the texts of the plays themselves she kindly directed me to the Antonio Pasqualino International Museum of Marionettes inasmuch as its director, Professor Pasqualino, and his wife, Professor Janne Vibeak Pasqualino, were attempting to provide audiotapes for all 270-odd episodes of this immense cycle which they were generously sharing with all interested scholars. Thus, with the advice of Marcella and the resources provided by the Pasqualinos, I was able to find the subject matter of my study: the place of Sicilian epic in the entire repertoire of Sicilian folktales, which notably included farce, saints' and bandits' lives, fairy tales, Christian myth and city legend.

When the Italian edition of the present volume was released, Marcella's insights on the chivalric tradition were invaluable to me. Whereas I was researching the place of epic in the realm of Sicilian folktales, Marcella was charting the historical development of epic in its various manifestations, literary and popular, throughout the sweep of Sicilian history. For instance, she looked at epic in the hands of both *cantastorie* (epic singers) and *contastorie* (storytellers who specialized in epic recitations) as well as puppeteers.

Whereas my own book, *Sicilian Epic and the Marionette Theater*, published—like this volume—by McFarland, explores epic in the context of Sicilian folk narrative, Marcella's study emplaces epic in its historical context, including not only the marionette theater, epic singers, and storytellers, but also popular festivals and art forms, most notably the brilliantly painted Sicilian carts that are richly depicted in this book's color insert. Thus, the two volumes act very much as complementary views of the brilliant tradition of Sicilian epic for—until now—the nearly neglected English-speaking audience.

Michael Buonanno is a professor of English and anthropology at the State College of Florida, Manatee-Sarasota. He has published articles in The Journal of American Folklore *and* New York Folklore, *and he is the author of* Sicilian Epic and the Marionette Theater *(McFarland, 2014).*

Foreword

by Christopher Kleinhenz

A few years ago, thanks to the remarkable generosity of Marcella Croce, my wife and I were able to participate in some of the activities of the Elderhostel in Sicily that Marcella and her husband, Giovanni Matranga, had organized. It was on that occasion, more than twenty years after having directed her doctoral dissertation, that I had the pleasure of seeing, for the first time, a performance at the Opera dei Pupi in Palermo. It was a marvelous event, full of drama, passion, sword fights and related acts of derring-do, and certainly no less interesting and exciting than what I had been led to expect. Indeed, as a student of early Italian literature, which had its auspicious origin at the imperial court of Frederick II in Palermo, I was also acquainted with the rich oral traditions of Trinacria and was eager to see how well they had survived into the early twenty-first century. I was not disappointed.

The power that a live performance possesses has been evident over the centuries, and its success depends in large part on the talents of the *canta-/contastorie* and their ability to communicate with and to win over their audience. In this regard I am reminded of the well-known story told by Poggio Bracciolini of the fifteenth-century *giullare* who so movingly presented the story of the death of Roland that one of the men in the crowded Milanese piazza was so overcome with emotion that he went home weeping, and, when his wife asked the reason for his tears, he responded: "But haven't you heard the news? Roland is dead, the only one who defended the Christians!" Such is the awesome power of live performances.

This anecdote of the affective nature of performance has played out many times over the centuries, and our common cultural heritage is the richer for it. The manifestations of these epic, chivalric tales are—or at least were, at one time—ubiquitous in Italy and particularly in Sicily. In addition to their oral transmission, these tales of adventure were presented in visual form for popular consumption on posters announcing the evening's show in the puppet theaters and on the *carretti siciliani* (and sometime more modern vehicles, such as on the side panels and rear doors of *api* and *furgoncini*). Moreover, the original stories involving Carolingian heroes were supplemented by those featuring more contemporary figures, as diverse as Garibaldi and St. Rosalia, whose images also adorned the Sicilian carts, as Croce notes in her very informative chapter on the *carretti.* The ways of keeping legends alive are many, and this sort of cultural adaptation is certainly one of the most effective, for it takes traditional elements and translates them into a cultural context that is immediately understood and enthusiastically received by contemporary audiences.

Two of Marcella Croce's earlier works—*Pupi, carretti contastorie: L'epica cavalleresca nelle tradizioni popolari siciliane* (1999) and *Pupari: Storia di Girolamo Cuticchio, dei pupi e di una tradizione* (2003)—form the basis of the current volume, which has been updated in terms of content and bibliography. For the first time, an English-speaking audience will be able to read about and become immersed in this vibrant cultural phenomenon known as the "puppet theater." In her engaging book Croce has given voice to the numerous, mostly anonymous carriers of the oral tradition over the centuries and has provided a meticulous portrait of the transformation of the medieval and Renaissance legends and heroes into tales and figures that have captured the imagination and admiration of countless numbers of spectators. This is an extraordinary feat, and one that could not have been accomplished without a rigorous scholarly approach combined with a native affinity for the stories, for the people who sing and tell them, and for those who work behind the scenes in the puppet theaters manipulating those inanimate *marionette* who regularly come to life, thanks to what we might call the *spirito vitale e geniale* of the Sicilian people.

Croce traces the history of the reception in Sicily of Charlemagne's Paladins whose exploits formed the basis of the Old French *Chanson de Roland* and, later, of the Italian Renaissance epics by Boiardo (*Orlando innamorato*) and Ariosto (*Orlando furioso*) and their retellings in the popular *Reali di Francia*. Episodes were altered and added, new themes (e.g., love) and characters (e.g., Rinaldo) were introduced, and all of these innovations kept the tales alive and meaningful for the ever-changing audiences. Crucial to the survival of these stories, of course, are the many talents of the storytellers themselves, and Croce also discusses the contributions made by historians of the cultural phenomenon (e.g., Pitré, Lodico). Her interests also extend to the presence of elements of these stories in popular dialect expressions, in toponyms and family names, and in traditional local folk celebrations. The artistic repertoire, stage techniques, and improvisational skills of the *pupari* are presented in rich detail, as are certain extraordinary practitioners (e.g., Giuseppe Argento, Emanuele Macrì, the Cuticchio family).

Marcella Croce succeeds most admirably in telling the complete, fascinating story of the literary and popular origins of Sicilian puppet theater, its protagonists and themes, its technical and artistic elements, its practitioners, entrepreneurs and audience, its varied impact on society, and the transference of its imagery to the Sicilian carts. Moreover, she provides a sensitive chronicle of the past glories of this art form and its perhaps inevitable—but lamentable—decline in contemporary society. Croce's detailed, engaged, and satisfying account has the great merit of introducing this unique art form to a large and appreciative audience and will remain its definitive treatment.

Christopher Kleinhenz is the Carol Mason Kirk Professor Emeritus of Italian at the University of Wisconsin–Madison, where he taught for almost forty years. Among his numerous publications are The Early Italian Sonnet, Medieval Italy: An Encyclopedia, *and a translation of Dante's* Fiore and Detto d'Amore.

Preface

Any research on Sicilian traditions must start from the work of Dr. Giuseppe Pitrè (1846–1916), a medical doctor from Palermo and Sicily's great ethnologist. Like other researchers active elsewhere in Europe and America he perceived the need for preserving and recording beliefs and examples of folk culture before they were forgotten or lost. To the infinite gratitude of all later scholars, he published what he had learned in his 25-volume series called *Biblioteca delle tradizioni popolari Siciliane* (Library of Sicilian folk traditions),[1] published from 1871 until 1910. He founded the *Archivio delle tradizioni popolari siciliane* (Archive of Sicilian folk traditions) and the objects he collected became a public museum. During his lifetime he arranged exhibits, corresponded with other scholars throughout Europe who were interested in similar topics concerning folklife, folklore and folk beliefs, and welcomed many visiting writers to Palermo.

Chivalric stories made a great impression and really struck a chord in the Sicilians' souls. In 1884 Pitrè wrote his essay "La tradizioni cavalleresche popolari in Sicilia" (Popular chivalric folk traditions in Sicily),[2] whose purpose was to demonstrate how and to what extent the chivalric stories of the Carolingian period influenced several aspects of Sicilian life, from toponyms to ways of speaking, from figurative arts to the famous puppet shows that became so common in Sicily in the 1840s.

This book traces the development and diffusion of the chivalric tradition in Sicily over the centuries and investigates how the situation has evolved in the more than one hundred years following Pitrè's essay. It also discusses the causes of the great success (and of the recent decline) of chivalric subjects. Through the analyses of its manifestations in various fields (storytelling, puppet shows, festivals, cart painting and other products of folk art), a good part of Sicilian traditions and culture is explored, with the goal of obtaining a multi-level portrait of an island which is unique for its geography and history, and which may have many surprises in store for researchers and readers who are interested in Italy and normally concentrate on more central parts of the country. The German poet Johann Wolfgang von Goethe in his famous book and reportage *Italienische Reise* (Travels in Italy),[3] written between 1813 and 1817, said Sicily was "the key to understand[ing] Italy," a sentiment that should be kept in mind by those who are willing and curious to investigate what lies "at the outskirts of the Empire."

The chivalric repertory (from *cheval*, which is "horse" in French) referred to the stories of Charlemagne (hence the name "Carolingian") and his knights, both before and long after their defeat at Roncevaux in the Pyrenees. The historical events had taken place during the ninth century and had become legends which inspired the *Chanson de Roland* written in Old French in the 12th century and which had later been elaborated upon in the Italian chivalric poems of the 15th and 16th centuries. It is believed that these stories traveled from France to Italy, from Northern to Southern Italy, and from the royal courts to the poor Sicilian theaters, through the storytellers, who unceasingly repeated them. As already mentioned, puppet shows with chivalric subjects started to be performed regularly in Sicily from about 1840.

This book analyzes how the stories were passed on, how successful they were, and how we know that the Breton cycle—that is, the stories of King Arthur and the Knights of the Round Table—was also known in Sicily, even if the puppet shows always had the Carolingian cycle as their subject.

Professional storytellers regularly told chivalric tales in Sicily until the early 1960s. Their techniques and repertory can be investigated through the words written by eyewitnesses. In the 19th century the stories belonging to the oral tradition of the storytellers were written down by various authors (especially in Giusto Lodico's *Storia dei Paladini di Francia* [History of the Paladins of France]),[4] and these texts immediately became the "bible" of both storytellers and puppeteers who followed them very closely. Some theaters are still active in Palermo.

The episode of the Rout of Roncevaux (*Rotta di Roncisvalle*), which is central in the cycle of the Paladins of France, has been chosen to show how its Italian remote source, Luigi Pulci's 15th-century *Morgante Maggiore*,[5] and its immediate one, Lodico's text, are related and how both were modified and adapted in the actual performances of puppeteers on various parts of the island.

Chivalric stories were also painted on the sides of Sicilian carts, swarming on the island beginning in the middle of the 19th century. The tales of adventure and daring have always had an appeal; the personalities, attributes and adventures of the knights were so widely recognized that a cart adorned with Orlando or Rinaldo was instantly appreciated.

This book attempts to explain, at least in part, the pervasive diffusion of the chivalric tradition in Sicily by the predominance of the so-called "sense of honor" that has permeated Sicilian life and has made chivalric stories appealing and fascinating to the Sicilian people to the present day.

Other information in the Appendix regards the story of Girolamo Cuticchio and his family of puppeteers, and sheds further light on the hardship and uncertain future of this art.

I became interested in this subject thanks to Professor Christopher Kleinhenz, who was my academic advisor when my husband and I were teaching assistants and graduate students in the French and Italian Department of the University of Wisconsin–Madison. In 1986, after seven years spent in our native city of Palermo, we decided to go back to Madison with our children in order to finish our Ph.D.s in Italian literature. Professor Kleinhenz, who is a renowned Medievalist scholar, proposed to me the subject of Sicilian puppets for my Ph.D. dissertation, since he was interested in how the Medieval repertory had made its way to Sicily.

I was immediately intrigued by this subject, which involved such an interesting aspect of the culture of my native island and which I knew very little about up to that moment, and accepted quite enthusiastically his proposal. I spent the following year (1986–87) doing research in Madison; the Internet did not exist or helped very little at that time, computers being used mainly for writing, but thanks to the interlibrary loan system with universities and colleges all over the United States, I was able to have in my hands precious articles and materials which would have taken me ages to find in Sicily.

During the following year I did the necessary field research in Sicily interviewing puppeteers, visiting museums, and watching and photographing shows, festivals and painted carts, and in the summer of 1988 I went back to Madison to complete and defend my dissertation. At first I was planning to look for an academic job in the States and was actually offered a teaching position at the University of Iowa, but I decided not to accept it for family reasons. We returned to Sicily where almost immediately we started a new career as coordinators and instructors of the new program that Professor Michael Campo, at the time director of all Italian Elderhostel programs run by Trinity College (Hartford, Connecticut), was going to start in Palermo in February 1989. In more than twenty years we have received literally thousands of Americans age 60 and over who spent two weeks on the island and were eager to learn all about its culture, history and art. For us that meant continuously researching in order to be ready to answer all sorts of possible questions.

In 1998 the Sicilian Region published a reduced and updated version of my dissertation, which was reprinted by the Palermitan publisher Dario Flaccovio in 1999 with the title *Pupi, carretti contastorie: L'epica cavalleresca nelle tradizioni popolari siciliane* (Puppets, carts, storytellers: Chivalric epic poems in Sicilian folk traditions),[6] and which is now offered to the American public for the first time in English, since both the original dissertation and the subsequently published book were in Italian. The text has not only been translated but also enriched with further information, some of which was contained in another publication of mine, *Pupari: Storia di Girolamo Cuticchio, dei pupi e di una tradizione* (Puppeteers: Story of Girolamo Cuticchio, of the Sicilian puppets and of a tradition).[7]

Since the end of the 19th century several books have been written about the Sicilian puppets, and they are quoted in the text and in the bibliography, but very few of them are recent, and none are in English.

I am hopeful that this book will be of interest to anybody involved in Italian studies, either for academic research or for interest in the Sicilian heritage. Since the book is related both to literature and to anthropology, it can be particularly suited to interdepartmental studies.

• One •

From the Middle Ages to the Puppets

Introducing Sicily—A Mosaic of Cultures

A triangle of land on which a long series of civilizations has left indelible traces: Sicily. The numerous tragic moments of its history and the few happy ones are unconsciously reinterpreted by local people in many different occasions: in religious feasts, which after so many centuries still retain the memory of a pagan world; in the expression of folk art in general, which shows the marks of the intense suffering historical events have caused on this island.

A natural bridge between East and West, North and South, Sicily, at 9,900 square miles, is the largest island in the Mediterranean Sea. In this relatively small space (about the size of the state of Vermont), history has crammed an extraordinary concentration, almost a palimpsest, of different cultures. Unique in the Western world, it may rightly be considered the *melting pot* not only of the Mediterranean, but of Europe. Or, even better, we should say the *melted pot,* since, unlike America, the melting *did* take place and happened many centuries ago, and most of the inhabitants have no idea (nor do they care) where their blood came from.

Because of its strategic position, Sicily was bound to be invaded and conquered by whoever intended to rule the Mediterranean. The list is long: Phoenicians, Greeks, Romans, Byzantines, Arabs, Normans, Swabians, French and Spanish, even the British and the Austrians briefly put their hands on it, while towns founded in the 15th century by the Albanian refugees fleeing from the Balkans in fear of the Turks are the only ones who never completely mixed and even today retain their particular culture in terms of language, religion and customs. Some Sicilians of Albanian origin immigrated to the United States and brought with them this peculiar language, which, having no contact with the Motherland for more than 500 years, had kept features no longer existing in modern Albania.

We can read the history of a place not only in the great monuments left by those who came before us, but also through the details of daily life, for example in the eating habits of its people. In Sicily foreign invaders brought and left some of the plants that nowadays we consider typical of the Sicilian landscape: with the Greeks, it was the olive tree; with the Arabs, the citrus groves; with the Spaniards, the prickly pear. But even the gestures of the people carry the taste of history: shepherds making ricotta cheese remind us of the Homeric tale of 2,500 years ago. It is believed that the present Capo, Vucciria and Ballarò historical markets in Palermo are on the sites of old Arab marketplaces and the way merchandise is exhibited is unmistakably Arabic.

The Sicilian landscape is almost entirely mountainous, and this has had an enormous effect on the local culture, making all communications and transportation tremendously difficult. Even today, many towns, even if accessible by asphalt roads, are remote and may require hours of driving to reach. A landscape, as Giuseppe Tomasi di Lampedusa says in *The Leopard*, is never boring, winding endlessly through innumerable hills, which, we can add, offers continuous change, like that of theater backdrops. That's where, up to World War II, only cart drivers succeeded in travelling regularly, bringing supplies and food that were not locally available.

The pivotal opposition in the entire chivalric repertory is that of the Christians versus the Muslims, usually called Saracens or Moors in this context. It should be noted that both puppet shows and cart painting reached the apex of their success in the second half of the 19th century, and by this time there were no more Muslims around Sicily. For at least five centuries and until about thirty years ago, most

Sicilians had no experience with different ethnic groups in their daily lives. The Muslims for them represented a foreign, non-Christian population living in distant lands, rather than people in flesh and blood to be feared. Aristocracy and social classes, rather than religious faith or color of skin, represented reasons for privilege or discrimination.

The Chivalric Stories Through the Centuries

The events enacted and narrated in the puppet theater performances of Sicily derive in great part from the chivalric romances of Italian poets of the Renaissance, which in turn derive from the so called *Matière de France* or *Chansons de geste* that grew out of the retelling of the *Chanson de Roland* ("The Song of Roland"), France's epic poem of the early 12th century.

"The Song of Roland" recounts the exploits of twelve Christian Paladins in their struggles against twelve Saracen soldiers of Islam. It culminates in the episode at Roncevaux when Charlemagne's army made its way from Spain to France by way of the mountain passes on the Pyrenees mountains. Through the treachery of their compatriot Gano di Magonza, a handful of the rear guard defenders led by Orlando, the emperor's most loyal and intrepid follower, were ambushed at Roncevaux (*Roncisvalle* in Italian) by overwhelming numbers of the enemy and ultimately annihilated. In real history it may actually have been the Basques attacking the French rear-guard in a minor skirmish. Through centuries of storytelling, reality was completely transformed into legends and Roncevaux became the pivotal episode of this saga.

Gano was a member of one of two rival clans currying favor with Charlemagne, known to audiences as the wicked Magonzesi (from Magonza—*Mayance* in French). Orlando, together with his boon companion Oliviero, and Turpino, the warrior archbishop of Reims, belonged to the loyal Chiaramontesi clan (from Chiaramonte—*Clermont* in French).

The tales of Charlemagne entered Italy by way of pilgrimage routes along which the populace would be entertained by storytellers or *cantastorie* (the Italian counterpart of minstrels and jongleurs).

From the outset the tales struck a responsive chord with the public and soon entered into the folklore traditions of the Italian people. Subsequently these stories were given more sophisticated literary treatment in the Italian Renaissance chivalric poems of Pulci (*Morgante Maggiore*), Boiardo (*Orlando Innamorato*) and Ariosto (*Orlando Furioso*).

Due to extremely popular retellings of the Carolingian tales in Italy (referred to as *I Reali di Francia*) the stories underwent a number of changes. They dealt in great part with imaginary events leading up to the defeat of Orlando and his fellow Paladins at Roncevaux. Episodes unfolded throughout Europe and Asia with action swinging back and forth from Paris to the Orient, the pretext usually being the pursuit of Angelica, the princess of Cathay, the rescue of damsels in distress, or the defense of Paris under siege by the Saracens.

The roles of some characters were expanded, and new characters are introduced especially heroes of Italian nationality like Rinaldo of Montalbano (*Renaut de Montauban* in French), who became the great favorite of puppet theater audiences and whose charm in great part lay in his amorous proclivities. Other characters included Rodomonte, the fearless champion of the Saracens; Agramante, the king of Africa; Ferraguto (also called Ferraù), the hot-blooded Spaniard; and the somewhat phlegmatic Astolfo.

Rinaldo became especially popular because he had had the courage to rebel for a just cause, unlike Orlando, who always respected the rules and seemed too obedient to the emperor's wishes, even when they were arbitrary or plainly wrong and unjust. Sicilians, who admire slyness, considered Orlando a bit stupid. Orlando is always cross-eyed in puppet theaters, although not in the original literary sources. His handicap may have been an attempt to make him seem more human, but it certainly rendered him slightly ridiculous. Orlando also becomes crazy or loses his wits (hence, the title of Ariosto's poem *Orlando Furioso* [The Furies of Roland]) when he sees the names of his beloved Angelica and the shepherd Medoro carved inside a heart on a tree. Astolfo, a Paladin of Anglo-Saxon origin, ultimately goes to the moon to retrieve Orlando's wits, lost over his jealous love of Angelica.

Along with the pixie-like magician Malagigi, Astolfo brought a comic element into the narrative. There were also giants, necromancers and magic rings like the one worn by Angelica that rendered her invisible. Angelica accounts for the innovation of an amorous element (conspicuously absent from the patriotically militant and religious *matière de France*) and represents the coveted prize for the Christian Paladins who forgot their duties to monarchy and God when confronted with her ravishing beauty that vanished at the twist of her ring.

The Chivalric Tradition in Sicily Before the Renaissance

The Medieval chivalric tradition was actually quite dissimilar from the Sicilian folk repertory, as declared by Pitrè in his essay *Le tradizioni cavalleresche popolari in Sicilia* (Chivalric folk traditions in Sicily) published in 1878: "What was left in Sicily of the Carolingian legends of the Norman times? Little, very little, if we are to rely only on historical sources and on living relics. No document I know of is describing the existence of this legend among us, no authority is supporting which facts had been widely understood or quoting the real and most important sources of the legends."[1]

Rather, most puppeteers were referring, more or less directly, to the chivalric romances of the 15th century for the choice of subjects. Even for the costumes and the armours, their models were popular prints from the Renaissance, and not the Medieval originals that certainly could not have been accessible to them: "Look for example at the typical Sicilian puppet: he does not wear the armour of a Carolingian hero. It is not the armour of the 12th or 13th century. His armour seems to come out from popular booklets published between the 15th and the 16th century."[2]

There are several reproductions of prints with knights, whose attire is strikingly similar to the Sicilian puppets' outfit, in one of the most important publications on popular prints, *Stampe popolari italiane dal XV al XX secolo* (Italian popular prints from the 15th to the 20th century),[3] written by Paolo Toschi, who was one of the first Italian scholars to dedicate his research entirely to the study of folk poetry and traditions.

However, not everyone agrees on the Renaissance origins of the chivalric tradition in Sicily. Luigi Natoli detected its roots much further back in time. In his article "Le tradizioni cavalleresche in Sicilia," (Chivalric traditions in Sicily), published in 1927, he asserted that although old chivalric poems (or fragments of poems) have not been found in Sicily, the tradition had never died out on the island since the Norman conquest in the 11th century: "Can we possibly exclude the well-founded hypothesis that the Normans took to Sicily the chants of their homeland? That troubadour Turoldo, believed to have authored the *Chanson de Roland* ("Song of Roland"), wasn't a Norman after all? How could the Normans, going overseas, have forgotten the national chants that were supposed to excite them before heroic battles and entertain them during their rest at camp?"[4]

A possible explanation for the lack of written texts observed by Natoli could be derived by some observations raised by Ettore Li Gotti. In his book *Sopravvivenze delle leggende carolingie in Sicilia* (Carolingian survivals in Sicily), he points out that chivalric literature belonged to a cultural milieu quite dissimilar from that of the Sicilian Poetry School, active at the court of the Swabian emperor Frederick II in Sicily in the 13th century: "Chivalric stories circulated among the popular or semi-popular public, probably through the storytellers, and never reached a higher status because, as it is well known, the poetry of Frederick's court, even if it may have accepted some echoes of the Arthurian courtly cycle, considered the Carolingian cycle (or *Geste Francor*) as the poetic expression of quite a different social class."[5]

It is significant that the only written text mentioning, although indirectly, Carolingian legends is *Il Contrasto,* a famous satirical poem of the 13th century, which was written by the Sicilian poet Cielo D'Alcamo in a language that is a mixture of Italian and Sicilian. Li Gotti points out that on line 136 the main character "tells his sweetheart that he loves her with *core paladino* ("with a Paladin's heart"),[6] but he fails to notice that these words of the *Contrasto* are actually pronounced by the female character. Either male or female, Li Gotti's conclusion is well grounded: by this early date, the expression had clearly entered the daily language of common people since, by general consent, the poem has a semi-popular origin: "There is no doubt as to the meaning of the phrase *core Paladino,* which is used by Cielo D'Alcamo as a proverbial expression, and thus proves the perfect knowledge of the Carolingian cycle in the cultural milieu above described. The word *Paladino* had already become a synonym for generous and loyal knight."[7]

Luigi Natoli, on the other hand, writing in the 1920s, thought that the very concrete reality of the recent wars between Muslims and Christians, and of the following Norman conquest, had produced among Sicilians a decline in the inspiration for the old French legends. He explains the lack of early chivalric texts in a completely different and not quite as convincing way: "This chronicle, which was so real, so recent, so rooted in history, could prevent the old French epic saga, which was so far and foreign, from becoming popular and widespread."[8]

It seems quite unlikely that a recent historical conflict could actually reduce the interest of the public on the matter; especially in the field of folk literature, just the contrary usually occurs. For example, at a time closer to us, in the process of the unification of Italy during the 19th century that took the name of Risorgimento ("Rising again"), the enthusiasm for the first revolutionary movements inspired several folk songs and poems, as it has been analyzed by Antonino Uccello in his book *Risorgimento e società nei canti popolari siciliani* (Risorgimento and society in Sicilian folk songs).[9]

Moreover, not everyone agrees on the very existence of a real religious conflict. The historian Virgilio Titone thus declared in *Storia, mafia e costume in Sicilia* (History, mafia and customs): "A real religious conflict between Christians and Muslims, a conflict that would assume the forms of fanaticism and intolerance found in other countries conquered by the Arabs, never existed in Sicily. On the contrary, it happened quite easily that, in view of the economical advantages that would derive, Christians did convert to Islam, just like Arabs who, after the Norman conquest of the island, converted to Christianity in good numbers and without too many scruples."[10]

Based on this information, we could produce a hypothesis that is opposite to Natoli's: The lack of texts could have been caused by an extremely low emotional participation of the people to problems derived from religious conflicts.

There are few certainties on these remote times and any hypothesis is bound to be shrouded in mystery. Li Gotti expressed the fascinating theory that chivalric tradition may have been employed by the German emperors Hohenstaufen (that is, Frederick II and his father Henry VI) to strengthen and establish their political power in Sicily in the 12th and 13th centuries. If this was the case, the vastly popular character of the tradition must have facilitated their task and been an excellent asset for reaching their goals.

Goffredo da Viterbo in his chronicle *Pantheon,* written in Latin between 1185 and 1187, mentions that Charlemagne coming back from Palestine had stopped in Sicily, and he provides an interesting detail in tracing the origin of the names of Capo d'Orlando and of Oliveri, a cape in the Northern coast of Sicily and a mountain respectively, today also names of the two nearby towns. Both of them would have been named after the two knights who were accompanying the Emperor Charlemagne: "Mons ibi stat magnus qui dicitur esse Rolandus. Alter Oliverius, simili ratione vocatus." ("There stands a big mountain that was named after Roland. And another one, Oliverius, thus called for a similar reason.")[11]

It's another useful piece to reconstruct the varied and complex puzzle of the Carolingian influences in Sicily. This legend could have been used to increase the national pride. Robert Folz in his book *Le souvenir et la légende de Charlemagne dans l'empire germanique mediévale* (The memory and legend of Charlemagne in the German Medieval Empire) maintains that the Swabians could have been able to justify the annexation of Sicily as a restoring to their Empire of a region that had already been part of it in the legend.[12] Sicily had been annexed thanks to the marriage of Henry VI Hohenstaufen, the Swabian emperor of Germany and last heir of the Norman kings of Sicily, and Constance of Hauteville.

All of these hypotheses are not real demonstrations, as neither Li Gotti nor Folz provide any kind of proof that the Swabians did actually try to put this demagogical strategy into practice. While Denis Mack Smith's seminal work *Storia della Sicilia medievale e moderna* does mention the diffusion of Carolingian and Breton legends in Sicily due to the French jongleurs, it ignores completely the theory about the Swabians' supposed plan.[13]

In order to complete the picture of these first misty centuries after the Middle Ages, we can add that after the 15th century the feeble traces of the Arthurian legend in Sicily were permanently lost. Giuseppe Pitrè,[14] and later Cecilia Wærn in her book *Mediaeval Sicily,* reported evidence of two extremely rare occasions in which the Breton legends referred to the presence of King Arthur on Mount Etna: "These tales were rapidly acclimatized, so that Gervase of Tilbury was told, when he was at the court of William II, that King Arthur was really still alive, living in a place of marvellous workmanship on the Mongibello (old name of Mount Etna), where he had been seen reclining in royal state, by a groom of the bishop of Catania, who had strayed there in pursuit of a runaway horse.... In the Italian anonymous poem *Il Detto del Gatto Lupesco* (The wolf-cat's saying) of about AD 1200 the author tells how he meets two knights from Brittany, who are coming back from Mongibello after a long stay there, hoping to learn the truth about their lost king."[15]

Pitrè drew the conclusion that the Normans, transferring to Sicily the lore of their epic legends, had also brought, at least in the earlier stage, the Arthurian stories. "They were not content with chanting only the deeds of Charlemagne and his Paladins, as their brothers were doing at Hastings where they had fought for their conquest of England. As we saw from Goffredo da Viterbo's passage, they rooted the Carolingian legend in their new homeland Sicily and added the Arthurian legend of the Breton Cycle, too."[16]

The issue of the diffusion of these legends in Sicily has thoroughly been analyzed by Arturo Graf. In *Artù in Sicilia Miti e Leggende* (King Arthur in Sicily—Myths and legends) Graf states that versions coming out later than Gervasio's, written by Cesario from Heisterbach and Stephen of Bourbon, stressed the diabolical and hellish elements of the tale and hypothesized that the Normans had been responsible for placing King Arthur's residence in Sicily.[17] The limited diffusion of the Breton cycle in Sicily is confirmed by the circumstance that the optical phenomenon observed on the Straits of Messina, which is called Fata Morgana (*Morgan le Fay* in the Breton cycle), is the only toponym on the island inspired by the stories of the Round Table.[18]

Two products of Sicilian figurative art have survived to our time and they demonstrate that the Arthurian legend was known on the island. Both of them have been dated before the 15th century, that is, before the Renaissance chivalric literature. The ceiling of the Steri Palace in Palermo was painted in 1380. Some of the subjects represented are inspired by Breton stories. Luigi Natoli thus describes them: "That ceiling is a real encyclopaedia: mythology, sacred history, Trojan wars, Queen Didon, hunting scenes and aristocratic life, the Sybils, the ancient sages, the Prophets, monsters, geniuses and, what interests us most, chivalric stories of the Chiaramonte (Clairmont) family, original owners of the palace, of the Charlemagne cycle and of King Arthur's."[19]

This is part of the evidence provided by Natoli to prove the vitality of the tradition before the Renaissance. The paintings of that ceiling were done by artists of semi-popular inspiration, and this helps demonstrate the diffusion of those legends among the lower social classes: "The list is long, but what is evident and certain is the richness of the chivalric subjects from which the painters took inspiration. They were certainly not scholars nor did they own a chivalric library; they were taking what was widely recognized and well known.[20]

In addition, the Bargello Museum in Florence owns two bed covers embroidered in the 15th century with Arthurian motifs and Sicilian inscriptions. Pio Rajna examined them in detail in his article *Intorno a due antiche coperte con figurazioni tratte dalla storie di Tristano e Isotta* ("About two old bed covers with images taken from the stories of Tristan and Iseult").[21] The two bed covers and the Steri ceiling are almost contemporary and they are quite similar to each other. Ezio Levi sees a strong link between these two artistic products: "Even a rapid comparison between the scenes of two embroidered bed covers and the painted scenes of the Steri Palace is enough to let us perceive that both relate to the identical iconographical tradition. We are in the same time, in the same train of thought and with the same images."[22]

Up until the 15th century the Arthurian cycle was known in Sicily: we must then conclude that in later times the Carolingian cycle gained a supremacy that was bound to stay unchanged for centuries.

The Success of Chivalric Romances in Sicily in the 16th Century

We know for sure that chivalric romances were quite well known in Sicily in the 16th century. We can quote two significant elements as signs of this popularity. Antonino Alfano in his poem *La battaglia celeste tra Michele e Lucifero* (The heavenly battle between Michael and Lucifer), dated 1568, had been complaining that the stories of Orlando had more followers than didactic and religious stories.[23]

There is also an ancient document about which Carmelina Naselli has dedicated her article *Figure e scene dell "Orlando Furioso" in un'antica pergamena catanese* ("Images and scenes of the "Orlando Furioso" on an ancient parchment document from Catania").[24] On this manuscript, which contained legal documents, a notary from Catania around 1550 amused himself by drawing chivalric subjects. Naselli points out that the author is not an artist, but simply one of Ariosto's enthusiastic readers, a fan of an extremely fashionable genre who liked to be updated on the latest literary trends. She carefully analyzes the drawings and observes a remarkable attention for mythological subjects (such as Ganimede's myth) beside the chivalric ones. This can be justified by the background of the author, which was learned, not popular, since the common people always remained indifferent to the Renaissance craze for mythology.

These drawings testify the *Orlando Furioso*'s diffusion in Sicily and also indirectly give evidence that tournaments, and chivalry in general, were still part of life in Sicily in those days. Naselli affirms that only one of the chosen subjects could have been known through prints, the duel between Ruggiero and Mandricardo, and she detects a link between these drawings and the narrative purpose that would have produced the painting of Sicilian carts three centuries later: "This testimony can give us the possibility of detecting at their origin a way to comment with pictures that from the higher classes would later be transmitted to lower classes and become, with the added appeal of bright colors, a genuine expression of the Sicilian soul and fantasy."[25]

Even popular poetry of the 16th and 17th centuries shows evident chivalric echoes, for example in some poems written in Sicilian dialect by the poet Antonio Veneziano, who lived between 1545 and 1592. These, however, are only fragments: as Pitrè noticed, even in the Renaissance period, Sicily lacks a corpus of chivalric popular poetry similar to what Costantino Nigra had gathered and examined in the Italian northern region of Piedmont. On the whole in Sicily, after the Renaissance boom, which must have taken place due to the publication of Ariosto's *Orlando Furioso,* chivalric tradition got lost in the myriad of small streams of oral tradition up until Romanticism.

Problems on the Origin of the Sicilian Puppet Show

It seems certain that the puppet show, in the form we know it today, is a relatively modern phenomenon. Giuseppe Pitrè, who had stated that "the puppet theater has offered shows to the lower classes for hundreds of years,"[26] was proved wrong by almost all of his successors, first of all Giuseppe Cocchiara, who explained Pitrè's incorrect deductions: "Here is Pitrè's error; on the one hand he goes on outlining, or at least sketching, the history of the puppet theater, while on the other hand he forgets that this theater, as a vehicle of the *matière de France,* does not have an ancient origin and cannot boast the nobility of 'hundreds of years.'"[27]

For Cocchiara the puppet theater was undoubtedly born in the Romantic age: "The puppet theater started to exist in Sicily at the beginning of the 19th century. We do not deny that already in Greek Sicily there could have existed artisans able to build and maneuver the marionettes. But the marionette-pupo, the marionette as a Paladin of France, appears in Sicily—as well as in Naples—in an epoch that was imbued by the most Romantic juices."[28]

Besides the general fascination for the Middle Ages that characterized 19th-century Europe, it was also the struggle for the unification of Italy (Risorgimento) that encouraged the interest for chivalric stories. A small example of this: On a small flyer in the 19th century, printed to publicize a choir of volunteer patriots significantly titled "La bandiera tricolore" (the three-color flag that is by definition the Italian flag), there are two knights in the perfect attire of Medieval warriors.

It is an indirect indication that people identified the fight for unification with chivalric battles. The origin of the puppet theater is still unknown, and it is shrouded by misty legends up to this day. Pitrè was not the only one who considered this tradition very old. Natoli, for example, thought the tradition already existed in the 16th or 17th century and that the model of the army had been copied from the tournaments that took place in Sicily during that time, or from the statue of Charles V in Piazza Bologni in Palermo. He explained the silence of 18th-century chroniclers, among whom was the Marquis of Villabianca, with the extreme frequency and ordinariness of the shows. Most scholars, however, agree with Cocchiara's statement dating the origin of the puppet shows to the 19th century.

• Two •

The Oral Tradition

Around the 1950s, those who had walked by Piazza della Vittoria in Palermo, not far from the Royal Palace, could have noticed a man who, accompanying himself with large gestures, would tell chivalric stories to groups of people. He was the last heir of a very long list of Medieval itinerant storytellers.

The tales of chivalry were familiar to Sicilians not only through the puppet theater, but also from the street performances of professional storytellers (*contastorie*) that attracted small crowds of *aficionados* every night. The *contastorie* were specialized in chivalry, while the *cantastorie* would keep people informed about striking news, recent or old, the story of the bandit Salvatore Giuliano being their *pezzo forte.*

The storytellers not only transmitted the stories and prepared the advent of the puppet shows, they also continued to exist even when the small theaters started to be full every evening with the usual daily show. Some people preferred storytelling to puppets and would wait for the storyteller near the same street corner where he, at the same time each day, would tell one of the episodes of the long cycles of chivalric stories.

The Chivalric Tradition Between Learned and Popular Literature

One of the main channels of circulation of chivalric literature among lower classes in Sicily, as in the rest of Italy, was represented by the storytellers who for centuries carried out that function in public squares. It is widespread opinion among scholars that in Italy, from medieval minstrels and jongleurs to more recent street storytellers, oral tradition had a pivotal role in the transmission and consolidation of chivalric traditions. Investigating how and when the mysterious oral and written transmission of chivalric tales took place is one of the most demanding and fascinating tasks for a scholar of ethnology and literature.

In the particular case of Sicily, for over eight centuries these tales were passed on from generation to generation, in a more or less subdued manner, before enjoying a sudden increase of popularity during the Romantic age in the 19th century, which gave birth to the relatively recent tradition of the puppet shows and to the development of folk art inspired by the same chivalric traditional stories.

The old French medieval repertory of the *Chanson de Roland* and the Breton stories of King Arthur and the Knights of the Round Table could not have been able to blend in the wonderful synthesis of Renaissance literature without the crucial role of storytellers. The eminent critic Pio Rajna in his article "I Rinaldi" (Neapolitan storytellers) in 1878 thus declared: "Had street storytellers not existed, Matteo Maria Boiardo would not have composed his *Orlando innamorato* (*Orlando in Love*) nor Ludovico Ariosto his *Orlando Furioso* (*The Frenzy of Orlando*)."[1]

In Italy during the Renaissance it became possible for the culture of the higher social classes to absorb elements from the lower classes, elevating their status and conferring them the prestige of the official culture. In Sicily in the 19th century the opposite phenomenon took place: at that time it was folk culture that was influenced by higher classes even if after three centuries. As already mentioned, this influence juxtaposed to and was highlighted by the prevailing Romantic atmosphere.

Not only in Sicily did chivalric literature enjoy great attractiveness among the most disadvantaged social classes: the same phenomenon occurred in many different places all over Europe. It is necessary to elaborate on this concept in order to clarify what role the storytellers had in this process of popularization.

The changing fortunes of the chivalric stories have often been taken by scholars as an example of the osmosis between erudite literature and folk popular narrative. However, according to the ethnographer Paolo Toschi, chivalric literature represents a quite unique phenomenon, since the cultural gap that opened with texts travelling up and down the social scale is very wide and its ultimate results are much more distant and diverse from each other than what normally happens:

> It is generally quite difficult and rare that the transmission and adaptation of a folk song or chant would produce such a wide discrepancy between the two cultural levels. However, under certain conditions, some songs, or types of poetry, may shift freely all the way from the highest to the lowest level or vice versa. As a result, refined chivalric poems were able to circulate among the populace, since the Carolingian epic tales were already quite deeply rooted in the culture of our masses. Even the humblest classes were very familiar with its heroes and, as far as poetry is concerned, there had already been a two-century-long tradition of chivalric songs which had prepared the advent of the great Italian epic literature of the 15th and 16th centuries.[2]

On this issue it can be of some interest a passage present in one of the *Trecentonovelle* (Three hundred short stories) written by Franco Sacchetti in the 14th century. Novella n. 15 has an unpretentious Dante who is listening incognito to a simple donkey man recite his poem and who is noticing some differences between what the man says and what he had written. Sacchetti points out that the donkey man did not know who Dante was. As a consequence we can conclude that there already was in the 14th century a wide circulation of the cantos of the *Divine Comedy* among illiterates and lower working classes.

In the case of chivalric poems, the phenomenon is exceptional: normally they do not include works of such high intrinsic literary value. The opposite phenomenon (i.e., folk narrative inspiring learned erudite literature) is well documented not only in a middle class author like Luigi Pulci, but also in an aristocratic poet like Ludovico Ariosto. This phenomenon is beyond the objectives of the present research, but it is important to keep this trend in mind while studying folk and oral literature. Toschi feels the need to stress the influence and the presence of the storytellers' language style in Matteo Maria Boiardo's highly refined 15th-century poem *Orlando innamorato (Orlando in love)*: "Stereotyped expressions, fillers, opening and closing formulas and so on: all elements of the storytellers' repertory survive in Matteo Maria Boiardo even if not with the intensity and power we found in Luigi Pulci."[3]

The "discrepancy between the two cultural levels" that Toschi referenced would not have been able to disappear without the presence of particular circumstances.

The Role of the Storyteller in the Osmosis Process Between Dominant and Subordinate Cultures

Since ancient times, the role of the storyteller in the interchange up and down the social scale has been pivotal. The Medieval epic poems did not have a popular origin as Arnold Hauser stated in his seminal book *Social History of Art:* "The rhetoric pomp of Romantic historiography did not originally have any relationship with the common people. The heroic and celebrative songs, from which that epic was derived, were the poetry of a caste, the purest ever produced by a ruling class. They were not created, sung, diffused by the common people, they were not directed to or tuned with their feelings. They were in every respect art poetry, of aristocratic inspiration."[4] The French minstrels of the Middle Ages made the Carolingian legends universally known among lower classes: they were "responsible for transferring the chivalric matter from the erudite feudal milieu to the popular one, making it attain a quite different tone in this passage."[5]

Who were the storytellers however? What was their role in society? These very peculiar characters acquired different functions through the centuries, going through incredible transformations and adapting themselves to the current trends and circumstances up to almost present times.[6]

Singers of tales have been surrounded by general esteem and consideration since the remotest times; in Homer's *Iliad* and *Odyssey* they were always highly regarded. Much more recently, several witnesses confirmed that, even after many centuries, the respectful attitude of the audience had not changed. Here is a quotation from a diary written in 1928 by a poor farmer in the small village of Borgetto, not far from Palermo: "People believe that the storyteller Benedetto Randazzo is a true magician, as he knows all the stories from hundreds of years ago, and tells about places he is the only one to know."[7]

In spite of this, according to Pitrè's statement,[8] the storytellers occupied a very low level on the social scale. In the summer, when people's interest in stories decreased, the storytellers were forced to earn their living as itinerant peddlers. Up to 50 or 60 years ago, storytelling in Sicily was still commonly done in the open air, and the storytellers' social condition and the fame surrounding them were unchanged.

Reverence and admiration of the public could be due to an intuitive identification of the storyteller as a mediator and interpreter of the official culture for the common people's benefit, as it has been expressed by Antonino Uccello: "Their activity was taking place at the border line between popular culture, whose main channel is the oral tradition, and the more highly structured and elaborate culture of the dominant classes."[9]

Cecilia Wærn, who saw the storytellers at work in Sicily at the beginning of the 20th century, immediately noticed their particular capacity of blending various forms of literature, both popular and erudite: "The tales represent a blend of Sicilian oral tradition and various literary sources incorporating accounts taken from the great poets of the Renaissance."[10]

"If I am allowed the oxymoron, the *cuntu* [Sicilian term for traditional epic storytelling] represents the 'popular aristocracy' of chivalric tradition in Italy"[11]: Li Gotti's statement is clarifying the definition of storytellers as the obligatory passage from the two "levels of culture" indicated by Toschi. They were the particular circumstances that made possible the merging of erudite literature and popular folk narrative.

Three Types of Traditional Storytellers: Chivalric Tales, Sacred Stories and Chronicles

Anthropologists have distinguished three quite distinctive types among traditional storytellers in Sicily. Li Gotti, in particular, as other scholars like Linares, Salomone Marino and Pitrè had already done at the end of the 19th century, made a distinction between "those who go around singing to the people stories and legends written in poetry" and "those who recite by heart accompanying their narration with vivacious gestures" (*cantastorie* and *contastorie* in Italian respectively, that is story singers and storytellers). He also distinguishes the geographic zones where the different types of storytellers were active,[12] stressing that in Naples storytelling had quite different characteristics. Modern scholars have maintained this distinction and Antonino Buttitta makes a distinction between storytellers who, like the poet Antonio Pucci in the 14th century, were narrating scenes and facts from everyday life[13] and those who never abandoned chivalric subjects: "Because of his function of journalist and people's informer, the traditional storyteller little by little tends to abandon the epic and chivalric subjects, which got handled exclusively by the *contastorie,* true teller of tales for the common people, who must always be distinguished from the *cantastorie,* and who was going to be the only one able and responsible to keep that narrative tradition alive, which was still true in Naples up to the end of the 19th century and still is true in Sicily."[14]

Given the subject of the present research, I am mainly going to deal with the storyteller of chivalric subjects (*contastorie*). This is how Buttitta defines different types of chroniclers (*cantastorie*):

> In Sicily today there are three types of chroniclers: one is more properly defined as a singer. He works either in cities or in the village where he lives, goes around clubs and shops, hops on and off public buses, singing songs of limited length, usually of comical contents. Another type, who is not as popular as he used to be, sings exclusively stories of sacred subjects and is called *orbu* ("blind" in Sicilian) because this kind of storytelling was typically done by sightless people. He has his own habitual customers, in Sicilian called *parrucciani* ("parishoners"), in whose homes he goes on predetermined days to sing the traditional sacred stories, usually prayers or novenas, which are prayers recited in installments for nine consecutive days. Like his 19th-century colleagues, occasionally the *orbu* may sing short comical songs upon request. A third type is the true storyteller, who tells stories of bandits, news and peculiar events, and who is active not only in the village where he was born, but also may go out of his province and even out of Sicily.[15]

*The Tradition of Blind Storytellers (*Orbi*) in Palermo*

The presence of blind storytellers in Sicily has been connected to the blindness of Homeric singers, and this interesting link with ancient classical authors goes well beyond the Medieval connections previously examined. There is a very important difference, though: while in ancient times blindness was considered a sign of divine inspiration—a gift from the gods—in times closer to ours, blind storytellers were justified by the necessity to offer blind people the opportunity to earn some money and make a living, as it was observed by Elsa Guggino.[16] Previous research in this field had been done by Leonardo Vigo in the 19th century.[17]

"The blind storytellers never dealt with chivalric stories," I was told by one of the last ones to survive, Fortunato Giordano, who was 82 when I interviewed him on March 14, 1988, a few years before his death. However, Giuseppe Pitrè had observed[18] that the Marquis of Villabianca, an 18th-century Sicilian aristocrat who wrote very accurate accounts and chronicles of all that was happening in Palermo at his time, seemed to assert quite the contrary. Villabianca included chivalric stories, such as Guerrino il Meschino and Orlando's story, in the repertory of blind storytellers in the 18th century, which means that in earlier times they were not limiting themselves to sacred stories. Several 19th-century researchers, including Leonardo Vigo, Salomone Marino and Giuseppe Pitrè, mentioned that the blind storytellers were also relating chronicles and news items. Pitrè in particular

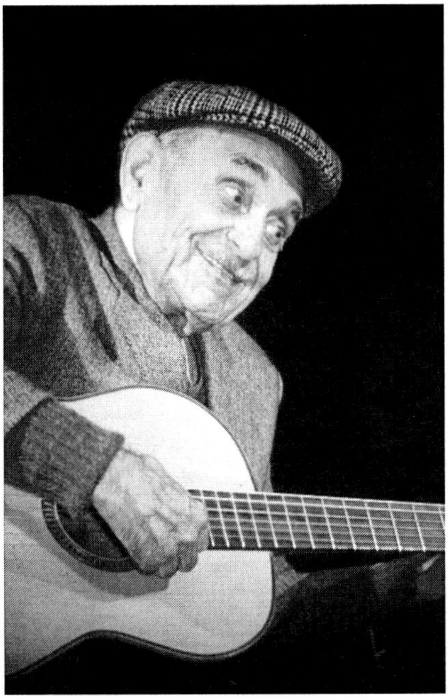

The blind storyteller Fortunato Giordano in 1988.

reported that they were accompanying puppet shows before the puppeteers decided to substitute them with a more economical barrel organ, which is still used today. We can then conclude that the repertory of blind storytellers must have originally been much wider, and that later on they specialized and restricted their stories to sacred stories, excluding everything else.

Up to the 1960s, the tradition of blind storytellers (*orbi*) singing sacred stories was thriving in Palermo. Two *orbi*, accompanied by a third non-blind person who helped them get around, would stop in front of one of the small votive altars that used to border streets or in front of the home of a client who was willing to pay them in order to listen to their musical religious stories, one piece at a time, always at the same time of the day. At night it was more expensive, because people could listen to the singing from their beds like a serenade, and sometimes the storytellers even went up the stairs.

There are documents indicating that, despite not being officially recognized until 1829, the Orbi (blind storytellers) Brotherhood was founded in 1661 under the guidance of the Jesuit Fathers of the Church of Jesus in Palermo, generally called Casa Professa.

"We were using a jargon (*baccagghiu* in Sicilian) that we had learned at the Institute for the Blind in Palermo," said Giordano, "according to which we were inverting syllables, so that words like 'basta' and 'ancora' became 'staba' and 'aranco'; if pronounced very quickly, the sentences became totally incomprehensible to the other listeners."

The Orbi Brotherhood was a mini society with a strict hierarchical structure. A real school was never established, but it was necessary to study very hard under the guidance of an instructor. When the Music School was created within the Institute of the Blind, the students who were not doing well enough to be accepted for the Music Conservatory higher courses were encouraged to continue their studies with novenas. In this way they were assured to have something in their hands to support themselves in one way or another.

This is how Giordano described the Orbi's yearly musical "season": They started on January 17, feast of St. Anthony the Abbot, with the seven Wednesdays of Saint Joseph, which ended in March with the so-called *triunfo* or *sciarra* ("triumph" or "brawl") di San Giuseppe, followed by a very fast-paced rhythm used to accompany a ball supposedly arranged in Heaven called *abballu di li vergini* ("the Virgins' ball"). It was a triumph for St. Joseph's miracles, a sort of great party organized to thank the saint for the vows he had fulfilled. Everything was concluded by a cheerful musical piece, the so-called "musica *a cumplimentu*," which was offered as a bonus to affectionate clients.

In July and in September, prior to the days of the celebrations in honor of Palermo's patron saints, the blind storytellers' *pezzo forte* was St. Rosalia's novena, whose 208 octaves Giordano remembered perfectly, even if he had not sung it for several years. Later novenas were the All Souls' novena (November 2), which he defined as too somber and gloomy, the Immaculate Conception's novena (December 8), and finally the most important one, the Christmas novena.

"To fill the gaps we did short pieces even in May and in other parts of the year," Giordano told me. "The so-called *rattedduzzi,* for example the *triino,* was sung for the Three Kings, on the Epiphany—January 6. On the days preceding June 13, the feast of St. Anthony from Padua, we would go to the small fishing village of Porticello, near Palermo, where people held an extraordinary devotion for this saint and where small altars were prepared in the street for this occasion."

The singing of the novenas was compared to a religious rite and in older times blind storytellers used to wear the tonsure, a special cut of some hair of the scalp as a sign of special devotion, in order to indicate they were to be considered like priests; others wore a skull cap similar to the one worn by bishops. They were sacred figures, and because of this they were often offered food considered sacred, often stewed fava beans with olive oil and garlic, but they were rarely able to accept, as other people were waiting for them elsewhere. "On the last day of the novena," Giordano remembered, "we would get paid an amount of money that was calculated with what had been written on the wall each night with a piece of carbon. Sometimes the payment could be done in nature, that is with food or other presents. Those of us who were doing too hasty of a job would be scolded by the clients who would teasingly call them *tagghiarini,* a nickname meaning 'those who like to cut short'—from *tagghiari,* that is 'to cut' in Sicilian."

In a strange and tragic coincidence, Giordano started his career as a non-blind singer accompanying the *orbi,* but later in life, he lost his sight himself. Sometimes the three persons were accompanied by a fourth person called *bilancino*, who was living in a faraway district and could help them find clients in different neighborhoods. "The term *bilancino* was also used to call the mule or donkey helping the horse to transport the heaviest weights," Giordano used to explain.

The blind storytellers used different musical instruments: the guitar, the violin and the cello, while the *azzarino* (or triangle) was used to mark the rhythm that was always the same no matter which text had been chosen. The *orbi* followed written texts and they were extremely jealous of them; as a consequence their texts were fixed and lacked the process of elaboration typical of popular poetry, which is typically continuously amplified or embellished by its users. While composing their stories they normally started from the Gospels, they also sometimes composed octaves about a miracle or event for which they had received a commission: in this case their singing assumed the value of an *ex-voto,* or thanksgiving for the fulfillment of a vow.

The blind storytellers were often invited to parties and weddings where they provided accompaniment for the dancing; they even went to play in brothels, as Giordano mentioned, even if it was forbidden by their statute. When the economic boom arrived in the 1960s, the blind storytellers' relatives, now fairly well off, started to consider this activity dishonorable, considering it similar to begging, and succeeded in convincing them to stop going around selling sacred stories. With the death of Fortunato Giordano, who in 1989 gave the last demonstration of his singing in a small puppet theater in Palermo, one of the last persons able to narrate and represent a piece of our culture has disappeared.

The Traditional Epic Storytellers in Sicily and in Naples

The repertory of epic storytellers used to be exclusively chivalric. In Sicily in the 19th century several epic storytellers were active both in Palermo and in Catania according to many observers, such as Giuseppe Pitrè who wrote a very detailed account of what he had seen in one of the chapters of the aforementioned essay *Le tradizioni cavalleresche popolari in Sicilia* (Popular chivalric folk traditions in Sicily).[19] This type of storytelling, like puppet shows, lasted a couple of hours and was practiced daily; two years were needed to complete the entire cycle. The tradition, quite widespread in the major cities of the island, continued to be very active up to the 1960s. After Don Tanu's death in 1946, Don Roberto Genovese had taken his place in Piazza della Vittoria in Palermo, the traditional setting where epic storytellers used to execute their tales. Genovese's performance was described by Rosalia Perret in 1956[20] and later recorded by a team of American researchers. The Italian writer Carlo Levi in his book *Le parole sono pietre* ("Words are stones") (1955) describes a storyteller in Palermo as "a man, seated on a low stool, who was telling stories...."[21]

In Naples epic storytellers used to be called *rinaldi*, from the name of the famous knight Rinaldo, the Italian name of Renaud de Montauban. The main difference between Sicilian epic storytellers and their Neapolitan colleagues is that the latter used to read (and comment on) the original chivalric poems, while the former, as already mentioned, used to tell the stories based on the prose books published in the second part of the 19th century. According to Pio Rajna, the Neapolitan *rinaldi* were proceeding at the speed of about 300 stanzas every day without taking into account the division of the text into cantos. Their tale was then interrupted by explanations either in Neapolitan dialect or in Italian:

> Their reading aloud, where the transition between one stanza and the next allows for an interruption, is quite often mixed with a sort of commentary partly in dialect, but more often in a language, which is hybrid but Italian in their intentions. These explanations sometimes show the feelings of indignation or joy caused by what is happening in the story and interpret the behavior of the crowd, who is following what they believe to be events that happened in real life; most of the times, however, it is only a free translation of the text. And the audience needs this help; it would have been absurd to expect them to understand a large quantity of poetical expressions and obsolete phrases and expressions.[22]

In Naples the public thought it was considered very important for the storytellers to follow the text word by word. Rajna reports that a *rinaldo* who had become blind pretended for a long time to go on reading in order not to lose his "post," up until the day somebody discovered he was holding the book upside down.[23]

As the Neapolitan philosopher Benedetto Croce wrote, *rinaldi* had already been noticed in the 18th century by another Neapolitan writer, Giambattista Vico, who ideally connected them with the poets of the ancient "heroic age."[24] When Rajna wrote his article in 1898 there were only three *rinaldi* still active, but only a few years later in 1885 there was only one surviving as reported by the dialectal poet Ferdinando Russo.[25] They completely disappeared a short time thereafter.

Sicilian Traditional Epic Storytellers in the Past and in the Present

The repertory of traditional epic storytellers had certainly been chivalric since very old times. Already in the 14th century in Tuscany: "Paladins and knights, noble women and aristocrats were the main characters of the same literature that constantly—maybe exclusively—made use of the chivalric deeds of the *matière de France,* of the love stories and adventures of the Breton tradition, and of the most inventive fairy tales of Medieval poetry.[26]

In Sicily the tradition had a much greater vitality and circulation than in Naples. In the 16th century there was a form of storytelling that probably was quite similar to the one observed in the 20th century. In the 19th century the tradition was revived and renewed by the advent of the puppet shows, which not casually had derived the repertory, the language, and, in part, the techniques from storytelling.

Giusto Lodico, a Palermitan school teacher and author, compiled a four-volume study of Charlemagne and his knights, the Paladins, published in Palermo between 1858 and 1861, transcribing in prose many of the Italian fifteenth- and sixteenth-century poems. As Lodico stated in the introduction of his three-thousand-page *History of the Paladins,*[27] all he had done was gather and put together in writing all the stories that were contained in chivalric poems and that had already been part of the oral tradition for a long time. The 3,922 pages appeared in installments, every two weeks, for sale to an avid audience. The publication by installments and the great success of his book (in Palermo there were more than three thousand subscribers), and later Leggio's and Manzanares's similar books, were an effect, not the cause of the extraordinary vitality of the tradition in Sicily in the 19th century. Giuseppe Capitò described the result as "ponderous," a thorough account written in a "flat and mediocre style." It was an incredible success as Sicilians were fascinated by the stories, even though they knew many of them already. For the storyteller, puppeteer, and cart painter,

Lodico's volumes were a true treasure, their "Bible," as many of them said.

Several witnesses report that traditional epic storytelling was deeply rooted in Sicily before 1861, when the publication of Lodico's book was completed. Among the *Racconti popolari* (Popular tales) written by Linares in 1840 there is one that describes the techniques of a storyteller named Mastro Pasquale and his great success with the public.

The storyteller Salvatore Ferreri, who was illiterate, started his activity in 1844. Here is was he declared to the ethnographer Pitrè: "In 1860 a friend showed to me the *History of the Paladins* by Don Giusto Lodico. I could not, and cannot even today, read or write, but someone read some pages to me. Now, would you believe it? Before my friend finished a sentence, I was saying what was to follow, and my friend exclaimed: 'Well, you know more than the book!'"[28]

From the description Pitrè made of the famous storyteller Salvatore Ferreri, we can become acquainted with the techniques this extraordinary mime used to keep his audience's attention. His performances involved his entire body, he often asked bystanders questions, and he referred to things he had already mentioned. He also used to change his tone from melodramatic to funny, from static to motion. His skillful use of suspense and his attempts to delve into psychology and the use of wonder kept his audience motionless, hanging on his every word. The extraordinary actor played the roles of his endless stories quoting proverbs and local idioms and, when possible, he used to use the Sicilian environment in his stories. For example if the actor said "under a carob tree," the audience could imagine a familiar place much more easily than if he just said "under a tree."

The storyteller usually relied on books and called upon their authority when the story seemed hard to believe. He was very careful not to lose the various story lines with a technique that is typical of the entire chivalric literature and which literary critics call *entrelacement* (French for "braiding" or "weaving"). By saying "*ora lassamu a chistu e phigghiamu a chiddu*" (Sicilian for "now let's set this one aside and consider the other one"), he was thus easily going from one side of Europe to the other. Notions about geography were approximate and the only object the actor used in his performance was a stick that could become a horse or any other object he mentioned during his tale.

Something more must be said about the typical mixture of pompous and middle-of-road languages that the storyteller, like the puppeteer, used in his attempt to imitate the literary language: many words were adapted from the local dialect, many others were entirely invented. The classic tale started with an account of the antecedent facts, followed by spoken parts alternated with narrative. This was still the same technique used, up to the 1960s, by storytellers such as Roberto Genovese and Peppino Celano. The latter, contrary to traditional storytellers, used a board and often wore a costume. Celano dealt also with every day facts. For this purpose he used to buy two newspapers a day, cut the articles he needed, and selected them according to the subject (e.g., "mafia facts," "stories of the bandit Salvatore Giuliano," "government facts," etc.).

My father-in-law, Francesco Matranga, and his brother Domenico remembered that in the 1930s, when they were working as masons, there were persons that were pleased to entertain their workmates during breaks, by telling them tales of chivalry. "They were even better than 'official' storytellers," they added.

The techniques of storytelling may vary considerably according to the public and the teller's personality. This ancient art, which is often considered the origin of theater, has been practiced for centuries without any theoretical basis in societies very different from ours where news and mass media had not heavily substituted the human voice and direct interpersonal communication.

Those who want to learn cannot observe their grandfathers or the village storyteller from the past but must look for a professional instructor who, through theoretical and practical lessons, can teach them more or less as you can teach someone how to write or to play a musical instrument. One of the basic problems is how to raise and keep alive the public's attention. Nowadays it is necessary for the storyteller to stand on a little platform so that everybody can see him. This was not the case in the past when he was an integral part of the social group to whom he was speaking. Today people should stand around him and it is preferable for the storyteller not to mix with the public and keep a certain charismatic distance from the spectators. This distance is naturally present in Eastern societies where actors are often considered owners of divine powers, but it is not as evident in Western societies where actors are considered normal people like everybody else, even if endowed with professional or artistic skill. Nowadays it is necessary to keep this distance and become a gigantic figure in order to dominate the space and not be overwhelmed by the number of spectators.

The puppeteer Peppino Celano started his activity as a storyteller in Palermo in the 1960s, even if with characteristics a little different than in the past. After his death in 1973 this ancient art risked being doomed to disappear, and it would have been the end of this tradition had his memory not still remained alive in the minds of many Sicilians who are in their seventies today. Celano was endowed with endless creativity in inventing his stories. He could practice his storytelling even while he was sleeping, according to those who knew him. Celano had in a way "stolen the trade" and initially had some problems getting known and accepted by a traditional audience who did not like their favorite stories told by someone different from the habitual person. Celano was a real "theater person," who, beside being a puppeteer, had also been an actor in plays written in Sicilian dialect. He had understood that crisis was threatening all these traditions; being a storyteller was how he had chosen to survive as a person. His extraordinary personality was able to adapt easily to novelties such as television, which he actively was exploiting as a source of inspiration instead of avoiding it. In this relentless search for innovation, he had "polluted the waters": he introduced novelties into epic traditional storytelling, such as explicative posters painted with the story to be told, which originally were used only by storytellers dealing with news and chronicles. He was improvising storytelling while wearing a costume, because someone had suggested it to him, mistakenly thinking costumes were typical features of epic storytelling. Instead of rejecting these mystifications, he was well aware of them and, in order to please whomever had invited him, he would wear a pair of black pants, a red cloth belt and a hat similar to Turiddu's, the main character of Mascagni's famous opera *Cavalleria Rusticana* (Rustic Chivalry). In other words, he tried to give the public what they wanted and expected, especially when they were more sophisticated than the common people in the streets. The audience was not aware anymore that a traditional storyteller would not use posters or costumes. Celano saw that his public was changing every day, while for an older storyteller like Genovese the same people came to listen to his tale every day at the same hour in

Villa Bonanno. Previous storytellers like Genovese were very serious and never used irony during the performance, while Celano did.

Today, Gaetano Lo Monaco, who is Celano's grandson (son of his daughter Emilia), has revived this art and performs as a storyteller, being able in the last ten years to give new life to traditional storytelling. Gaetano was only six when his grandfather died, and he remembers he would continuously tell stories of chivalry not only in the public square, but also in daily life, such as at the dinner table with his family. Celano's storytelling used to take place in a square near the Courthouse in Palermo, and it was mainly attended by local workmen during their lunch break, while his puppet theater was in Vicolo Pilicelli 5, a small street nearby, exactly the same place which, after having been closed after his death for about 20 years, was reopened by his grandson, who uses it as a workshop for building puppets. Gaetano learned the art of storytelling mainly from his grandfather's brother Rosario, who is still alive. He does not perform as a storyteller every day as his grandfather used to do, but whenever he is asked to do it. The storyteller who once was the intermediary in the osmosis process between dominant and subordinate cultures, between learned and popular literatures, has now become protagonist of a refined recovery of an age old art.

Traces of the Chivalric Tradition in the Language of the Sicilian People—Idiomatic Expressions and Proverbs

There are several expressions in the Sicilian dialect that indicate the diffusion of the chivalric tradition at the popular level. Pitrè noticed several of them: for instance, *Carrumagnu cu lu pugnu chiusu* (Charlemagne with a tight fist), meaning "a stingy person"; *Farinni quantu Carlu 'n Francia* (To do as much as Charles in France), meaning "to do great and memorable things"; and *Chi ti senti Rinardu di Muntarbanu?* ("Who do you think you are, Renault de Montauban?"), an expression used while talking to an arrogant person. The legend of Buovo d'Antona was mentioned in *Fari lu Bovu d'Antona* (To act as Buovo d'Antona) and *Facitilu pi l'amuri di Diu e di Bovu d'Antona, ch'era un bravu cavaleri a stu munnu* (Do it for God's love and Buovo d'Antona's who was a good knight of this world), which was said when teasing a person who was asking a favor in God's name.[29]

My husband, Giovanni Matranga, remembers that his parents and grandparents would use these expressions commonly, often without realizing their origin. Nowadays they are not used, though, and the majority of Sicilians have never heard of them.

Felice Cammarata in his book *Pupi e carretti* (Puppets and carts)[30] quotes other expressions that point to the amazing success of puppet shows among lower social classes in Sicily. *Immiscare a Franza ca' Spagna* (To mix France with Spain) means "to put together two subjects that are totally unrelated." *Chi aiu u saccu chi pupi ca ti fazzu ririri* (Why are you laughing? Do I have a sack with puppets?) means "Do you think I am a puppeteer?" Very famous and common even today is *Fazzu l'opira* (I am going to do a puppet show), which is "I am going to throw a tantrum."

It's interesting that the names of many chivalric characters became synonyms for people with certain distinct characteristics. It's once again Pitrè giving us detailed accounts of these mostly lost appellations. Beside *Trisullina,* which derives from Drusiana and indicates a vulgar and nosy woman, he lists many others:

> The awful fame of the Magonza (Mayance) family is transferred into the terribly offensive qualification of *Magonzisi* or *Cani di Magonza* (literally "Mayance's dog"—which is also a play on words between *cane* ("dog") and Gano—the first name of the traitor), which is the worst insult because it is an accusation of betrayal, the most infamous sin even for Dante as it is for our people. *Re Pippinu* (King Peppino) means a hunched back person; *Pilucane* is a person who goes around looking and sniffing everywhere; *Giganti Ferrautu* (Ferraù Giant) is an incredibly tall and coarse man, *Malagigi* is a nickname for a priest who is extremely thin, wearing a very short robe and glasses, who looks like a necromancer the way he walks and talks; and *Brunello* is a sly, untrustworthy and distasteful man.[31]

This last expression is still rather commonly used in Sicily today, and *Cani di Magonza* is often abbreviated into *Canimanza*; most Sicilians use these two idioms appropriately and in the correct context but do not have any idea about the origin of these expressions. The others are very rare as a consequence of the decreasing success of the puppet shows in the local culture and of the interference of the Italian language used on television and in schools with the Sicilian dialect.

Toponyms and Family Names

The names chosen to indicate people and places are always indications of an extensive use in the spoken language that later crystallized. For example in Sicily names of places frequently carry traces of the different denominations that have been alternating on the island, in particular the Arabic one. The success of the chivalric stories could not help but leave traces there too.

I have already mentioned the legend about the knights Orlando and Oliviero arriving by ship near Messina. From this legend came the name of the town of *Capo d'Orlando* (Roland's Cape), and some of its inhabitants are probably only vaguely aware of it. The Cape was believed to have taken its triangular shape from Roland's magical famous sword (called Durendal; *Durlindana* in Italian) having cut a rock out of a nearby mountain.[32]

As Li Gotti noticed, other places taking their names from chivalric stories are la *Sella di Orlando* (Roland's Pass) and the *Purteddi di Orlando* (Roland's valleys) near the towns of Aidone and Canicattì respectively,[33] while Pitrè added more details: "A *Turri d'Orlannu* (Roland's tower) is in the Island of Lampedusa, and the *Oliveri* Castle is between the towns of Patti and Milazzo. *Massa Oliveri,* also called 'the island' by people in Syracuse, is the Plemnirium promontory Ptolomey mentioned, a small peninsula protruding into Syracuse harbour. The river Oliveri, which starts from the Pulvirello spring, is about five miles above the Montalbano (Montauban) Castle in the province of Messina. Montalbano is also the name of a large town in the Messina province, the name of an old tower in Palermo, and the last name of a great number of families all over the island."[34]

Montalbano is also the last name of the policeman who is the main character in a famous series of detective stories written by Andrea Camilleri, which have been best sellers in the last fifteen years and are now translated into English and many other languages. Several other last names of chivalric origin are extremely common all over the island. Here is the list given by Natoli: Brandimarte, Brandaleone, Merlino, Tristano, Marfisa, Galasso, Angelica, Orlando, Orlandino, Argalia, Ferrauto, Fioravanti, Rizieri, Oliveri, Viviano, Carlomagno, Palmerino, Altobello, Gerone, and Milone.[35]

The very length of this list indicates the size of the phenomenon described above. Consulting the Palermo phone book we can find many more last names of chivalric origin: Rinaldi, Ruggeri, Ruggero, D'Antona, Ronsisvalle, and Paladino. The greatest majority of Sicilian people carrying these last names are not aware of their origin.

• THREE •

The Celebrations

The chivalric tradition has had an outcome in popular theater, whose most renowned and manifest examples are the puppet shows. Some traditional folk celebrations can be considered forms of dramatization, particularly the Mastro di Campo (Master of the Field), which takes place in the small town of Mezzojuso in the Palermo province on the last Sunday of Carnival.

Hundreds of interesting traditional celebrations annually take place in Sicily. Beside the Mastro di Campo in Mezzojuso, Pitrè indicated two other events, the Taratatà and the Madonna delle Milizie (Virgin of the Armies), celebrated in the towns of Casteltermini and Scicli respectively, which he considered aspects of the everlasting love of the Sicilians for the chivalric world.

In all three of these traditional pageants the fighting is identified with the usual opposition of Moors vs. Christians, on which the entire chivalric tradition in Sicily is based. Due to the Saracens' presence and to the mimic element, these dances with swords can be considered part of the *moresca* tradition, a pantomime dance in which the executants used to wear Moorish costumes and which was performed in various parts of Italy from the Renaissance on.

On these occasions dances with swords are executed and Toschi in his seminal work *Le origini del teatro italiano* (The origins of the Italian theater)[1] considered them dramatic actions inspired by the battle theme, which in the Master of the Field is combined with the nuptial theme, according to a pattern common to many popular celebrations all over the world.

According to Toschi's theories,[2] the struggle between the two opposite factions repeats the contrast of winter vs. summer which recurs every spring, and results in summer's victory, and which in societies based on agriculture all over the world has a particular importance within nature's annual cycle. The opposition of winter vs. summer gave origin in Italy, and particularly in Tuscany, to the tradition of epic sketches, short dramatic actions called Maggi, because they took place in the month of May (*maggio* in Italian), and which later gradually disappeared. It may then not be by chance that both the Madonna delle Milizie and the Taratatà take place in May.

A Carnival Pantomime with a Knight: The Mastro di Campo

Let's examine the celebrations that interest researchers who look at traditions from an anthropological viewpoint.

The *Mastro di Campo* (Master in the Field) is a pantomime that has been acted in the main village square in Mezzojuso since the 17th century. Nobody is surprised by the numerous oddities happening and everything is justified by the particularly permissive atmosphere of Carnival, which is the time for joy and transgression before Lent, forty long days of fasting and mourning that start immediately afterwards and which in the past used to be strictly observed. It is useless to ask the local people the reasons for the actions put on stage: the inhabitants of the town have never raised such a question; that is the way the pantomime has always been represented, they like it and have fun.

The event starts around 2 p.m. with a short farcical parade of people wearing 15th-century costumes: the so-called king and queen, followed by the baron and baroness, the master of ceremonies, and various court dignitaries. Up to about thirty years ago all the female characters were played by men, a detail that recalls all forms of theater in the past—from ancient Greek time to Elizabethan age—when it was not proper for a woman to act. Then follows a knight in love with the queen, the Mastro di Campo, who wears a curious red mask and shows off on his horse. The fact that he is a knight armed with a sword has suggested to numerous experts the connection of this celebration with the puppet shows. Pitrè reports that in the past a celebration very similar to this one was performed also in Palermo in the Albergheria district. The knight begins his attempt to conquer the "castle," represented by a framework where the king and the queen are supposed to be at a ball. He has the help of the so-called engineers who with gigantic compasses measure the square in order to decide the proper strategy for the attack.

Recent studies have denied the "historical" explanation of this strange farce that found a likeness between this celebration and the story of Bernardo Chiabrera and Queen Bianca of Navarra, which really took place in 1412. At that time Bianca, after the death of her husband, King Martino the Young, refused to concede the Regency of the Kingdom to Chiabrera, count of Modica, who asked for her hand in order to win her resistance. On the 12th of January, Chiabrera attacked the Steri Palace in Palermo to find Bianca, but she had been warned and had fled with a barge to take refuge at Solanto, a few kilometers out of the city. The story goes that Chiabrera, terribly upset for not being able to find the queen, would sniff at her empty bed exclaiming: "Yes, I have lost the partridge, but I still have its nest!"

But there are a few major differences: Bianca hated Chiabrera and found him a disgusting man, while the queen in Mezzojuso really likes the knight who is pursuing her and is trying to climb the "castle" with a ladder against the king's opposition. Every time the king turns his back, the queen smiles at the knight and tries to attract his attention by waving her handkerchief among general laughter. There are so many important differences with real history, that Antonio Pasqualino considered such a relationship nonexistent.[3] In my opinion, it is not so important to establish the nature of the relation of the farce with the historical facts, but it is highly significant that such a link has indeed been operated, though often half consciously, by the people or by the local learned men. This history-making process, common to many popular celebrations all over the world, is fundamental and masks the original reasons for the fight that tend to fade from memory.[4] I personally witnessed a type of armed dance during a trip to Guatemala in 1978. Some people belonging to a native ethnic group were wearing blonde wigs and were impersonating the Spaniards that arrived in Guatemala with Pietro de Alvarado and conquered it in the 16th century. Obviously some Spanish people had blonde hair and that must have impressed the native people, who still remember that after so many centuries.

In Mezzojuso there are many other apparent "oddities," for example the arrival of Garibaldi and his *picciotti* (boys), a presence added in the 1920s, certainly before 1926, according to the description given by Ignazio Gattuso.[5] The introduction of Garibaldi in this context is totally anachronistic since he arrived in Sicily in 1860 and actually visited Mezzojuso in 1862. Someone must have thought it was a nice idea to add the participation of the Hero of the Two Worlds, as he is called, since he also fought in South America, and now he arrives every year to complicate a little the scene of this fascinating Sicilian tradition. At the deafening rhythms of the drums, Garibaldi's boys start fighting with swords against the Saracen guards of the castle, impersonated by young men with their faces painted in black, which brings us back once more to the *opera dei pupi* (puppets opera), as the puppet shows are commonly called. According to Pasqualino, the Mastro di Campo's struggle is revolutionary and can thus easily be associated with the Red Shirts, or the Mille (the "one thousand"), as Garibaldi's boys are popularly called in Italy.[6] Garibaldi would thus represent the revolution, like the so-called group of the Foforio formed by individuals masked with dark skins who probably embody brigands, charcoal burners, and warriors, who are allies of the Mastro di Campo and who struggle to maintain an alternative order and overthrow the constitutional power of the king's court. In order to enforce the "law," the Foforio jokingly "kidnaps" wealthy people to ask for a "ransom," such as sweets or liquor. At this point another odd character arrives, the Diavolo Pecoraio (Shepherd Devil), covered with sheep skins, the true adversary of the hero, who is also his double. He is also characterized by rudeness and animal-like behavior and now and then falls to the ground seized by what looks like an attack of epilepsy.

At the end, after several exchanges of messages between the queen and the knight and written challenges between the knight and the king, the Mastro di Campo climbs the castle and the two contenders begin to duel. The hero is wounded in his forehead and defeated twice while the drums beat feverishly and the group of the Foforio has to help him while he is falling from the ladder. But it is only a temporary defeat: in the second part of the show, exactly as with most typical story patterns,

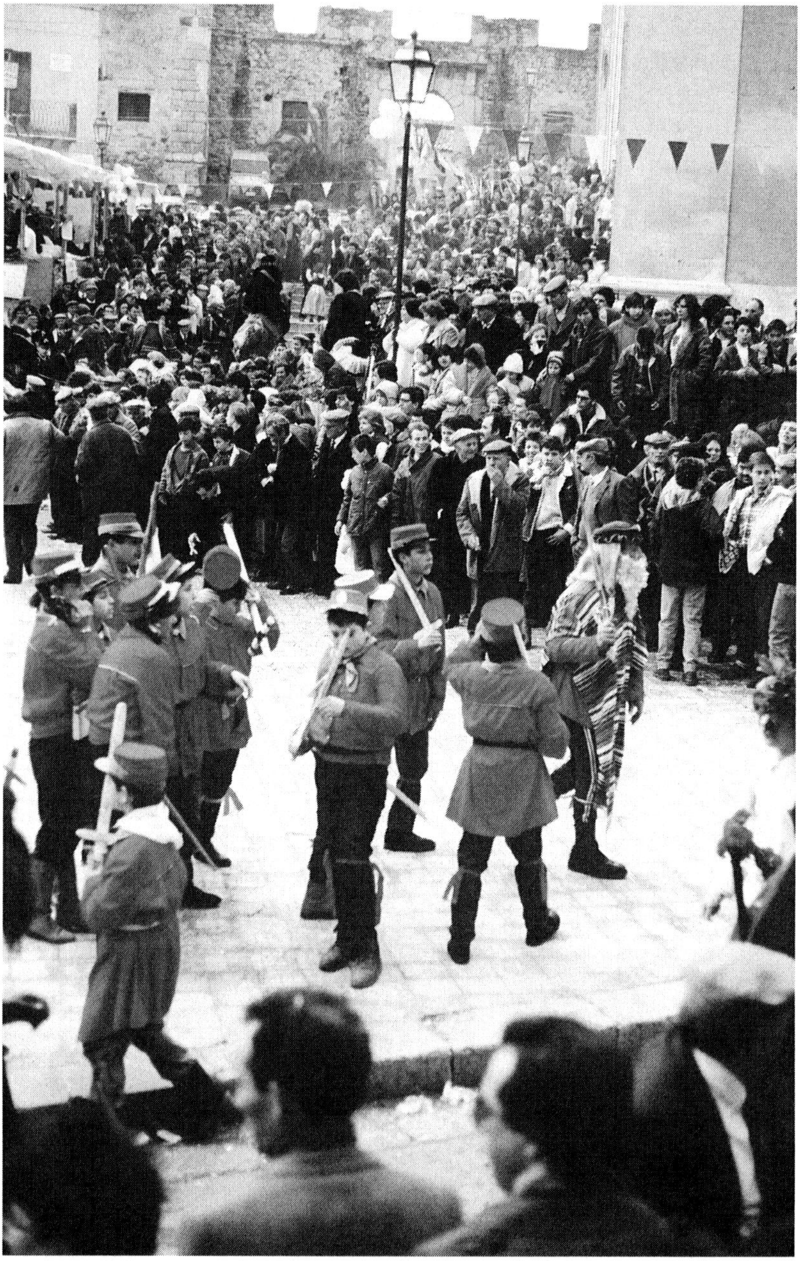

Garibaldi and his Red Shirts (popularly called *picciotti*, i.e., "boys") during the *Mastro di Campo* festival in Mezzojuso, a presence added in the 1920s.

the knight will rise again, recover from his wounds, come back with his army, sneak into the castle, take off his mask and finally win the queen's love, a happy ending for all, except for the king of course.

The feast of the *Mastro di Campo* may be subject to a multilevel analysis that goes well beyond the appearances: there is a fundamental opposition between the court (that is, the city) and the country, represented by all the others and especially by the *massari* (farmers) who symbolize the tie to the soil and to agriculture. There are quite a great number of people in the crowd who hand out products of the country (cheese, salami, bread) and start violent battles with oranges and sugared almonds, in Italian called *confetti,* a typical feature of many Carnival celebrations all over Italy. There is the cosmological and agricultural level of spring represented by the so-called gardeners, people crowned with green leaves who offer flowers to the ladies with the help of wooden extensible instruments called "ladders." There is the sexual level with the struggle between the two males (the knight and the king) and with the war the Mastro di Campo engages against the supernatural obstacles posed by the Shepherd Devil. And there is finally the level of magic with strange characters wearing pointed hats; they are called *maghi* ("wizards") and pretend to dig under the castle looking for the treasure (*trovatura* in Sicilian), which in reality is a big chamber pot filled with spaghetti dressed in tomato sauce with sausages, which they start eating with their hands and offering to the crowd. This last detail stresses the subversive and intentionally disgusting nature of Carnival.

After an interruption of a few years due to an accident that occurred during the 2008 celebration, the *Mastro di Campo* is enjoying new popularity in Mezzojuso, where young boys never stopped playing in the streets wearing a red mask and acting as a knight fighting against Saracens, and where the expectation of the *Mastro di Campo* celebration is similar to the eager anticipation people experience for the important events in life.

Dancing with Swords and a Holy Virgin in Arms

In Casteltermini in the Agrigento Province, the swords for the Holy Cross celebrations are clanging, in memory of a historical fact:

the finding of a cross three miles from the town, which was immediately considered a miracle. The strange letters incised on the cross have been interpreted in various ways: some faithful believe they indicate that the cross was used as an instrument of martyrdom during the persecutions of Christians imposed by the Roman Emperor Decius who ruled between AD 249 and 251.

This celebration has his most intense moment with the Taratatà dance, which is performed with swords and takes place on the last Sunday in May. The strange movements of the dancers can remind us of a typical Arabic dance called *fantasia;* according to Toschi, once again the original reasons for the fighting are the pagan propitiatory rites for the fertility of the soil. The Christianization process probably used the story of the cross to mask the eternal conflict theme: the opposition of summer vs. winter. It is not coincidental that many celebrations of ancient origin, such as the Christian Easter, take place in the spring: after winter, which means darkness, death, mourning, and grieving, we must hope and believe that summer will be coming, a concept of basic importance that is common to all agricultural societies in the world where seasons play a pivotal role.

The Taratatà sound of swords and drums (the name of the dance is obviously an onomatopoeia) can remind us of the puppeteer beating his clog on the stage during the battle scenes in the puppet shows.

On the same days of May in Scicli, a beautiful baroque town in another little known corner of the island in the Ragusa province, the statue of the Virgin of the Armies (*Madonna delle Milizie*) is riding her beautiful white horse. She looks almost like a reincarnation of Bradamante, the female Paladin who is a heroine of the Sicilian puppet shows. In Pitrè's time (the end of the 19th century) the statue, which probably is the only armed Holy Virgin in the world, was carried on the shoulders of the faithful up to the shrine of Donnalucata, nowadays in ruins. He adds that this celebration used to take place on the eve of Palm Sunday, while now, as already mentioned, this festivity and the Taratatà are both celebrated during the last weekend in May.

The most interesting moment is the Sacred Representation that reenacts the arrival of Saracen pirates in 1091: when the ship called *Stambul* (corruption for Istanbul) comes threateningly close to the coast, the arrival throws the Norman inhabitants of the castle into panic. The large crowd watching the show intensely sympathizes with

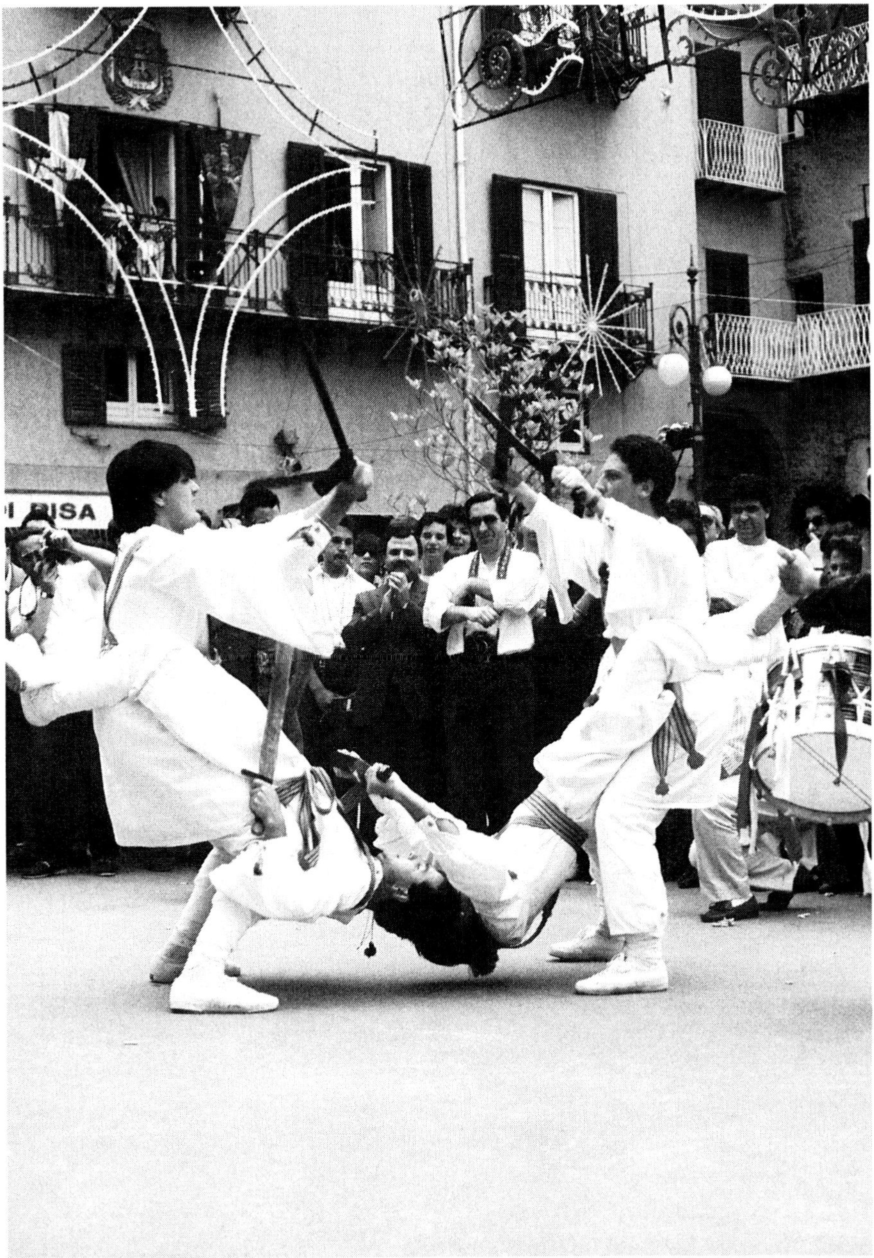

Dancing with swords: the Taratatà festival in the town of Casteltermini in Agrigento.

the Christians in this moment of extreme danger which certainly was quite real for long centuries. Count Roger and the Saracen leader Bel-Kan have a famous argument at whose end the two opposite armies start fighting on the platform that has been raised in the middle of the village main square. The Christians are about to be defeated when the *Madonna delle Milizie* is carried on a wheeled vehicle into the scene of the action. She can thus intervene in the Christians' favor; riding her white steed with a sword in her hand, she is accompanied by the music of the band, an intensely blue smoke and the blasting of many firecrackers. The fighting on stage stops, and all the actors kneel down thanking God and the Virgin for the miracle.

Many celebrations in Sicily are traditionally accompanied by the eating of specific foods that are eaten only on these occasions. Cannoli and cassata, two of the world famous Sicilian sweets, were originally eaten only for Carnival and Easter respectively, until they became so popular that they are now available all year, except for summer when the climate is too hot for ricotta cheese, which is the main ingredient of both. It is interesting that for the *Madonna delle Milizie* festival the specialty is called *testa di turco* ("Turk's head") quite cogently with the Christian vs. Saracen theme, which accompanies as a *leit motif*, all that regards the chivalric tradition in Sicily. It is a giant puffy cake filled with custard and chocolate, whose shape is meant to resemble a head surmounted by a turban. In his book *L'Antico Carnevale nella contea di Modica* (Old Carnival in the Modica county),[7] Serafino Amabile Guastella refers to a cake called "Turk's head" that used to be eaten in Modica, not far from Scicli, on the last Sunday of Carnival; several other towns in Sicily have cakes that may be quite different from each other, but all have names that have something to do with Turks, Arabs, or even Ethiopians, and all have in common the vague resemblance of a turban, and sometimes the color of a Muslim's darker skin. Eating these foods originally meant eating, and thus eliminating, the enemy. It's the same reason why Jewish people during Purim festival eat a cake called *Amman's ears,* and this is the way found by a Sicilian mother (more precisely, my mother-in-law) during World War II in order to neutralize those who were keeping her husband away from home: "In Sicily in 1943—remembers my husband, Giovanni Matranga (class of 1939)—for years we had been eating only very dark bread done with who knows what legumes; my mother would make gingerbread men with that dough, and would tell me they represented Hitler and Mussolini. She told me to eat them so that my father would come back from the war, I ate so many of them, that he did come back from the war."[8]

Chivalric Stories with Drums and Bells in Monforte San Giorgio

The town of Tortorici in the Messina province was very famous for its foundry that provided bells for numerous Sicilian churches. Two of them are still tolling today in the church of St. Agatha in the nearby town of Monforte San Giorgio. Both towns are nested in the Peloritani mountains, which run parallel to the northern coast of Sicily; they are not far from each other by air, but travelling from one to the other by road requires long detours since they are in different valleys and many mountain roads are only dead ends.

Every year from January 17 to February 5 these bells were used to narrate the Normans' arrival and their conquest of Sicily in the 11th century, a saga described in all possible media; storytellers would narrate it, puppeteers would perform it, painters would paint it on the sides of Sicilian carts, and so on. Twice a day for twenty consecutive days, at 6 a.m. and at 7 p.m. drums and bells (*tammuriniata e campanata*) would play together for about half an hour to offer an unusual musical homage to St. Agatha, who is the patron saint of the town. Every day 25 different rhythms would suggest the messenger announcing the arrival of Hauteville leaders, the trotting of horses, the pace of the camel on which, according to the legend, their leader Count Roger was advancing, and finally the Saracens' retreat.[9] Perched on the bell tower flogged by the wind, the last two interpreters of this old tradition, Piero Catanese at the drums and Giovanni Giorgianni at the bells, watched by a couple of boys who wanted to learn this refined art, would take out a musical script that, they said, was quite reduced compared to the past when over a hundred rhythms were available, and which would flood the valley with sounds that could be pressing, cautious, turbulent, and finally triumphant.

From their homes the inhabitants of the town would listen silently to this fascinating serenade without words, called Katabba: several etymological explanations have been tried for this mysterious term, either from Greek *katabasis* (descent) or from Arabic *qataba* (large meeting). Even the presence of these two instruments has been interpreted as the hundredth proof of Sicily's diverse souls: the drums would represent the Arabic heritage, the bells the Christian one.

In recent times the Katabba has acquired a renewed popularity because elements have been added that did not exist in the past, such as the parade in Medieval costumes and the showing of flags. The drums and bells rhythms, unfortunately, are losing importance.

• Four •

The Puppet Shows

The Sicilian Puppet Shows in a Nutshell

The tradition of the Sicilian puppets had its origins in the middle of the 19th century when small theaters in Sicily started to present chivalric stories. The repertory referred to the legendary deeds of Charlemagne and his Paladins, the shows were held daily and the entire story lasted two years.

Besides the Carolingian tales of the *Matière de France,* medieval French literature offered another repertoire of chivalric stories called the Breton cycle, better known in the English-speaking world as *Stories of King Arthur and the Knights of the Round Table.* As already mentioned, the Breton cycle was known in Sicily; there are stories of King Arthur painted in the ceiling of the Steri Palace in Palermo (1370) and in two Sicilian blankets of the 1400s, belonging to the Bargello Museum in Florence. However, in the puppet shows that became extremely popular in Sicily from the 1840s on, the Carolingian cycle was the only one represented in the two-year series of daily shows. King Arthur may have never been so popular because he was judged to be too intellectual and interested in love rather than fighting, and for this reason Orlando and Rinaldo became the Sicilians' favourite heroes: "Orlando is bringing pasta to our table," the puppeteers would say.

Between two long cycles, the puppet master put on brief cycles of one or two months with completely different repertoires and characters—for example the stories and adventures of the bandits Testalonga and Guarnaccia who, like Robin Hood, were considered "heroes" and were believed to steal from the rich in order to give to the poor. Other shorter cycles had stories from Shakespearian tragedies like *Romeo and Juliet*, stories of Garibaldi, of St. Genevieve and of St. Rosalia, the patron saint of Palermo who, according to legend, descended from Charlemagne.

Contrary to what normally happens nowadays with most puppets and marionette plays, Sicilian puppet shows were not considered comic or particularly suited to children: the traditional public who attended the daily shows were adult males, attending every single night and participating passionately in what happened on stage. They believed the shows depicted true stories and they were keenly interested in the characters' destinies. Chivalric stories were very important for the traditional public who thus expressed their love for the heroic; that is why people violently inveighed against traitors with scurrilous language. Women, therefore, preferred (or were expected) to remain at home and only attended stories of a religious nature. Chivalric stories were so popular that they started to be painted on Sicilian carts. Men, of course, were also the cart drivers and cart makers.

Action consisted of raging battles and fierce duels which became the high point of every evening's puppet theater performance. The clanging of swords on the metal clad armor of the marionettes was augmented by the rhythmic stomping of the puppeteer and his crew.

The puppet theater afforded conditions for a thriving craft activity. The puppeteer himself more often than not was a many talented craftsman who, in addition to manipulating and making the puppets (the word *puparo* originally denoted just the person who made them), knew how to paint the backdrops, the sceneries, the stage settings and the playbill posters displayed outside the theater publicizing the performance. The *puparo* (literally "puppet maker") was then not only handling but also building the puppets: he would sculpt the wooden heads and model the wonderful metal armors. The making itself of the puppet called for a considerable familiarity with sculptural art and metal work; it was the puppeteer who dedicated himself to such activities while his wife made the costumes.

Puppets from Palermo are much smaller (80 cm) and more

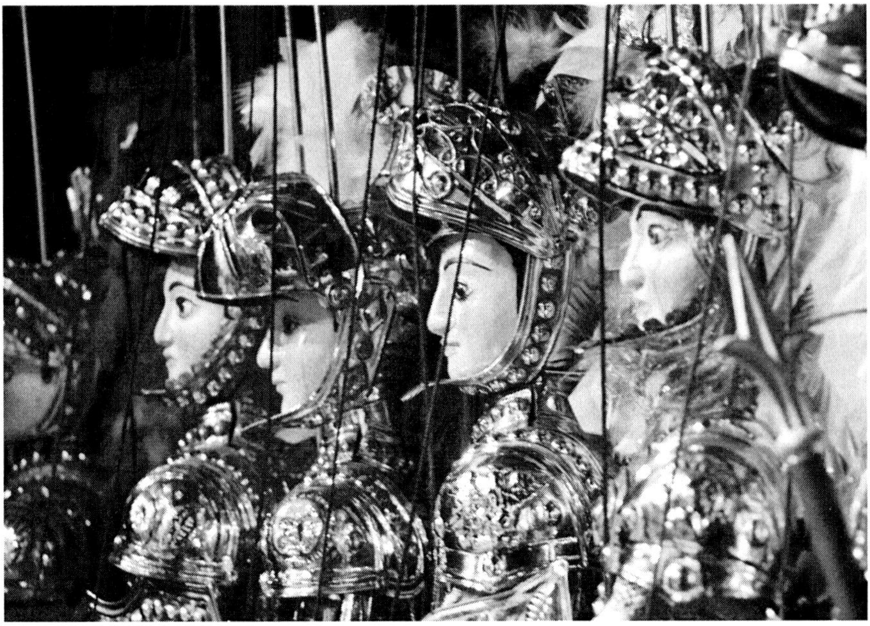

Christian Paladins, Palermitan puppets of the Franco Cuticchio theater.

maneuverable than the ones from Catania (120 cm). Consequently the theaters in Catania were larger and addressed a more sophisticated public. On the other hand the theater in Palermo is deeper and it allows the representation of even three duels at once, and the show has a greater level of improvisation.

The *puparo* used to put all the good puppets on his right, and the evil ones on his left. Indonesian shadows (*wayang kulit*) are similarly divided by the puppeteers (*dalang*) into good ones on the rights and bad ones on the left, even if there was not any direct connection between Sicily and far away Oriental cultures. As in fables and rites of passage, in these adventures, similar to those of ancient gods and heroes, there are a series of tests, each presuming that the Paladin has overcome the previous one. The fundamental opposition was between friendship, strength, astuteness, faith and honor (Orlando and Rinaldo) on one side, and betrayal (Gano di Magonza) on the other. The martyrdom of Orlando was compared to that of Christ. Rebellious barons like Rinaldo are poor adventurers, resourceful and cunning, not very respectful of legality but always fundamentally loyal, and for this reason greatly admired for their shrewdness. Orlando instead, even if loved, was judged too faithful to the king up to the point of stupidity. To make him more human, he is always represented cross-eyed, a strange detail existing only in the Sicilian puppet shows.

Each puppet was perfectly recognizable to the audience from the coat of arms on their helmets or shields. Facial lineaments, clothing and armature were strictly codified with distinctive features: the members of the *Magonzesi* (*Mayence* in French) clan wore beards, the shields of the Saracens bore a crescent and so on. The puppets were almost looked upon as flesh and blood creatures and objects of considerable fetish attraction.

Saracens were also characterized by turbans—a threatening aspect—oriental clothes, darker skin, bent swords, pointed helmets, and big moustaches. Even today in several Islamic countries like Iraq or Jordan most men wear moustaches as a sign of virility. The Saracens of the Sicilian puppet shows are strikingly similar to the so-called "Moors" sculpted on the Porta Nuova ("New Gate") in Palermo, built in 1535 to celebrate the victory of Emperor Charles V over the Muslims of Tunis. The Moors represent the Muslims portrayed with their arms tied or cut in a sign of submission to the Spanish power.

The Sicilian puppet shows took from the French and Italian chivalric poems the presence of female knights among the armored puppets; for Bradamante, the most famous female knight, a special armor was made, which was suited to the body of a woman. (In the appendix of this book there is a short guide to recognize some of the most famous characters.)

In addition to the individual puppet character themselves, each theater had a myriad of other characters, monsters, animals, angels, devils and so on. Each theater was also equipped with large quantities of material that included the whole gamma of playbill-posters and stage sets for the basic cycle of the Paladins of France and for other shorter cycles. The theater and all that it contained was referred to with the overall term *mestiere*, the "work that we do."

The *pupari* did not use any scripts, but only rough outlines of every single episode, called *copioni*. They were patiently handwritten in copybooks, considered the precious containers of all their knowledge, and jealously handed down from father to son. They did not have the characters' dialogues, but only the main facts and they were

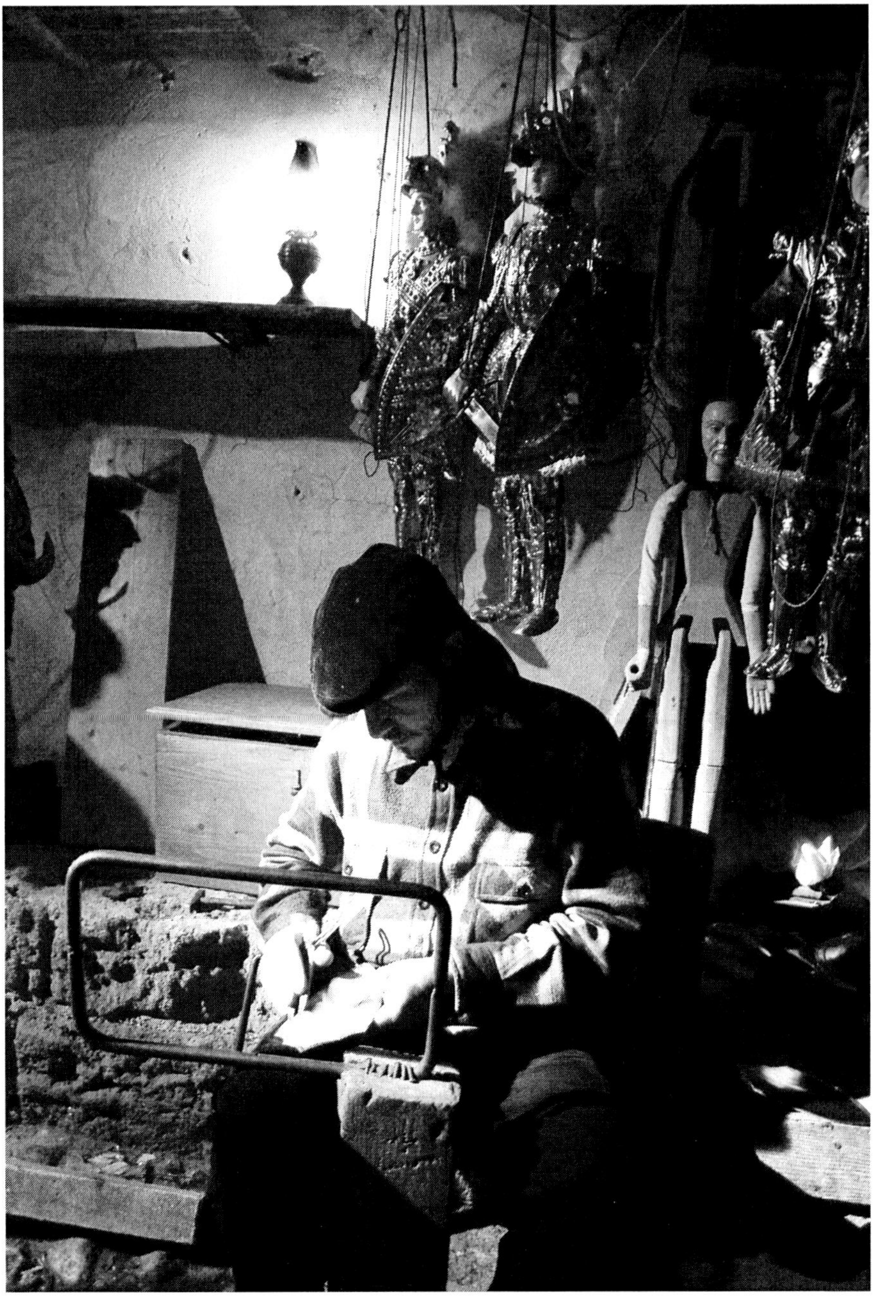

A builder of Palermitan puppets. The *puparo* (literally "puppet maker") was not only handling but also building the puppets: he would sculpt the wooden heads and model the wonderful metal armors.

divided into acts (normally three acts for each evening, each divided into two scenes). The experienced *puparo,* however, knew everything by heart and seldom looked at the *copioni,* as he only needed to consult them in order to have a few brief notes in hand to remember the most difficult names or the most complicated scenes.

For economic reasons, the musicians who originally accompanied the shows were replaced by small player-pianos or barrel organs, which are still used by the puppeteers active today. Musical overtones changed according to the type of scene represented and are mostly adaptations of famous operas: the so-called "Christian march" (that is, the *ouverture* of the William Tell opera) is played during the council the emperor (or Christian leader in general) calls in order to meet his best knights and decide which strategy to use against the enemy, while the so-called Turkish March accompanied the Saracens' analogous meetings. Two melodies composed specifically for the Sicilian puppet shows, the "battle" and the "complaint," were particularly appreciated by the audience. All battle scenes are accompanied by the rhythmic beating of a special clog on the stage and the puppeteer uses *macchine di scena* (stage machinery) to obtain the sounds of rain and wind. In recent times puppeteers have used more new special effects to obtain smoke or fire, in order to increase their appeal to the public.

The *pupari* realized that the public needed to relax after the great suspense of the show and they used to improvise short sketches in dialect concerning facts that had occurred in the neighborhood, which are called *farse.* Perhaps the *farse* go back to the *vastasate* of the 1700s (stories of *vastasi*, that is "laborers" in dialect), which derived from the *Commedia dell'Arte.* The only written text of a *farsa* that we have is *Lu curtigghiu di li Raunisi* (Sicilian for "The Courtyard of the Aragonese"). The public laughed because they recognized themselves in these puppets without armors called *paggi,* and particularly in the famous couple Nofriu and Virticchiu. If someone had had the electricity cut off because they could not pay his bill, that evening the puppeteer would improvise a *farsa* about it; everybody knew who he was talking about, and everybody laughed. The puppeteer would often go around the poorest districts of the city in order to get inspiration from episodes of real life that could become the subject of the *farsa* in the evening's performance.

After shutting down because of World War II, the small puppet theaters re-opened even if the short cycles were almost completely abandoned. The real crisis arrived with the opening of cinemas and the advent of television in the 1960s. Some puppeteers, Mancuso for example, tried to attract the public coupling their show with an 8-mm film. It was only a temporary stage after which many of them, but fortunately not all, sold their "trade" (*mestiere*), which consisted in the theater together with all the puppets, backdrops, instruments for the building of the puppets and play bills. At the beginning of the 1970s there wasn't even one theater regularly open in Palermo. Today there are more than twenty puppeteer companies active in Sicily.

The late Prof. Antonio Pasqualino, author of one of the most important books on the Sicilian puppets,[1] purchased several puppet theaters with all they contained in the 1960s and founded the International Puppet Museum in Palermo in 1975.

Puppets or Marionettes? The Opera dei Pupi *and the Sicilian Dialect*

Even if the Sicilian puppets should really be considered marionettes since they are operated from above and not with hands, they are normally called puppets in English to assimilate to the current Sicilian term *pupi* (which means "dolls"). The puppet shows are called *opera dei pupi* ("opera of the puppets") in imitation of the contemporary melodrama that raged among upper classes at the time puppet shows started to attract crowds among the lower classes.

The most important source for the *pupari* was the already mentioned book by Giusto Lodico that, together with other similar publications, was printed around the middle of the 19th century and had enormous success. The *puparo* tried his best to imitate the literary language, deriving it from Lodico's book and various chivalrous texts published toward the middle of the 1800s, adorning it with stereotyped phrases. This type of language is defined as "courtly popular" because of the frequent dialect expressions that the *puparo* or storyteller could not help interposing to the story in his attempt at copying literary language: many words were taken from Sicilian dialect, and many others were utterly invented. This type of language is somehow similar to the language used on similar occasions in other parts of the world, for example during Serbian and Croatian storytelling, which was described by Albert Lord in his book *The Singer of Tales*.[2]

The narration that accompanies the stage action is then declaimed for the most part in the standard Italian of passages excerpted from the above mentioned romances of chivalry, a stately language far removed from the dialect spoken daily by the youthful members of the audience, even more removed than that of say, Tennyson's *Idyls of the King*, from the everyday spoken idiom of the children of Appalachia. Because most puppeteers had very little education, this language is interspersed with dialectal terms and it's full of grammatical mistakes.

The Sicilian dialect, and all the other Italian dialects, from the linguistic point of view, are really different languages, since they are not mutually understandable. The only one that is quite close to standard Italian is the Tuscan dialect, from which the national language is derived. Tuscan became the national language thanks to the importance of the writers Dante, Petrarch and Boccaccio (14th century). Before them, important poets at the court of Frederick II of Swabia (13th century) in Palermo wrote in Sicilian dialect, which could have become the national language if the Tuscans had not done better than our poets.

As one might expect, the Sicilian dialect has many words borrowed from Greek, Arabic, French, and Spanish, due to the different peoples who ruled the island over the centuries. Today Sicilian is quite "polluted" by standard Italian and few people now speak the pure dialect. School teachers and parents (especially middle and upper class parents) seek to prevent children from using Sicilian by saying it is "bad language." In northern Italy the dialects are not so stigmatized, so people often switch from dialect to Italian without feeling ashamed. The arrival of television in the 1960s taught everyone in the country at least to understand, if not to write and speak, Italian properly. Sicilians who emigrated to America are often speaking a much more archaic kind of dialect, as it always happens when people are not in contact with the motherland anymore, detached as they are from the natural evolvement of the language. For the same reason American English has some more archaic features than British English.

The Climax of the Sicilian Puppet Shows: The Famous Legendary Battle of Roncevaux

The Sicilian puppet shows had an extensive and well assorted chivalric repertory. I have chosen to analyze the particular episode of the Rout of Roncevaux because all puppeteers without any exception indicated it as pivotal in the cycle of the Paladins of France. Already in the 19th century the Sicilian ethnographer Giuseppe Pitrè observed this phenomenon, and thus described the particular attitude of respect the audience held during the evening when Roncevaux was put on stage:

> I have never seen the Paladins' death without being deeply impressed by the audience behavior. It's rare, extremely rare for the audience to keep such complete silence as on that night. Sadness is on everybody's face; every single word that spectators exchange is spoken in an extremely soft voice in sign of respect for the place and for the sacred and solemn moment. Even the snack seller coming into the theater between acts does not shout, does not yell, does not even whisper. As soon as the angel appears to the dying Rinaldo di Montalbano, or when the archbishop Turpino blesses the count Orlando, everybody takes off his hat as they do on the evening of Good Friday for the procession of Dead Christ. Actually between Jesus Christ's procession and the Paladins' death there is so much similarity that I couldn't think of anything so much alike. Both representations are equally magnificent, mournful, heartbreaking.[3]

This comparison between Roncevaux and the Passion of Jesus Christ became almost obvious common place. The twelve Paladins, re-incarnation of the Twelve Apostles, betrayed by a reborn Judas, that is Gano di Magonza, were exhaling their last breath in front of extremely enthused spectators who, in order to see them that night, were willing to pay a price even double than normal. Starting from Pitrè's observations, Antonino Buttitta has reinterpreted the episode of Roncevaux stating that the famous battle would satisfy a need for rational justice which is innate in humankind. The holocaust of the Paladins, like the sacrifice of Jesus Christ, would represent the restoration of order and the beginning of a new life:

> Pitrè's words establish a strict connection between the Passion of Jesus Christ and one of the main and essential functions of the narrative legend of the Paladins. He stresses the value that its theatrical representa-

> tion had for the traditional audience satisfying some of their deepest ideological needs. The Holy Week celebrations have the function to restore the year cycle from *caos* (disorder) to *logos* (order) through the ritual repetition of God's Death and Resurrection which happened so long ago. Likewise, the representation of the Paladins' death, always ending with the triumph of Good prevailing over the forces of Evil, would make equal and just at a mythical and ritual level what in the real life of listeners was neither equal nor just, and would rationalize what in their experience was permanently threatened by the upsurge of irrationality.[4]

Beyond and beside any possible scholarly interpretation, Roncevaux held an undoubtedly deep emotional impact on the traditional public. Here is what Pitrè reports hearing from two habitual spectators on October 14, 1878: "What can I do about it? How many times have I listened to this? And every time I can't help feeling overcome and shuddering...." "And am I not the same as you? Seeing the best Paladins over there? Trapped in an enclosed place? I feel like crying...."[5]

In order to carry out my research, I read the cantos of the *Morgante*, which regard the pivotal battle of Roncevaux, and the corresponding chapters of Lodico's book, the former composed in the 15th century by Luigi Pulci, the latter compiled in the 19th. Then I listened to many recordings of puppet shows putting on scene this famous episode. The goal was to see how a certain episode has been "transplanted" from chivalric literature into the Sicilian puppet theater.

Roncevaux in Lodico's Book

In the mid–19th century, Giusto Lodico assembled his famous *Storia dei paladini di Francia* (History of the Paladins of France),[6] which was printed and published in installments in Palermo between 1856 and 1860. As already mentioned, this book enjoyed enormous success and immediately became a real "Bible" for storytellers and puppeteers alike.

As he stated in the preface of his long work, Lodico did not invent anything; he only wrote a "summary" of approximately 3,000 pages, re-elaborating in prose a great number of chivalric poems. His tone is intentionally impersonal; he never intervenes or comments on facts in the first person or mentions his own role in the narration.

There are remarkable differences between his book and Luigi

Pulci's *Morgante,* which was his main source for the Rout of Roncevaux, mainly because Lodico's work lacks any intrinsic literary value. Reading Lodico is important though, in order to determine its influence over the tradition of the puppet theater, since none of the puppeteers or storytellers ever read the *Morgante* or any other Medieval version of the Rout of Roncevaux. As a consequence, analyzing Lodico's work becomes mandatory for whoever intends to study the repertory of the puppet theater.

On the whole, the plots, the main features and even small details of the stories in Lodico's book are quite faithful to the *Morgante.* Ricciardetto's and Rinaldo di Montalbano's deeds are introduced with the technique of the *entrelacement,* a characteristic of all chivalric narrations, which involves "interlacing" stories of different characters happening in different places at the same time. (For example: "Now let's leave those two over there, while we take the time to tell about the pilgrim we had left...." "Now let's go back to Rinaldo who was coming along with his companion Ricciardetto....") It seems that both Pulci and Lodico realized that the connection of Rinaldo's stories with Roncevaux was a bit awkward and felt the need to introduce them with special conventional expressions. Like Pulci, Lodico uses comparisons as literary devices ("giving him two blows in his chest, he opened it like an apple," p. 295; "the paladin cut him as if he were a frog," p. 286), but they are fewer in number and lack the humorous and vivid immediacy of the *Morgante.* Lodico is often hasty and superficial: entire duels are bluntly reduced to one single line: ("Having Rinaldo meet Gallerano, he deprived him of his life," p. 297); his tale is often filled with obvious, commonplace statements ("A fox never lacks slyness," p. 279).

Lodico's use of the language is neither particularly inventive or brilliant. There are several highly erudite words, and the linguistic register is rather monotonous: the narrator and all his characters talk with the same learned and refined manner, at least in the author's intentions. The characters' personalities are not well outlined. Astarotte is not present at all, so the humorous vein is practically absent.

There is very little reference to the classical world of antiquity, which in Italy is always associated with a good level of education: Lodico was an elementary school teacher without having received official certification, and also his readers had received very limited (if any) schooling. There is no attempt to use the Latin language either in the religious context or with Pulci's highly literary intentions. What prevails is the didactic and edifying vein: those chivalric deeds were to be an example of dazzling glory for the readers and consequently also for the puppet theater audience. There are frequent obvious commonplace assertions such as "Goodness at heart is rewarded both by people and by God" (p. 286).

The greatest majority of the audience were very superstitious people and the key role of magic in the chivalric tales was one of the most important reasons for their success among lower classes who always operated a peculiar syncretism between magic and religion. As it was to be expected, there is a strong and important presence of charms and supernatural signs in Lodico's book. When Gano di Magonza concludes his infamous pact with Marsilio, thus betraying the French Paladins, "the sky frowned, with terrifying thunderbolts, and the carob tree started to sweat blood.... A lightning exploded, whose powerful blast left them speechless for a quarter of an hour" (p. 278). Magic can be either good or bad; Malagigi (*Maugris* in French), the Christian sorcerer, intervenes with apparitions and prophecies; Ricciardetto "remembered that on another occasion Malagigi had predicted that, because of Gano's betrayal, the Paladins of France were to die in Spain.... He had a dreadful vision, and in his dream he saw Malagigi laughing and touching him with his right hand to reassure him" (p. 283).

An angel appeared to Rinaldo, who had become a monk, to encourage him to take up his weapons again and fight. Another angel appeared to Orlando as he was dying after blowing his horn too hard in order to ask for Charlemagne's help. The lengthy discourse the angel gives Orlando in the *Morgante* is reduced to one single line: "Orlando, said the angel, do you want to live or to die?" (p. 296). There is no existential crisis here; Lodico is the interpreter of a world whose values are permanently clear cut, sound and clear.

His readers did not discuss basic and fundamental truths, they only wanted to see them represented on stage and to identify themselves with the characters of the puppet shows. Here is how Buttitta explains this point in his work *L'opera dei pupi come rito* (The puppet show as a rite): "The puppet theater did not offer a show in the sense we commonly think of this word, rather it was a ritual ceremony where the public could find their own perception of the world, and meditate over it."[7]

Lodico's prose is plain and basically monotonous: he describes a world of clear oppositions (good vs. evil), which lacks any shade of chiaroscuro in between, in spite of the fact that, like in the *Morgante,* cruelties are committed equally by Christians and by Saracens. Strangely enough, Lodico goes back to a feudal and nationalistic vein which Pulci, who had written so many centuries earlier, had already abandoned. The epic feeling that is innate in the masses made them identify themselves in the book of this humble elementary school teacher, and the triumphant and pompous atmosphere of the upcoming Italian nation, which was to be unified in 1861, must have contributed to increase his influence and success.

Roncevaux on the Stage of the Sicilian Puppet Shows

The archives of the International Puppets Museum in Palermo keep several recordings of puppet shows that have the Battle of Roncevaux as their subject. The chart below lists the puppeteers who put up each show, the year and the city in which the recording was done, and the catalogue number in the above mentioned archives:

Puppeteer	*Year*	*City*	*Catalogue Number*
Giuseppe Argento	1969	Palermo	128–129–130–131–132
Emanuele Macrì	1967	Acireale	175–176–61
Napoli Bros.	1977	Catania	201 e 34
Gesualdo Pepe	1978	Caltagirone	48 e 49
Argento/Cuticchio/Mancuso	1980	Palermo	58

The last show on the list is a coproduction of three Palermitan puppeteers, each of them accompanied by all their sons for a total of 10 persons, a circumstance that had never taken place before.

First of all we should point out that these versions follow a fixed pattern, since all of them have Lodico's book as a common source. Only Macrì from Acireale is a bit different because, as he had stated in a recording done by Antonio Pasqualino, he was following directly the text of the *Chanson de Roland* after some professors from the Sorbonne and Grenoble Universities had remarked that the episode of

Rinaldo and one of his brothers, Ricciardetto, as reported by Lodico, did not exist in the French poem. Macrì had thus decided to modify his performance and do something really "classic" and pure. All the other puppeteers include Rinaldo and Ricciardetto in the Roncevaux episode.

As already mentioned, three Palermitan puppeteers accompanied by their sons were able to work together even if among several disputes: this would have been impossible without a common source, the famous Lodico's book. The three father puppeteers would often be angry at each other when they did not agree on how to proceed. They would argue for more than half an hour on how to do a certain scene: Argento said he was using his father's written outline (*copione*), and Cuticchio as a retaliation would say he was working on books (that is, on Lodico's book), meaning he was working with real facts, not invented like the *copione*. Their sons would then try to convince them to make peace, telling them that the modern public was not interested in who had been hitting a certain blow to whom, or other minor details like these, as it happened 50 years earlier, and they would reiterate that they had to place all their efforts on the quality of the acting, the skill of the maneuvering, and on the speed of the action. Amid all of these quarrels, the show did take place though, and this would not have been possible without the amalgamating influence of the famous book.

In spite of these similarities, there are remarkable differences among the shows examined. First of all the length of the show is not the same: Argento's version was done in two consecutive evenings as it would happen in older times, while all the other puppeteers had succeeded in condensing the subject in only one evening, thus adapting themselves to the taste of the modern public.

As far as the musical accompaniment is concerned, the traditional barrel organ is used in all the Palermitan shows; the music is almost joyous and very fast, which contrasts sharply with the tragic character of the episode. On the contrary Gesualdo Pepe is accompanied by a small orchestra of three people who are introduced at the end of the show. This used to be very common before the puppeteers, for economical reasons, would opt for the cheaper and more practical barrel organs.

It's interesting that in Pepe's show there is also symphonic music and even Neapolitan music accompanied by mandolins, which do not sound very well suited to the show. In any case this does indicate a concern for novelty, a desire for innovation, and an understanding of the importance of the soundtrack, which older puppeteers would not have had, even if one might not agree on the chosen type of music.

The Napoli brothers in Catania used the recording of Wagnerian music and of sacred music, especially in particularly pathetic scenes. The puppeteer Macrì from Acireale never used music for an episode supposed to be too tragic. With his typical tendency to try and arouse laughter in the public, Macrì throws a short joke in Sicilian even during the intermission between one act and the next, when he says that the puppeteers need some free time in order to "take the dead to the cemetery." Macrì's interpretations are full of sighs, hiccups, screams and beastly cries (at a certain point a Paladin tells his enemy: "Your blood is not better than a beast's"), which together with the extremely slow pace contribute to the particularly static and tragic atmosphere of the show. The Napoli brothers proceed very slowly too, and this contrasts sharply with the brief and plying scenes of the Palermitan shows, where the battles are raging more and more, the beating of the heels is faster and faster, and the war cries stunning (especially Argento's): it really seems that there is a huge army on the stage.

Before Macrì's show, there is a long introduction of all the characters and a prologue explaining both what had happened in the previous episode and what was about to happen in the next. The great number of the puppets and their huge size (in the Catania province the puppets are 120 cm tall) implied a bigger size of the theater, which in Eastern Sicily would often contain between 200 and 250 people, while Palermitan theaters held no more than one hundred. In Catania the same theater would often be used for other types of show, and actors were often also puppeteers, like Giovanni Grasso, who used to be very famous in the Catania area. One of the consequences was that in Catania both the puppeteers and the public belonged to a slightly higher social class than in Palermo.

In Argento's show it is Charlemagne in person, not the puppeteer, who provides information on the previous episode during the initial scene of the council with the Paladins. Since his version of Roncevaux is divided into two evenings, at the end of the first installment the puppeteer gives a summary of the second. The choice and the sequence of the scenes, especially the initial and final ones, vary considerably:

contrary to what all the others do, Argento includes the scene of Gano's betrayal and his agreement with the Saracen King Marsilio, and the Napoli brothers have Orlando's wife Aldabella entering the scene in despair over his death.

Argento starts in the middle of the action with Charlemagne already quite close to Roncevaux, while the Napoli brothers start with the pivotal scene where Charlemagne and Gano are listening to the sound of Orlando's horn while they are playing checkers. When the Christians had been treacherously attacked at Roncevaux, Orlando blew his horn (which was called Olifante) to ask for help from Charlemagne but had waited too long and had blown it too hard, and his veins burst causing his own death. As a result he had not died because of an enemy sword, and this was very important in the spectators' eyes, as we shall see. Like for Achilles who had to be hit in his heels, the only part of his body not protected, they had to find a very special way for Orlando to die.

The participation of the public is much greater for the shows of the Palermitan theaters than the Catanese. If it were not for the clapping halfway during Macrì's show, one would think the recording had not been done live. The Italian language used by the puppeteers is generally acceptable; already gone were the times when the puppet shows were famous for the puppeteers' colossal grammatical mistakes.

Even in this respect there are remarkable differences between the eastern and western parts of the island. In Catania it seems that improvisation was already out of fashion: the Napoli brothers had been using for years texts written by Nino Amico, while Macrì seems to be reading too, as his Italian is quite correct and even sophisticated. He uses courtly words, certainly derived from Lodico's book, and several comparisons ("as cruel as a tiger"), which are a typical feature of chivalric literature. The linguistic register is always very high, with an extensive use of the subjunctive tense, which in Italian is usually dropped by people with little education, and there are no grammatical mistakes. This was not the case in the interviews recorded by Prof. Antonio Pasqualino and by the film director Angelo D'Alessandro, where Macrì's Italian is very poor, but in both cases he still does not abandon his heroic and solemn tone, which apparently was one of his characteristics. In the interview he is telling the story of his life, starting when he was only two months old and was miraculously rescued from the ruins of the 1908 earthquake, which totally destroyed the city of Messina and killed the rest of his family. He was later raised by his adoptive father, Mariano Pennisi, who was a puppeteer, and he substituted him one evening taking all his courage *con un cuore d'asino e uno di leone* ("with a donkey's and a lion's heart," which means "having a chicken's and a lion's heart at the same time, but taking all his courage in his hands"); in these words we can feel the same slow and solemn rhythm used for Orlando's death. On these occasions he was not reading though, and his grammatical and syntactical mistakes are innumerable.

It is significant that Macrì is the only puppeteer who in the interviews above mentioned does not indicate Rinaldo as the public's favorite character. His personal predilection was for the loyalist Orlando rather than for his rebellious cousin Rinaldo. This may be due to the traditionally conservative inclination of Acireale, the only Sicilian city that in 1860 voted against the annexing of Sicily to the newly unified Kingdom of Italy; as a consequence the entire country would be ruled by the Piedmontese Savoy Royal House. In his exasperated ideal of chivalry, Macrì would extend the concept of chivalry to the knights' wives as well: upon his moment of death, Oliviero reminded Orlando to tell his sister Aldabella not to cry, because the wife of a Paladin should never surrender to grief.

Argento makes several grammatical mistakes during his show; for example, he uses the conditional tense instead of the subjunctive and distorts or invents words altogether. Argento has very vague geographical notions; for example, Rinaldo went to Armenia to retire and become a hermit, as if it were not too far from the Pyrenees. Similarly Orlando had blown his horn in the Pyrenees and Charlemagne was supposed to be in Paris when he heard it.

In Palermo the puppeteer, usually with one person helping him, would manipulate and interpret the puppets at the same time, while in Catania, because of their heavy weight, this was not possible, and speakers and manipulators were always different people. Macrì's interpretation, because it was mainly based on his voice, really sounds like a type of epic storytelling—you can't even hear the movements of the puppets on the stage, which on the contrary is quite clearly heard in Palermitan shows. Macrì knows quite well how to adapt his voice to the various characters, the traitor Gano di Magonza utters real asides like the characters of a Shakespearian tragedy. "From Roncevaux nobody will come back, he says, I sold them to the Saracens and not much later I will be the king of France," thus denouncing his nature of villain even in his low tone of voice. It may be worth mentioning that also in operas the *basso* (which in Italian means "low") traditionally interprets the villain's part. Being able to adapt one's voice to the character is a typical attribute of the Sicilian puppeteers in general: for example the voice of Rinaldo in Argento's show is very different when he is a hermit in the cave and when he decides to come back to action and intervene in the battle.

In Cuticchio's show, which has a remarkable mixture of traditional features with modern ones, the characters are rather problematic and obey peculiar strategic and political rules. Astolfo doubts Gano's sincerity and Gano is very cunning when he prepares his trap for the Christians, and then with good strategic policy he states that what most interested him is to have been able to conquer a people to Christendom. These features are already present in many chivalric poems.

All the shows stress the religious nature of the Paladins' sacrifice. Macrì points out that the battle took place in 778 on August 15, which is the day of the Catholic celebration of the Assumption of the Holy Virgin. Repeating a Christian and literary recurring theme, the earth trembles and a terrible thunderstorm bursts after Orlando's death, as it happened after Christ's death. It is not by chance that his soul is taken to paradise by an angel. Argento defines Rinaldo as "filled with grace." In the Palermitan co-production Orlando is thirsty like Jesus Christ on the Cross, and we could give many more example of this.

In Palermo the shows are improvised, not read like in Catania, and this circumstance creates a much greater immediacy; in Cuticchio's show the atmosphere is immediately produced by the numerous yells that accompany the entrance of each Paladin into the scene. Argento's show is put together on the spot: in the recording you can hear his instructions to his helpers about which puppet they should pick up and about what to do with him/her: the stage director is participating actively and immediately.

As it is traditional in Catania, the Napoli brothers' show has a female voice, but even in Palermo the three puppeteers' version is entrusting to a woman with the voice of an angel who in the end is asking Orlando if he wants to live or to die and who pronounces the final words, which are the same as in Cuticchio's show: "Covered with flowers your pale face/I take with me your soul to paradise."

These two lines rhyme in Italian and give the Palermitan shows a slightly comical tone, which is totally absent in the eastern part of the island, because they are pronounced with a strongly ironical tone and they are immediately followed by the public's laughter. Even one of the sins Orlando confesses to the Archbishop Turpin on the moment of his death, that is to have left his bride a virgin, stresses the semi-comical character of some parts of the Palermitan shows, which is confirmed by the immediate feedback of the public. Today this tendency toward the burlesque is much stronger than in the past.

For the Napoli brothers, the scene of Orlando's choice whether to live or to die is stretched quite considerably, while in Palermo it is much shorter. In Catania the lack of action in general makes the show similar to a sort of meditation upon Roncevaux, sealed by Rinaldo's crying over Orlando's body.

Up until the arrival of the crisis, the interest of the traditional public was always very strong: the story was always the same, but the habitual spectators did not miss one evening, and some of them, in order to be sure to have a seat, would bring a sandwich to the theater, as in 1971, when D'Alessandro realized the TV show *The puppet opera.*

The Rout of Roncevaux in the Ideology of the Opera dei Pupi

From the recordings of interviews kept in the archives of the International Puppet Museum in Palermo several observations can be made about the different interpretations given to Orlando's death in the Rout of Roncevaux. Some puppeteers (for example Macrì) think blowing the horn was the only possible way for him to die because he could not be killed by anyone; others (like Argento) think it was a shameful death because he did not die fighting.

The death of Orlando had assumed a particular significance in Medieval European literature. In Antonio Pasqualino's book *Le vie del cavaliere* (The Knight's Roads) the author analyzes the causes and the consequences of this episode and of others similar to this in other French Medieval poems (*Chanson de Roland, Chanson Guillaume,*

Chanson d'Aspremont), in the chronicle of the Archbishop Turpin, in Scandinavian texts, beside Italian Medieval songs (*cantari*) and romances. Pasqualino points out that the death of Orlando is part of the recurring theme of the glorification of the personal sacrifice of the hero.[8]

The so-called Rout of Roncevaux was actually a secondary historical episode that was transformed in a sort of Holy War: what really happened in Roncevaux was that some Christian warriors, probably Basques, attacked the French arrière guard who had been invited by a Saracen leader to come to intervene in Spain against other Muslims. The sanctification of the war, which ended up with barbarian warriors disguised as Medieval knights, resulted in a total misinterpretation of the principles of the Christian faith and consequently in the glorification of the religious war and of the irrational sacrifice of the hero. Orlando, like Vivien in the *Chanson de Guillaume* and the antihero Aumont in the *Chanson d'Aspremont,* is a victim of his own excessive pride, that is of his *hybris,* which prevents him from crying for help by blowing his horn and which drags the entire army into total destruction.

The consequences of the death of the hero are not a total and definite disaster like the effect of the death of the antihero Aumont, after which the Saracen army will not be able to go back into action. The defeat of the Christian army, on the contrary, is only temporary and only after Roncevaux law and order will be restored, either thanks to a mature hero like Carlemagne or by means of a new hero like Amerighet, who was the son of Arnaud de Bellande in a Venetian version of the French poem. These "heroes of the impossible loyalty," as Pasqualino defines them, indicate in a certain sense the decline of chivalry which entrenched itself behind extremely strict rules and which would lead directly to the choice of a losing position. In the same way, as Pasqualino points out, in the Aspromonte poem, Ruggero di Pisa, who in the Italian romances would become the founder of the Estense family who was to rule over Mantua during the Renaissance, repeatedly gave up the advantages obtained in the war, as if he were fighting in a tournament.

The *Opera dei Pupi* has stressed the desire of Orlando for martyrdom instead of the gravity and the danger of his carelessness. As already mentioned, Macrì was proud of following directly the original

Chanson de Roland, even if he was not aware of the differences with the various Italian versions of the story. He entirely shared the warrior ideals that became a fundamental characteristic of the *Opera dei Pupi,* and which were thus described by Pasqualino: "Even today when we would think that the prevailing pacifist ideals would devaluate the war theme (and many puppeteers have Charlemagne or Orlando pronounce various speeches against war), the most persistent element of the legend of the death of Orlando keeps on being the religious extolling of the death of the warrior, a far away echo of the religious ideology against barbarians, enlivened by the Medieval ideal of the glorious heroes."[9]

I listened to some recordings of interviews released in the 1960s by the puppeteers Macrì and Argento to Prof. Antonio Pasqualino and to his wife Janne Vibaek (catalogue n. 290 & 292 in the archives of the Puppet Museum). It was exactly the defense of one's own honor up to the extreme point of what fascinated Macrì as it appears from this conversation:

JANNE VIBAEK: "And now we have arrived in Roncevaux. How come Charlemagne did not realize Gano's betrayal?"

MACRÌ: "If God had sensed Judas's betrayal, would he have ended up on the Cross? As the proverb says, 'God should save me from my friends, because I know how to save myself from my enemies.' It was Gano, the one who betrayed them."

VIBAEK: "But why did the Paladins trust Gano? Because Charlemagne, we know that, has always taken Gano's defense, but the Paladins hated him...."

MACRÌ: "The Paladins did not fear death; for them death did not exist. They had orders to go to Roncevaux, and in order not to be considered cowards, when Oliviero invited Orlando to blow the Oliphant (that was the name of his horn), in order to ask for help from Charlemagne, Orlando refused to deprive the Paladins of their honor. I learned from birth that death saddens only cowards, and we never were such. We must face our enemies and punish them for their wickedness. As soon as the Paladins entered the valley, they were surrounded, they were overpowered by the enemies, they had not realized they were in such a number. There were 300,000 Saracens on one side and 12 Paladins with 20,000 soldiers on the other. What could they do? They surrounded them in a circle and they killed them, they massacred them; then Orlando blew his horn, which caused his death, but he was not killed by the sword of the enemy."

> VIBAEK: "Do you think Orlando did the right thing by not blowing his horn sooner?"
>
> MACRÌ: "He did well not to blow it, yes, so that he did not dishonor the Paladins. Otherwise the Saracens could have thought they were afraid. The Paladins were never afraid of anyone or anything. It was an act of courage on Orlando's part."
>
> VIBAEK: "Did Orlando do the right thing even when he told the angel he wanted to die?"
>
> MACRÌ: "No, here I don't agree. I disapprove of that because when Christ was nailed on the Cross of the Golgotha, the Eternal Father did not ask him if he wanted to live or to resurrect. We humans must die, all of us who are people of the earth must die. What is life, madam? It's a gift that we must return, in one way or another we must return it; this addition of the angel asking Orlando whether he wants to live or to die, I think it is useless. Orlando had to die because on the stage he represents a man like any other and he must give life back to Whom so generously gave it to him. Do you agree on this?"
>
> VIBAEK: "I agree."

These words confirm our impression that Macrì was deeply fascinated by the pure heroism of the Paladins. He must have had a very strong character, not willing to lean towards any compromise. We can notice many mistakes of grammar, lexicon, and syntax, which confirm our impression that he would not have been able to improvise his acting in a language as perfect as the one he used during the shows. In the interview there are several sentences without a beginning or an end, subjects that do not agree with the verbs, words used inappropriately, or mixed with Sicilian, and so on (which is necessarily lost in the English translation).

Macrì's views are for many respects opposite to Argento's, the latter considering the death of Orlando the only possibility for him, since he had been left alone:

> PROF. ANTONIO PASQUALINO: "Was Orlando right when he decided not to blow his horn?"
>
> ARGENTO: "Well, in my opinion, yes, at the beginning he was right since he had won all the battles in his youth and, besides, he always felt the best, so he was ashamed to blow his horn and ask for help, and then he preferred to die and not to ask for help from Charlemagne who was six miles away down the valley."
>
> PASQUALINO: "Was he right telling the angel he wanted to die?"
>
> ARGENTO: "Well, since all his mates and his relatives had died, he wanted to complete the total disaster with his own death."

PASQUALINO: "What does the public think? Do they get very emotional about it?"

ARGENTO: "On this occasion they certainly get emotional, they really cry for Orlando's death, which is definitely not a glorious death, definitely not."

PASQUALINO: "So you think it is not a glorious death?"

ARGENTO: "Yes, because Orlando does not die in the battle; from what Lodico says, he does not get killed, first of all because he is invulnerable, then because he had magical weapons, and in the end he was alone and desperate, frantic because he could not avenge the Paladins, and then he prefers to die...."

Of course we can imagine that Macrì would have been very surprised to hear Orlando's death defined as not glorious or utterly shameful. Macrì considered not having been hit by the enemy's sword as a sign of glory and distinction. On the other hand, both puppeteers see close links between the puppet shows and life. For example Macrì declares to be willing to teach young people to consider the puppets as real men when they are on the stage and expresses his disappointment in seeing his efforts go vain and in being surrounded by indifference. His complaint is typical of older gentlemen always complaining about the current times:

MACRÌ: "You see these modern guys, most of them are superficial and are only able to catch a bunch of flies. I wanted to have them come to the theater in order to get them used to understanding what life really is, not only to learn about the puppet shows. I wanted to instruct these guys to manipulate the puppets as if they were real men, to build them and let them understand that puppets behind the scene are only wood coated with brass, but that on the stage they are real and alive men.... I wanted to succeed, but they cut my feet, and ... once I am dead, the world dies with me...."

Argento chose the betrayal of Gano to demonstrate that the changing fortunes in life are similar to the ones represented in the *Opera dei Pupi*.

ARGENTO: "For Gano's death the public intervenes because they see the end of a real traitor ... although also today there are similar ones ... terrible spies...."

PASQUALINO: "Like Gano di Magonza?"

ARGENTO: "Even worse! Maybe they keep apart, hidden, but they are real traitors, worse than him."

PASQUALINO: "There are always traitors...."

ARGENTO: "Yes, always traitors, there may be more now than in those times … because now there are more people in the world…."

PASQUALINO: "This may be the reason why the public is interested in these stories, because they see in the puppet shows the traitors that they see in real life…."

ARGENTO: "Exactly, they see them on the stage. It's something authentic, really authentic, what you see today in real life and in the theater, it will be like this until the end of the world. Gano was acting quietly and without danger of being discovered because he had Charlemagne's power behind him who was helping him, who would cover him and would warrant for him, and then he had the possibility of being able to…. He had the time of thinking it over and deciding how to get rid of his adversaries as soon as possible…."

From these words it is clear that the public of the puppet theater was watching on the stage stories that were somewhat similar to their own every day life experiences and this is one of the most evident reasons for the success of the puppet theater. As Prof. Antonio Pasqualino has well pointed out in his seminal work *L'opera dei pupi*, the opposition of loyalty/disloyalty is of basic importance for understanding the ideology of the Sicilian puppet theater and it can explain the persistent success of chivalric literature among common people and particularly the lower social classes.[10] The episode of the Rout of Roncevaux held a particular importance for the traditional public from this viewpoint.

The Puppet Shows as "Necessary Art" of the Sicilian People

Peter Schumann, founder of the Bread and Puppet Theater of New York, in 1968 referred to the Sicilian puppet show as a "necessary art."[11] He had previously called in this way his own theatre in order to distinguish it from bourgeois art that was "superfluous." What does this mean for Sicilian puppets and folk art in general? For example it was necessary to paint and decorate carts in order to protect them from the vagaries of the weather and to attract new customers at the same time. As for the choice of chivalric subjects, it should be pointed out that the tendency to transfer real facts and people into a mythical level is universal, and so is the opposite phenomenon, that is, for legendary events and figures to become real in the minds of people.

Puppet shows with chivalric subjects were once common in many parts of Italy, including Rome, Naples and Apulia; later on when Sicilians emigrated to different countries in the world they introduced them wherever they went, either leaving the tradition unchanged (in New York, Tunis, Buenos Aires) or giving it other characteristics (in Belgium). Chivalric tradition was then by no means unique to Sicily, but in Sicily it throve, always at the popular level, deepening and widening its roots much more than elsewhere.

There are many reasons why the legends of Charlemagne and his knights acquired such vast fame. They became emblematic of Sicily and René Bazin was puzzled by this popularity in the island since, in France, the interest in the stories of the knights had faded long before the 1890s.[12]

As already mentioned Sicily has known a great deal of impositions and vexations, but not the might of a power with which the Sicilians could identify. The historian Virgilio Titone stated in his *Storia, Mafia e costume* in Sicilia (History, Mafia, customs)[13] that a real Sicilian people does not exist, but only a series of people fighting against each other. In such a state of anarchy, the weak ones were not protected; their rights, when stated, remained on paper and never enforced in spite of the countless revolts. People were then looking for a kind of "personal" justice; this is one of the reasons for the beginning of the Mafia, according to old and recent researchers.

In 1886, in his book *La Maffia nei suoi fattori e nelle sue manifestazioni* (The Mafia in Its Aspects and Manifestations), Giuseppe Alongi described organized crime on the island, which he had dealt with as a policeman and highlighted the Sicilians' proclivity for personal justice rather than legal justice, which was normally felt as something alien and suspicious.[14]

Illegality and abuse of power have always been accepted as inevitable evils in Sicily. Shortly after the establishment of the unified Kingdom of Italy, two university professors and politicians, Leopoldo Franchetti and Sidney Sonnino, came to Sicily to conduct an unofficial investigation into the state of Sicilian society and published their research in 1876. Franchetti's report, "Condizioni politiche e amministrative della Sicilia" ("Political and Administrative Conditions in Sicily"), was an analysis of the Mafia in the nineteenth century that is still considered authoritative today, while Sonnino analyzed the tremendous lives of the island's landless peasants and described the illegality pervading every aspect of Sicilian life and the resignation of its inhabitants to this state of affairs.[15] The appalling poverty of the Sicilian peasants had also been analyzed by Salvatore Salomone Marino, one of the most important and authoritative ethnologists of the 19th century, in his well known book *Costumi e usanze dei contadini in Sicilia* (Customs and Traditions of Peasants in Sicily), published in 1897.[16]

In order to defend themselves from the abuses of power, the historian Salvatore Romano maintains in his *Storia della Mafia* (History of Mafia) of 1963 that lower classes could only choose between the Mafia, a sort of alternative law that detained power and assured order, and brigandage, which openly opposed the law.[17] Several outlaws had become brigands because they were rebelling against forms of injustice. As a consequence they had become extremely popular with the poorest people who transformed them into living legends. According to Romano, the spirit of the Mafia consists in the necessity, in order to fight against the violence and injustice whose victim one is (or can be), of using violence as a support and basis for one's own personal prestige.[18] In the Sicilian peasants' eyes, the Mafia "man of honor" was the one who knew justice and could impose it to the official power.[19] The brigand would not give in to the abuses of the unworthy. In spite of the means he used and the crimes he committed, he was attributed, while being persecuted and chased, superior qualities of a leader and warrior.[20] In Sicily the Mafia man and the brigand were equally admired. Both had in common the respect for religion and women, one's own mother in particular. Mafia essence and crime got confused; Franchetti stated several times he was not able to distinguish between the two.

The connection between chivalric tradition on one side and perception of the Mafia on the other, already suggested by Li Gotti in 1959,[21] was confirmed by Romano, who stressed that the identification or similarity of the Medieval itinerant knight with the brigand is historical and well documented.[22]

It seems obvious that for the Sicilian people chivalric stories represented their own tragic situation projected upon an ideal level. Isn't Rinaldo similar to a Sicilian Robin Hood, defending people who are weak and poor and rebelling against the authority of the State (i.e., Charlemagne)? The huge personal success of Rinaldo di Montalbano in the Sicilian puppet theatre, while he held only a secondary role in the *Chanson de Roland,* can be understood only if we keep this relation in mind. It is not a coincidence that the repertory of the puppet theatre evolved up to including stories of bandits like Guarnaccia and Testalonga, whom De Maria defined as "Rinaldo di Montalbano's apprentices."[23]

The swords of the Paladins were like Sicilian knives (*cutieddi* in Sicilian)—a bit longer than usual. Turiddu, the main character of *Cavalleria Rusticana,* was a modern Roland; the knights of Charlemagne were doing in the open and in a chivalric manner what the Mafiosi were doing in silent darkness, what every Sicilian male (and it is to be kept in mind that puppets shows were operated and watched only by males) would have liked to do in a strongly idealized vision of society. "The Paladins must not bend their knees in front of anyone!": showing a misunderstood "sense of honor," thus the puppeteer Macrì from Acireale would justify the greater stiffness of Catanese puppets compared to Palermitans. A connection between puppets and the Mafia was established by Alongi, who thought puppets were causing an increase in crime.[24] Precisely for this reason, the police prohibited the stories of bandits to be put on stage and Pitrè himself intervened to defend the puppeteers on this matter.

This art, which we have defined as "necessary," was adapted to any kind of topic. It was updated to almost contemporary times, up to include Garibaldi, the new modern Paladin, considered the real heir of Charlemagne, the war of Albania, and even the Spanish Viceroy Uzeda, transformed into a hero. In the religious sphere an extraordinary syncretism took place: the Holy Week and St. Geneviève were dedicated very popular brief series of shows; they even considered Rosalia, patron Saint of Palermo, a descendent from Charlemagne!

It's an art that achieved very good technical results: the puppets could move their eyes and mouth; the Palermitan ones could take the sword out of the sheath and bend their knees. The Manteo family, whose puppet theatre was for awhile very active in New York, was able to obtain particular special effects, like real small explosions, beheading of knights, blood shedding, and so on. It was an art that, at least in the first stage of its decline, did not surrender to technology and actually tried to use it: in certain towns where cinemas had not opened yet, the puppet shows were presented together with an 8mm film in order to attract customers, as the puppeteer Mancuso did in the 1950s.

In spite of its vitality, in the second half of the 20th century this tradition had to surrender to the wild consumerism that starting in the 1960s, Sicily embraced unconditionally in a way that often characterizes developing countries. Why should people be interested in the stories of Rinaldo when television was keeping them busy without even going out of the house? Why should the puppeteers' sons attempt to engage in an artistic job when they could make a much easier, but also much more anonymous and ordinary, living, as a doorkeeper at the City Hall or at the Courthouse?

Puppet shows were really a "necessary art" in the past, as demonstrated by many episodes quoted by Pitrè and other witnesses showing the intense emotional participation of the public. There were students who did not want to study in order to go and see the puppet shows, illiterate people who would nevertheless buy Lodico's book, fathers who would hire puppeteers to come to their houses in order to keep

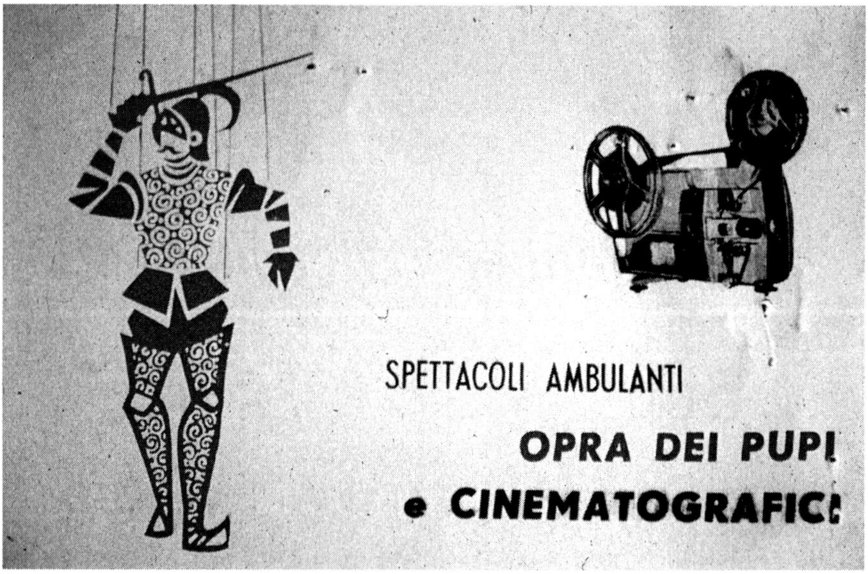

The visiting card of the Palermitan puppeteer Nino Mancuso in the '60s when he was offering puppet shows together with 8mm films in order to attract an audience that was starting to abandon the evening shows (Pasqualino International Puppets Museum, Palermo).

their children at home at night, people who would start a brawl in the street to demonstrate the superiority of one puppeteer over another one, *aficionados* who could not sleep at night and would wake up the puppeteer in the middle of the night in order to force him to free Rinaldo who had been left in a dark prison the previous night, and so on. Endless discussions were started among the public to distinguish what was fake from what "had really happened."

Hearing all this, it seems impossible that a few years of relative affluence would succeed in modifying one of the most typical characteristic traits of the Sicilian culture, a tradition that Pitrè, a little over a hundred years ago, judged timeless.[25] A prediction that has been, we are sorry to say, proven to be blatantly wrong.

The first symptoms of the crisis were already present at the end of the 19th century, as shown by the short story *Don Candeloro,* written by Giovanni Verga in 1894, whose main character is a puppeteer forced to move continuously because the public preferred vaudeville shows.[26]

Real crisis was still far away though, and it arrived with the advent of television in the 1960s, when most puppet theatres closed down. Some puppeteers like Nino Mancuso started to offer puppet shows coupled by 8 mm films in order to survive. In the last thirty years, thanks to the Association for the Preservation of Popular Traditions, which manages the International Puppet Museum in Palermo, there has been a revival of the puppet shows, and some of the children or grandchildren of old puppeteers have taken up the puppet art again, even if the public is very different, mostly consisting of tourists, students or local amateurs who do not and cannot attend shows regularly, but only every once in a while.

In February 2014 most of the Sicilian puppeteer companies still active on the island gathered for a ceremony held at the International Puppet Museum in Palermo and were awarded a certificate stating their belonging to this tradition, which in 2001 had been included by UNESCO on the List of the Intangible Cultural Heritage of Humanity. On the same occasion Rosario Perricone, director of the Museum, announced that the museum's website, www.operadeipupi.it, would inform tourists and amateurs about the times and locations of the shows.

• Five •

A Family of Puppeteers

Presentation of Girolamo Cuticchio and His Family

Girolamo

Born in 1933 he learned the art of manipulating and interpreting the puppets at a very young age and he opened his first theater in 1954. After a period of crisis during which he worked as a lorry driver, he started to work again as a full-time puppeteer in the 1970s, founding the Teatro Arte Cuticchio Company in 1975 and starting together with his children an intense collaboration with the International Puppet Museum in Palermo, which lasted until 2004.

Teresa

Born in 1960 and daughter of Girolamo, she collaborated since a very young age with her father's activity working at the cashier together with her mother and manipulating puppets and moving the backdrops. She organizes shows and makes costumes. Besides maneuvering the puppets, she interprets and gives her voice to the female characters. For several years together with her father and brothers, she actively worked for the realization of puppet shows in the town of Cefalù in the small theater which had been given the name of Corte delle Stelle and was well attended by students and tourists before its closing in 2010.

Franco

Born in 1964, and son of Girolamo, at a very young age he learned from his father the art of maneuvering and interpreting the puppets during the shows. An excellent manager of theater settings and builder of sceneries, he worked at the Biondo and the Massimo theaters in Palermo and on the building of the triumphal pageant which occurs every year for the festivities in honor of Saint Rosalia, who is the patron saint of Palermo. He builds the "soul" of the puppets, that is the wooden interior structure, and he is also a good carver of the puppets' heads. He has recently renamed their company Franco Cuticchio Figlio d'Arte and after some years of limited activity because of the lack of a theater, the company will start offering shows on a regular basis in its new location opposite the church of St. John of the Hermits in Palermo. See https://www.facebook.com/pages/Cuticchio-Franco-Puparo/236214673200496.

Giacomo

Born in 1967, and son of Girolamo, he is the stage director of the company and he also makes the puppets' armor. He manipulates and interprets the puppets, and he is actively looking for old and new outlines (*copioni*) of the puppet shows. He worked for the Biondo and the Massimo theaters in Palermo for a long time and also for the realization of the shows of several other theater companies. He is also a music composer and writes lyrics for songs.

Girolamo Jr.

Born in 1987, and son of Franco, since the age of 12 he has helped his father and grandfather during the puppet shows, and he is now devoting himself entirely to this activity.

Story of the Family—Girolamo as a Puppeteer's Apprentice

Puppets in the blood. Evening after evening, Girolamo attended the puppet shows in his neighborhood and, after the little curtain went down, he went up on the stage to hug and kiss his beloved Angelica whom he called his fiancée. It was 1936: Girolamo Cuticchio was only three-and-a-half years old, and he was already interpreting the little angel who was taking to Paradise, one after the other, the souls of all the Paladins. At the end of 1935 a puppeteer had opened his theater near where Girolamo lived with his family: every evening he watched that little guy who was not missing a single word of the daily saga, and he knew that the child could not wait to interpret those Paladins. The puppeteer would have liked to have little Girolamo next to himself, and he knew that he would have been ideal to give him a hand. The child was crazy about the puppets but, since he was so young, not even with the help of a stool could he have reached the belts hung above and across the stage that could have helped him to ease the weight of the puppets. Not even from the second wing of the theater could he manipulate the puppets; he would have fallen on the stage together with the puppet.

For a few years his master had to work with another apprentice who, however, did not have enough self confidence to actively participate in the show and feared having anything to do with the public. Another apprentice of the puppeteer was his sister who, as a woman, had to hide while she was entering the stage, and she was obliged to go to the theater hours ahead of time, so that nobody would see her. Her hair tied under a cap, wearing wide trousers under her jacket, she succeeded in going into the small theater without being seen by the inquisitive eyes of the people in the neighborhood, and thus without causing a scandal. The theater was not for women. She was fascinated by the show and spellbound by the adventurous deeds of the Paladins, and for a certain period nobody knew there had been a woman behind those colored curtains.

In the meantime the war broke out, so the puppets and all the material for the show had been stored in a garage, because the puppeteer had been conscripted in the navy. The Cuticchios, after a few months in Alia, a small village about 100 miles from Palermo, taking refuge from the heavy bombing Palermo was suffering in 1943, had come back to the devastated city like so many other Palermitans, and the master puppeteer had started offering the evening shows again in 1944. Little Girolamo started to play the barrel organ and to sell water and toasted seed snacks to the spectators. The master puppeteer still badly needed a helper and offered Girolamo bed and full board and a little pocket money to do that, exactly as it used to happen in all the artists' workshops from the Middle Ages on.

Girolamo, at the age of eleven, could not wait to start becoming a real puppeteer. Even if he was doing quite well in school, so much so that his teacher was willing to pass him directly from first grade to third, he had to work in order to help his father with the selling of fruits and vegetables, and he attended only one year of primary school. But what he had done in school was enough to allow him to read the written outlines for the shows (*copioni*) and the famous "book," that is the chivalric stories collected by Giusto Lodico, endless and authoritative source of information for all the puppeteers. Little by little Girolamo was able to find a dozen small puppets made of tin; it was only junk for tourists, but it was enough to establish a mini theater in the house of one of his friends. In such a way he was able to earn his own pocket money, his first income as a mini puppeteer.

A Puppeteer Is Born

In 1947 Girolamo had already been officially promoted as assistant puppeteer, and with his "master" puppeteer he would move from town to town in the interior of the island to always find new customers. In each place they stayed about one year, the time necessary to finish all the story, and then they would move on to find a new place. Finally at the end of 1948 a great opportunity happened: in the town of San Cipirrello his master was very sick and was not able to do the show. The public was disappointed and started to complain and to inveigh against the puppeteer who in the meantime had fallen asleep and was crouching in a corner of the small theater.

At this point Girolamo was perfectly able not only to maneuver the puppets, but also to do the so-called "preparation," which consisted of reviewing the subject of each evening show, reading the written outline (*copione*) of the story, and preparing everything that was necessary to do the show: backdrops, puppets, and so on. Girolamo took the opportunity with both hands. Reassuring the puppeteer's wife, who did not feel so sure he was up for the job, he invited a spectator who was particularly assiduous to be his assistant and started the show by himself. Talking in Sicilian dialect through Virticcho, the most typical character of the comical sketches (*farse* or *vastasate*) that accompanied the puppet shows, Girolamo said what everybody had already understood: "Well, dear gentlemen, this evening my boss is feeling very sick. Instead of him his apprentice, Girolamo Cuticchio, will present the show, and since this is the first time he faces the stage by himself, he hopes to leave all of you happy with it." Everybody laughed getting ready to listen and after only a few minutes they had already forgotten something new was happening behind the curtain: the warm final applause marked with a standing ovation the official birth of the new puppeteer.

Girolamo was still a teenager and he had asked his father to buy him a puppet theater, instead of a motor scooter as young people do today. He was so insistent that in the end he won. His father, with great perplexities, finally gave in to his son's persistence, and had his son "examined" by a "committee" of old puppeteers. "Now we shall see if he really has the knack for this job," he had concluded. As a test they had chosen *La morte di Milone* (Milone's death) for the difficulties that putting on stage this particular episode presents, and Girolamo had done quite well. At that point his father could not refuse any longer to fulfill his son's desire; he waited for a good bargain and, with enormous financial effort, he bought him the *mestiere* (job), that is, the theater with everything necessary for the puppet show: puppets, backdrops, sceneries, posters, and so on. He never regretted it, since Girolamo's shows went very well and, even if he was one of the youngest puppeteers in Palermo, they were always very well attended. It was 1954, his first theater was in Corso dei Mille in Palermo, and that was the beginning of his professional career.

Evening after evening the aficionados were always there and never missed the appointment with the usual two hours of fabulous adventures and of intense fighting, betrayals, love and magic. Women stayed at home: husbands, fathers, and brothers certainly did not want all those swear words that were flying around the theater to reach any delicate feminine ears. There was also a sort of "policeman," an old man who volunteered to do that job, and was watching that nobody would disturb the women of the puppeteer's family who would normally stay behind the counter, taking the money for the entry tickets. But some women were curious to access that forbidden place, so on Sundays the puppeteer would put on shows, called "special evenings," that were suited to families. There was an entire series of stories suited for that purpose: stories of St. Geneviève, stories of the bandit Musolino, stories of lovers like the unfortunate Tullio Frecciato, who had been condemned to die, and of his lover Adelaide, for whom everybody shed tears when she killed herself jumping down from the window. On those evenings no man would dare come to the theater without a woman, so as not to be mistaken for a crazy guy coming only to disturb women.

In the 1950s Girolamo took his theater to towns around Sicily. He let many boys come in to see the show without paying; others paid something "in nature" with eggs or bread pinched from their mothers' kitchens. In spite of this, things went well, so much so that his father in the winter gave up his job of itinerant vendor of fruits and vegetables in order to help him. Girolamo always had great success. In 1955 in the town of Mezzojuso in the Palermo province, he had been woken up in the middle of the night by a dozen distinguished gentlemen, the head of the local police and the town doctor among them, who forced him to put on stage a short show just for them. In order to see Orlando and Rinaldo in action, they were willing to pay quite well.

In 1958 Girolamo had in the meantime gotten married in Termini, a big town 30 miles from Palermo. His wife, Enza La Corte, belonged to a well-to-do family and she had had problems convincing her father to give his consent to the marriage: the main reason for his objection was exactly the future bridegroom's job, which Francesco La Corte thought was similar to the circus acrobats. But in the end Enza got what she wanted, and with the help of her mother who, like many Sicilian women, had a very strong will, and who had taken a great liking for Girolamo, succeeded in convincing her father. And from then on, like all the other wives of the puppeteers, for her husband's love, she would work as a theater cashier.

One day a small group of three old puppeteers decided to test him: "We heard you are doing pretty well. Let us see one scene of your choice," they said. The three puppeteers were Peppino Celano, Tano Meli, and Francesco Fiore—they were called the Spaniards. This nickname was certainly an indication of bad temperament, since the Spaniards of the puppet theater were the Saracens themselves, and they had very little to do with the nation we call Spain today. Girolamo chose the episode of the story of Cladinoro, who went around looking for Clarinda, Rinaldo's daughter. Just a few minutes were enough to have one of the puppeteers exclaim: "That was very very good!" and another one added that one day he would have done better than all of the other puppeteers, a prophecy that one day would prove true: in 1979, during a real tournament a jury of experts at the Sicilian Puppets Festival (*Rassegna dei pupi siciliani*), organized by the International Puppets Museum in Palermo, declared Girolamo the winner among all the other puppeteers, including the three who had tested him.

Crisis and Return of a Passion

Suddenly, immediately after the arrival of the economic boom of the 1960s, a crisis arrived under the form of a devilish object, the television, which kept people stuck at home or at the local coffee bar. Girolamo got discouraged and in 1960, for 180,000 lire (about the average monthly wage of an employee at that time), sold his puppets to a dealer from Porticello, who sold them to tourists. He started to work as a truck driver to support his growing family, and he thought he had definitely ended his puppet theater career.

But you can't give orders to your heart. Girolamo could not forget the first passion of his life, and from 1965 on he started to buy posters and backdrops from the famous painter Giovanni Salerno, who lived in a building in Via Colonna Rotta in Palermo, which had been abandoned because the fire brigades had declared it unfit for human habitation. He started to buy puppets again through monthly installments. He bought them from Luciano Bumbello and from Ciccio Sclafani, who were building puppets near the Capo market. He bought them from Paluzzo, called *'u marmuraru* (the marble cutter and/or vendor), who had his shop near the Chinese Pavilion. He bought the puppets from anybody who was willing to sell them. He would often go and visit Paolo Di Giovanni, a puppet builder who had chosen a very strange place that he used as *casa e putìa* (a common Sicilian expression for "workshop and living quarters at the same time"): he lived and worked up in a belfry of a church in Via Rocco Pirri, near the central Railway Station in Palermo. Even Girolamo's son, Giacomo, today an excellent puppet builder, would go up those steps years later in order to learn the job from this incredible person, who between one puppet and the next, would tell the terrible story of his wife, which sounded like a horror movie. Her husband, like all puppeteers, was often away and she had suspected him to be unfaithful, so she asked a woman who practiced magic to do something in order to take away the evil eye from her. The sorcerer inserted a needle into her head which caused her insanity. Paolo had kept faithful to her and he did not remarry; like the Baron in the Trees (in the novel *Il barone rampante* by Italo Calvino), he lived perched on that belfry and every Sunday went to visit her in the mental asylum.

For a short while all those puppets that Girolamo had with such effort put together again stayed silent, hung one next to the other over a staircase in his house in the town of Montallegro in the Agrigento province, where he had moved in order to work for the transportation of salt extracted from the mine of Cattolica Eraclea. He was working there in order to pay back the debt he had contracted for the purchase of his vehicle. From 1970 on, a double life started for Girolamo: truck driver during the day, puppeteer at night, a life that was tiresome but also rewarding. In the summer he would also offer bus transportation services for the tourists who were staying at the resort of Città del Mare, 20 miles from Palermo. Thanks to the local tourist office that offered him a free location for holding the puppet shows in the nearby town of Terrasini, these tourists became his first clients for the new puppet theater he had opened. The real connoisseurs knew his puppets were neither the best for quality nor for quantity and, because he did not have enough puppets, during some shows he had to "multiply" the puppets by reusing them for different characters by changing their heads. But the local *aficionados* would attend the shows in great numbers anyway, "because they liked how I would tell the stories," Girolamo says. When for the first time a really beautiful puppet, a Ruggero in full array, complete with a magnificent armor and colored feathers, arrived on the stage, the audience applauded for at least twenty minutes.

When he moved to the town of San Cipirello, Girolamo was authorized to use the bus he drove during the day in order to transport to a new residence, during the night, his theater belongings. The market required him to move quite often, and in 1975 together with his wife and the five children that had been born in the meantime (Teresa in 1960, Carmelo in 1961, Franco in 1964, Giacomo in 1967, and

Michele in 1970) he went back to the town of Termini where his wife's family was still living and where he could hang up posters to advertise the show exactly on the same hook he had taken it from in 1957: for almost twenty years, that hook had incredibly been left there, stuck in the exact same place in the so-called Strada della Verdura (Vegetables Street). It was an almost tangible sign of the real and final return of Girolamo to the art of puppets. And the new theater was finally inaugurated on March 23, 1975. From that moment on, everything was easier; in 1974 he even succeeded in selling his truck, and that meant being able to dedicate himself full time to the puppet theater. Around that time something happened that can be useful in giving an idea about the emotional involvement the puppets were able to arouse in the public. In Termini Imerese a group of angry people obliged Girolamo, threatening to beat him up if he refused to burn the puppet of the traitor, the dreadful Gano di Magonza, the personification of Evil itself and who was directly responsible for the death of the best Paladins of France. Girolamo could not do anything except obey the orders of these hot heads and, after that unusual *auto da fé,* he had had to buy a new puppet.

In those years the most important event was meeting Professor Antonio Pasqualino, who often came to see Girolamo's shows together with his wife Janne Vibaek and their children. Pasqualino, who has been the most important expert on Sicilian puppets in recent times, had just inaugurated in Palermo the International Puppet Museum, which now bears his name after his death in 1995, and is the leading institution for the preservation of this tradition. Girolamo started a very fruitful collaboration with the museum which lasted for more than twenty years. At the end of the 1970s the Cuticchio family moved to downtown Palermo and, with the suggestion and encouragement of Prof. Scaletta who was teaching at the elementary school in Bagheria, they started a very intense collaboration with schools in the entire Palermo province. While in 1960s the headmasters of schools would not have been pleased by the sight of a puppeteer in their institutes, but now many schools were requesting the shows.

Originally when a puppet theater started to offer shows in a town, it stayed there for about a year, the stage was fixed to the walls, and the entire business of putting up the theater required about two weeks. Now Girolamo and his family were constantly moving and Girolamo invented a type of stage that could easily be dismantled and reassembled again, which is still used by the company for their shows.

They still had the problem of transportation. At first Girolamo used for this purpose a little Vespa that he had purchased with the money of his wife's dowry (even if she would have preferred to invest it in a refrigerator), then he bought a van with a kitchenette, and finally a real caravan. The first travelling show was offered at the Fiat factory in Termini Imerese. "For schools we always chose one with a particularly fast pace, for example *The siege of Paris,* and every child would pay 300 lire," Girolamo remembers, "but I often had to ask for some money from teachers. Usually I parked the caravan in the school's courtyard, giving a tip to the custodian, but in a school in Caltanissetta the doorkeeper said he could not accept it because he saw the harsh life we were living."

Little Puppeteers Grow Up

The caravan with everything it contained must have looked something like the famous cart of Zampanò (the itinerant street performer interpreted by Anthony Quinn in Fellini's 1954 film *La strada*). Still Girolamo was happy and his children were growing up—the puppets were their brothers, friends, and guardian angels. The children were forced to change school every year, and they still remember how their wealthier school mates looked at them with a certain disdain, while the poorer ones held them in great consideration. Endless afternoons were devoted, after completing their homework, to copying the notebooks (*copioni*) that other puppeteers had loaned to their father. The puppeteers were very jealous of their *copioni*; it was believed that all their knowledge was contained in them, but every once in a while they lent them to each other as a sign of great respect and consideration.

Girolamo offered puppet shows in the public squares without asking for tickets, but only for voluntary donations, and in the summer he would perform also in camping sites in different towns: in San Nicola l'Arena, in Casteldaccia, in San Vito Lo Capo. He had been neither a painter nor a puppet builder, but he did everything possible to allow his children to learn these arts. Giacomo at the age of only nine years would very often go by himself from Trabia to Palermo by train and spend a lot of time in the workshop of Paolo Di Giovanni in order to learn how to build a puppet. A few years later many other trips would be necessary for his apprenticeship as a painter of posters and backdrops in the workshop of Giovanni Salerno. Even Teresa gave a hand to her father and brothers when their assistant was late.

During the show Franco, still too young to manipulate the puppets, would go up a small stool and, from a hole in the main curtain, would watch the audience who, according to what was happening, would rejoice for the death of the traitor Gano or shed warm tears for the death of their favorite Paladins. And when he, exhausted, would fall asleep on the benches, his father would take him home in his arms. The same hole in the curtain was used by Girolamo to check that the audience was behaving correctly towards his wife and his daughter who were present in the theater. Teresa still remembers the sudden outburst of his father when he caught her turning a bit too often towards a spectator who was insistently watching her.

The life of puppeteers was certainly very uncomfortable. One evening in Caltanissetta Girolamo slept in the truck and left his son Franco, who was only twelve years old at that time, sleeping all alone on the desks of the school where they were to offer a show the next day. It was so cold and there was so much silence: the young boy used the posters for the puppet show as blankets and fell asleep hugging the puppets in order to find relief for his loneliness.

Girolamo was very strict about cleanliness and tidiness in the theater—everything had to always be in perfect order. The armors were continuously polished; it was not necessary to say anything about it, as one glance was enough to let the children understand something had not been done properly. He never stopped being concerned about his children's training: the "lessons" were taught both at home and on the stage. One of the most complex and difficult maneuvers to learn was the so called "squadron," which precedes the real battle. Beside the various types of maneuvers they also had to learn the particular techniques of recitation. As the Cuticchios say, the recitation is the most difficult art of the puppeteer's job.

For all three of Girolamo's children, for a certain period of time being a puppeteer was a second job, but after the founding of the Teatro Arte Cuticchio Company in 1989 all their efforts concentrated in one direction: Teresa gave up a secure job with the Sicilian Region, which is what many Sicilians dream about, and Giacomo quit his job as a stage director in the Massimo opera theater in Palermo.

Two Artisans' Workshops in Giacomo Cuticchio's Memories

Giovanni Salerno, a Painter with a Good Deal of Disorganization

Every morning the late Mr. Salerno arrived in his "studio," which was only an abandoned house that had been declared in danger of collapsing by the local police. According to what he proclaimed himself, the head of the police gave him the keys so that he could be able to "earn his bread, i.e., his living."

In the morning, when he arrived early enough, it was almost impossible to recognize him. I could not believe my eyes. He would show up in his best clothes. I remember him always with the same navy blue suit, carrying a stick, putting up the air and the elegant pace suited to a real gentleman. He was a low stature person, but dressed like that he looked at least twice as tall.

After having gone up the very steep external staircase (which needed careful handling, otherwise you could end up in the hospital, to say the least) he would open the door, which was all smeared by the stains of different colors that represented the tangible signs of his profession. The first thing he did was take out an electric lamp he was keeping jealously hidden in a drawer; he would go up a little stool and he would screw the lamp on the electric rope hanging from the ceiling. The first day I looked at him in astonishment. I really could not understand why in the evening he would unscrew that lamp and then in the morning he would screw it in again. He caught my inquisitive glance and going down from the stool he told me: "Ehhhh, it could get stolen...."

Immediately afterwards, he would take off his show costume very very slowly, and he would put on a working suit, which consisted of an old shirt and a pair of pants made from jute sacks for coffee beans, which, instead of a belt, were held up by a rope around the belly.

This is how his working day would start. Or I'd better say, maybe it would start.

I am going to explain better.

The life of Mr. Salerno, as I called him in a sign of respect and politeness, was characterized by a great deal of bad organization. First of all I should start by saying that he had quite a lot of customers, and all of them were in a hurry.

A puppeteer would come who urgently needed a backdrop for his show and he would say: "Come on Tuesday"; another puppeteer would commission a poster, and he would say to him too: "Come on Tuesday." A third person, who already knew him and his ways, wanted him to paint the *masciddaru* (side panel) of a cart: "*Zu* (Sicilian for "Uncle") Giovanni, I would need it in a hurry," and Salerno would tell him: "Come on Tuesday"; and the other one: "For sure?" Salerno, rather annoyed and raising his voice a bit: "Come on Tuesday!"

Let's go on. When the famous Tuesday finally arrived, of course nothing was ready, except one painting only. I felt very bad for him.

As soon as the customers came and did not find what they needed, it was the end of this world. But, who knows why, he was always lucky. Almost impossible to believe. The first customer to arrive was always the one whose work was the only one ready.

And what would Salerno do? Knowing very well what he would have to expect, he would hurriedly close the workshop and he would go away. This could even happen at 9 a.m. "It does not matter, my working day is over," he would tell me.

But once it did not go so well. I had forgotten that order too, and that was the one I was not allowed to forget. Yes, because the puppeteer in question, a certain Cacioppo, was a real hot head and he had a very frightening look; he always wore a suit, dark eyeglasses and a moustache that made him look like someone from a Mafia movie.

He had ordered Salerno a little stage curtain with the story of "Death of Manfrino," recommending to him it was absolutely indispensable for a show to be held in Catania.

Both Mr. Salerno and I had totally forgotten about it. As he always did when he was painting with oil, he had put the colors, the palette, and the piece of the cart to be painted right across the door.

When we saw the dark silhouette of this puppeteer Cacioppo, Mr. Salerno's face turned white. The more Cacioppo's face turned dark, the more my dear Mr. Salerno's face would turn pale.

Cacioppo told him abruptly: "Get the curtain Giovanni, I am in a hurry to go to Catania."

Salerno was getting paler and paler and he was totally silent; he did not have the courage to answer him. "Giovanni, the curtain, because I am in a hurry."

"Curtain? What curtain?" he stammered. At those words Cacioppo understood his curtain was only virtual, and stopped being a man to become a devil. He threw a tremendous tantrum.

I only remember that all the painting materials belonging to the poor Salerno were thrown into the air: brushes, colors, the piece of cart he was painting, everything....

"I am not going away until you paint my curtain," thundered Cacioppo.

That's all, to be short. Salerno had to paint immediately that curtain for the "Death of Manfrino" and he was so scared he did not even remember how to do it.

It was Cacioppo himself who suggested the characters and their postures.

In one word, as one of his customers would say, Mr. Salerno was a painter famous for *farne di tutti i colori* ("doing things of all colors") with a play on words with this idiomatic sentence, which in Italian means "to be into all sorts of mischief."

Poor Mr. Salerno. But he was good at heart.

In the neighborhood where he worked you could see and feel hunger around.

Every day at the same time a boy about five years old would always come up to his workshop. He would come in and say quite politely: "Good morning, Mr. Salerno, good morning."

Recognizing his voice, he would not even turn and would answer: "Hi!" and would go on painting. The boy would not utter a word. He would not stir. He would only throw an intense glance at him. Salerno pretended to be absorbed in his painting but I noticed that with the corner of his eye he knew he had the eyes of a child stuck on him.

The boy looked like a lion watching his prey.

Salerno was resigned that the boy would still not go away, and what would he do?

He would put everything aside, get a one hundred lire coin and he would give it to him.

And the boy: "Thank you, Mr. Salerno," gave him a little kiss and off he would go.

And Salerno would look at me and would say the same thing every day: "And does that not mean three thousand lire a month?"

Paolo Di Giovanni, a Life Perched on the Belfry

In Paolo Di Giovanni's workshop, builder of armors for the Sicilian puppet shows, the atmosphere was much more serious. But maybe even stranger.

He lived perched on the belfry of a church in Via Rocco Pirri in a room of about 10 square meters. Here too the staircase did not help. It was a snake of steps twisted around the corners of this belfry. When I finally got to the top, I looked outside the window. It was so high I thought I could see the island of Ustica 30 miles away, but first of all I had to recover my senses after that zigzag ascent that made my head turn.

My father sent me there when I was eight or nine years old. He literally sent me. Because at that time we lived in Trabia, a small town about 25 miles east of Palermo, and even if I was so young, like a "little man" as they called me, in the summer when my school closed, I commuted to Palermo. But the commuters, the real ones, did not want to believe that I was going to learn a job. At first they thought I had escaped from home.

I was too young and "it could not be true" as they would say, and they would add: "But … do you have a mother?"

At these horrible questions, I understood they felt pity for me. To worsen the situation, I was so thin I looked even younger. But I succeeded in setting their minds at rest, and in a short while they were all very fond of me. I had become a "little man" for them too.

The armor builder Paolo Di Giovanni was someone who had gone through all sorts of troubles and hardships.

His voice and his face were worn out because of the fumes of the acids used during the welding of the armors of the puppets.

Not to talk about his teeth. He had only a few left.

I remember the few times he would actually talk to me, I had to adjust my ears to his shrilling voice in order to understand what he was saying.

One thing he repeated very often was that I should not have done that job. If I really insisted on that purpose, I should have done it only for "amusement."

I did not really understand that word, but I guessed right; it meant for fun, for one's own pleasure.

In that room he had all his world.

The bed, the toilet, a small desk with all his instruments. The toilet was only a hole in the floor with a piece of wood on top to separate it from the rest of the room, and the smell would make you faint if you got a little closer.

It was all there. Actually not.

There was also a she cat. Yes, there was a she cat who came especially at lunch time.

Zu' (Uncle) Paolino, as they called him, always got angry with her because, instead of catching the mice that were around the room, she wanted to eat our pasta.

And what pasta! One day dressed with canned ragout, another with a bit of butter.

Always the same for the entire three summer months.

Either ragout or butter.

And the best thing was that every once in a while one of his nephews came up; he was working at the ironworker's shop nearby. When his nephew was given his plate of pasta, at the first bite he would say: "It is overcooked." At those words, my goodness! His uncle would go completely mad.

Di Giovanni's daughter was staying in a mental asylum. Once a week she was given a free day and she would come to see her father.

She was fat. I would sit on the bed to watch and to learn.

She would raise her foot on the bed and, as if it were completely normal, she would raise her skirt, and she would put up her stockings, saying always the same sentence: "It's so hot!"

Once upon a Time at the Corte delle Stelle Theater in Cefalù

From the 1980s on, if anybody walked by Corso Ruggero, the main street in the beautiful Medieval town of Cefalù, s/he could not have helped noticing an ultra modern architectonic structure, with large arches, whose strange dark red color, which may have been Pompeian in the intention of its designer, was in a violent contrast with the characteristic houses of the historical center of the town. It was supposed to be a multifunctional center but, like so many other sad skeletons of unfinished modern buildings in Sicily, had been immediately abandoned to mice, garbage and carelessness. A street sign was indicating the existence of a "Roman road" of the 2nd century AD, but nobody was able to see it, or to guess where it could be: How could the passersby guess that those archaeological remains were, as they still are, inside a room of the mysterious building?

In the summer of 2001 this location, poetically baptized Corte delle Stelle (Courtyard of the Stars), had finally obtained a good use since the mayor of Cefalù had given it in concession to the Teatro Arte Company of Giacomo. Franco and Teresa Cuticchio had invested not only their financial resources but also their time and personal commitment, in order to get rid of the garbage that had accumulated there, to erase the innumerable obscene graffiti that had been written on the walls and to make the building aesthetically acceptable as much as possible. This authorization was cancelled by the administration of the Town of Cefalù a few years ago, thus depriving the town of a structure that had proved to be a highly positive addition to its natural beauties and a first rate cultural and touristic attraction.

The Cuticchio brothers, together with their father Girolamo, who is today the oldest puppeteer still alive in Sicily, had started in July 2001 to offer three puppet shows a week, but it was such a success that they soon started to do two shows a day. The performance was particularly interesting because the audience had the possibility to see the stage and the manipulation of the puppets from a sort of raised platform. The Cuticchios had used the space at their disposal as best as they could, transforming part of it into a small museum where part of the collections that belong to the family had been exhibited. The exhibition was divided into six sections, five of which were devoted respectively to backdrops, to puppets, to posters, to heads and wooden structures of the puppets, to barrel organs and to handwritten outlines (*copioni*). The sixth section was the reconstruction of a real laboratory for the building of a puppet. Most of the puppets exhibited were "armed," that is showing off in their armors, like the legendary Paladins

Orlando and Rinaldo, or like the Saracen warriors Rodomonte and Ferraù. There were also the characters of the comical sketches (*farse*) which are called *in paggio*, which means "without armor" in the puppeteer's jargon, among them the famous Nofriu and Virticchiu, who were personifying the people on the street. The puppeteers never had real scripts for their shows—the ones that belong to the Cuticchios' collection and that were exhibited in the museum were the outlines of the shows (*copioni*), handwritten in copybooks, which for every evening were reporting the division in acts and scenes and the summary of each show. Among the section of the museum, maybe the most important for the rareness of the objects exhibited, was the one dedicated to the pianole, among which was one built in Nice in 1840. They are all in working condition: the Cuticchios are the last ones in Sicily able to repair these musical instruments. Two of them were purchased in a workshop in Madrid, which today does not exist anymore. The other one used to belong to the theater of the puppeteer Canino; it was fortuitously found by Girolamo Cuticchio in a garage in Alcamo, and restored. The Cuticchios have also arranged for the coming of Vittorio Bonafede from Rome in order to let him mark the battle music on a roll: today he is the only artisan in Italy able to do such work.

"It was necessary to rent a truck in order to take away all that stuff that is now in a storage place," says Teresa Cuticchio today. "We already had contracts to offer shows to students coming from schools all over Italy and to groups of tourists, and we were not able to maintain them. To go away from Cefalù was a real disaster for us." All of a sudden it was the end of an excellent cultural activity, which without financial support of public money was also a good business: the company had sold thousands of tickets, especially to foreign tourists who otherwise would not have had the chance to know this aspect of Sicilian culture, which is so peculiar and unique.

Because of the extraordinary emotional participation of the audience to the chivalric stories, in 1968 the Sicilian puppet theater was defined "necessary art" by Peter Schumann, founder of the Bread and Puppet Theater of New York and, as already mentioned, in 2001 it received the important international designation of being included by UNESCO in the List of the Intangible Cultural Heritage of Humanity. "I tried to contact UNESCO so that they could intervene on our behalf. What is the use of this recognition," Franco Cuticchio wonders, "if the

Sicilian puppet theater is then mistreated in this way?" The highly positive closing balance of the Teatro Arte Cuticchio Company did not move to pity the administration of the town of Cefalù, which has evicted them. A success story that has been suddenly cancelled. And the Corte delle Stelle went back into carelessness and abandonment for the following four years.

As already mentioned, after some years of limited activity, Franco Cuticchio has recently founded the new Franco Cuticchio Figlio d'Arte Company and, with his son Girolamo Jr., will start offering shows on a regular basis in their new location opposite the church of St. John of the Hermits in Palermo. See https://www.facebook.com/pages/Cuticchio-Franco-Puparo/236214673200496.

C1

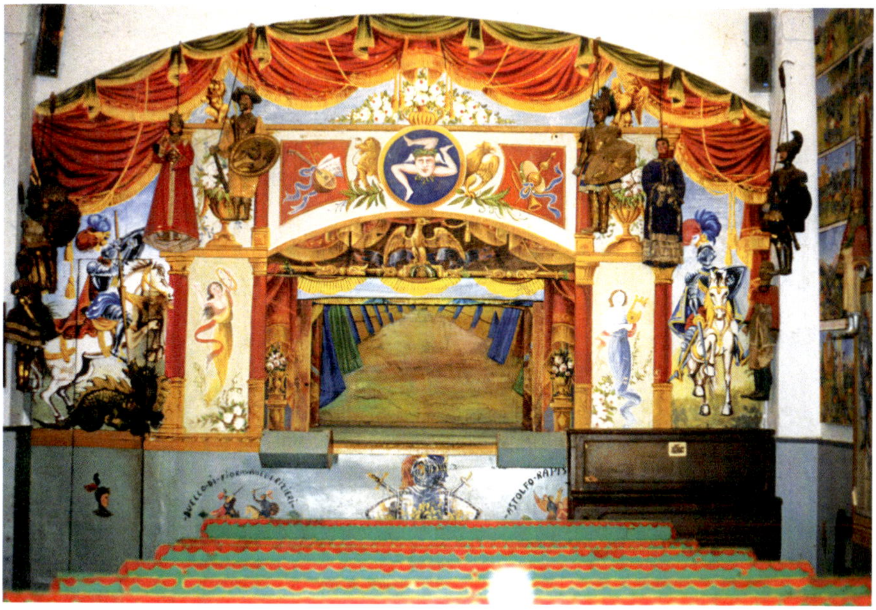

Puppet theater of the Palermitan type, Pitrè museum, Palermo.

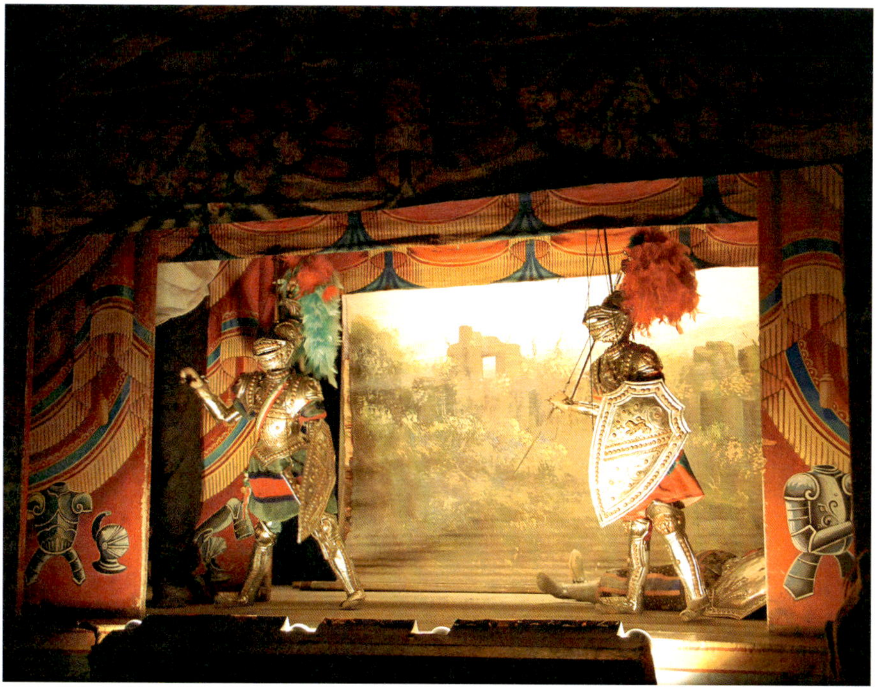

Palermitan puppets during a show.

C2

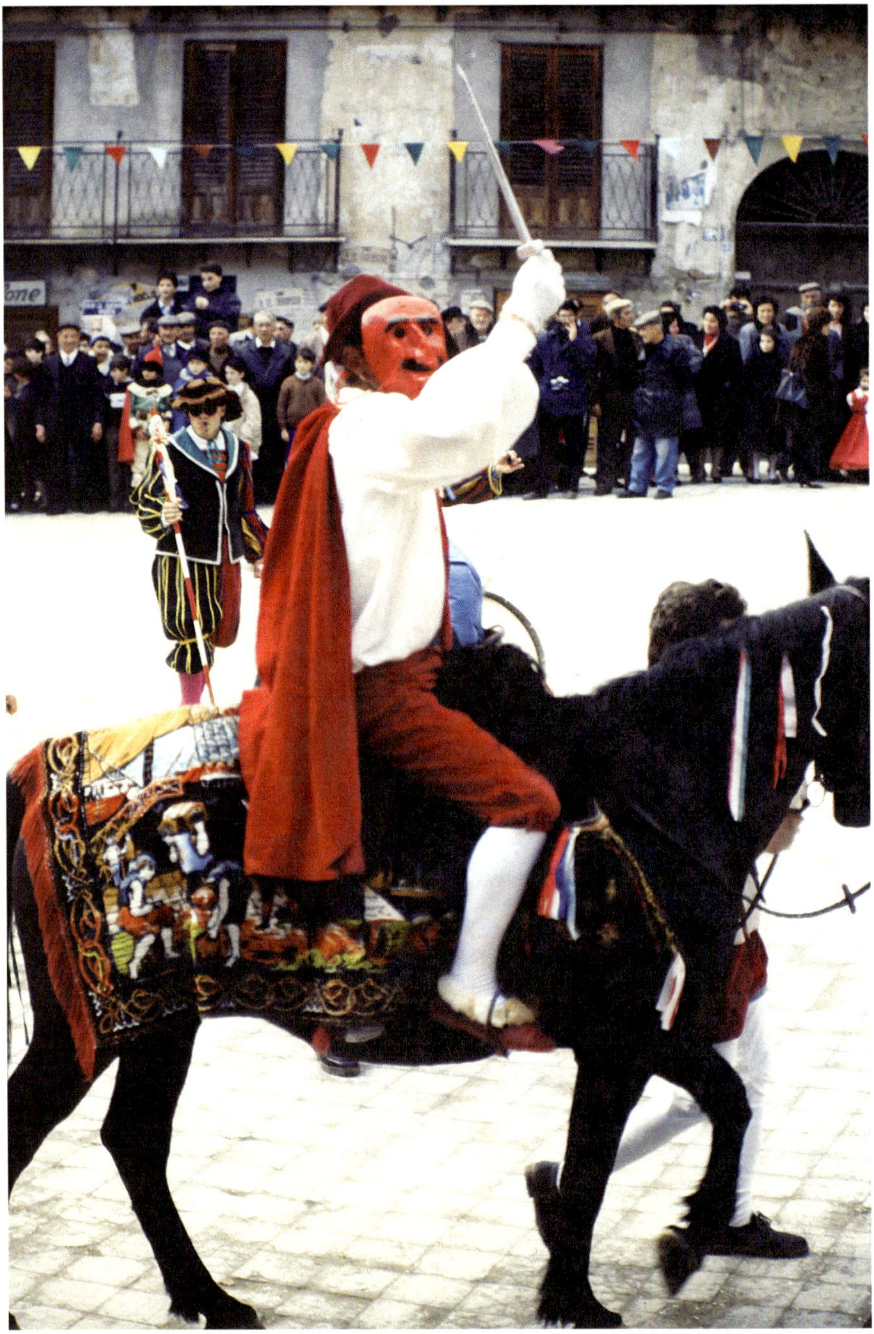

A Carnival pantomime with a knight: the *Mastro di Campo* (Master in the Field) in the town of Mezzojuso in Palermo.

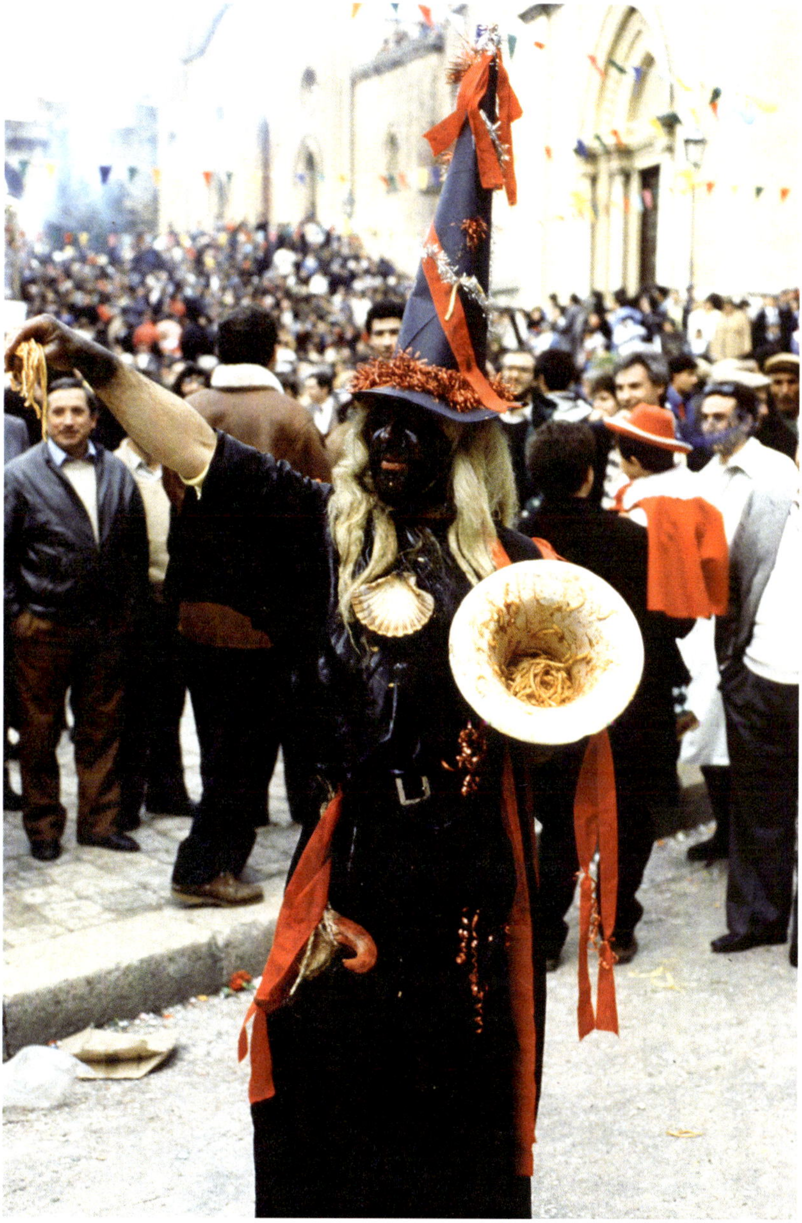

During the *Mastro di Campo* festival the so-called *maghi* ("wizards") wear pointed hats and pretend to dig under the castle looking for the treasure (*trovatura* in Sicilian), which in reality is a big chamber pot filled with spaghetti dressed in tomato sauce with sausages, which they start eating with their hands and offering to the crowd. This last detail stresses the subversive and intentionally disgusting nature of Carnival.

C4

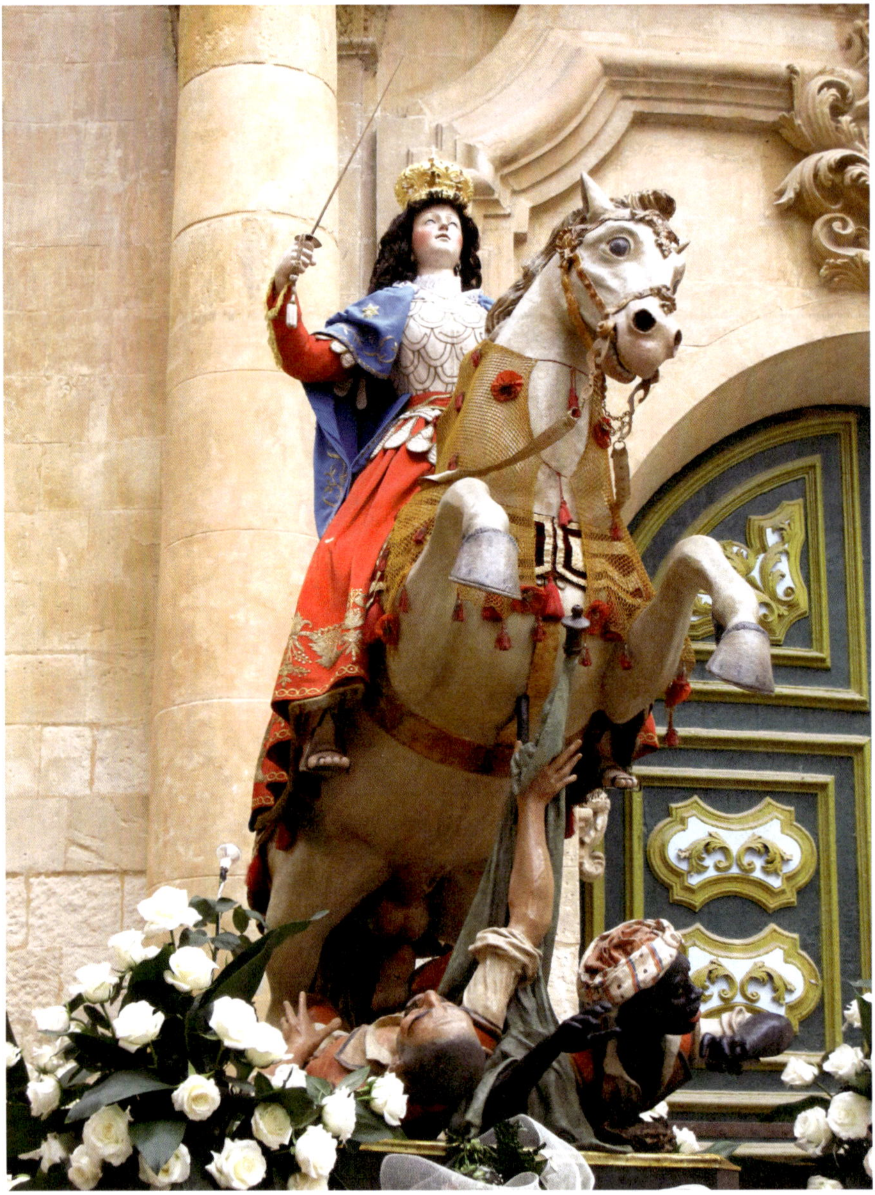

Above: The Holy Virgin in arms: the *Madonna delle Milizie* in the town of Scicli in Ragusa.

Opposite: The Sacred Representation during the *Madonna delle Milizie* festival in Scicli re-enacts the arrival of Saracen pirates in 1091: when the ship called *Stambul* ("corruption" for Istambul) comes threateningly close to the coast, its presence throws the Norman inhabitants of the castle into panic.

C5

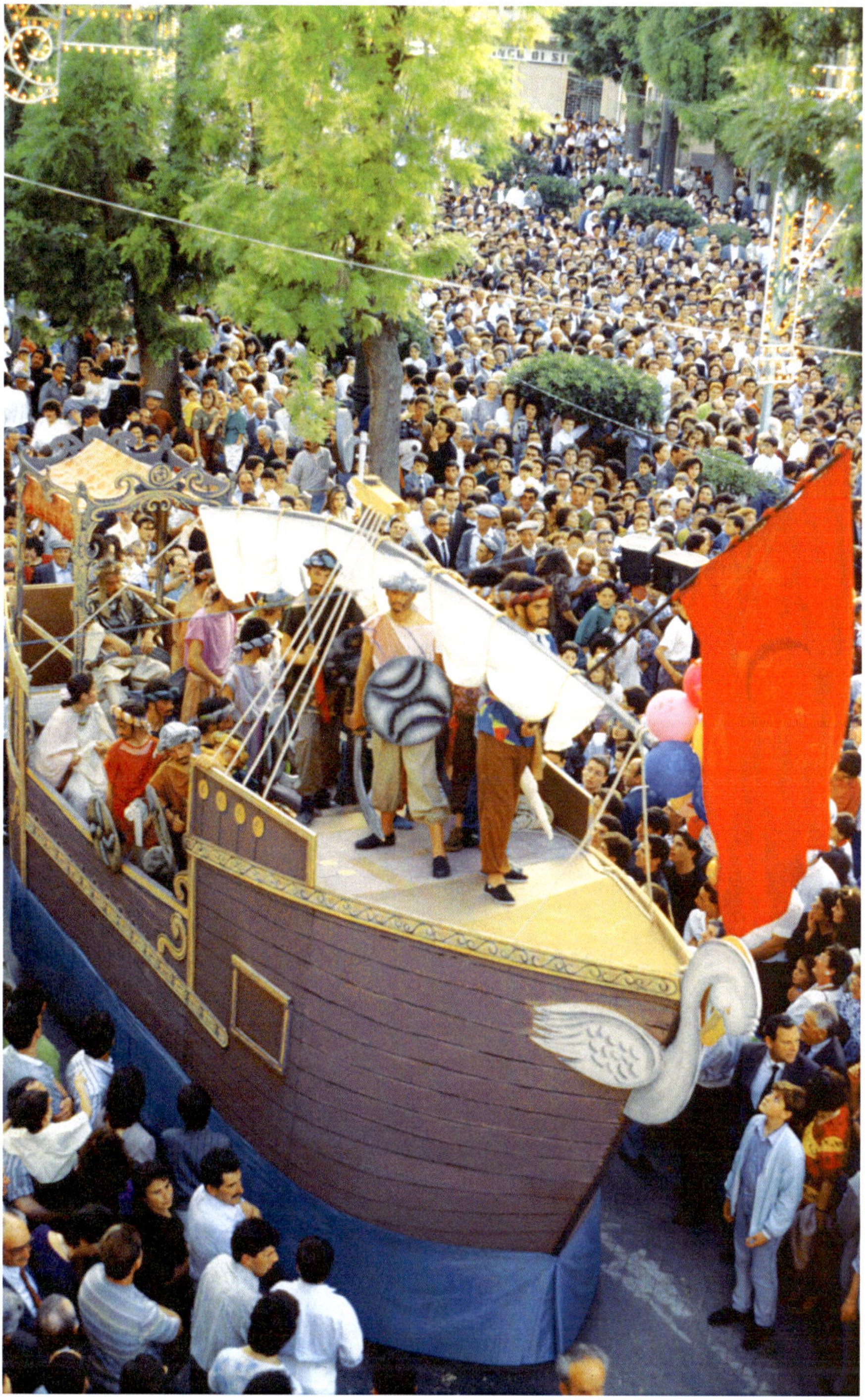

C6

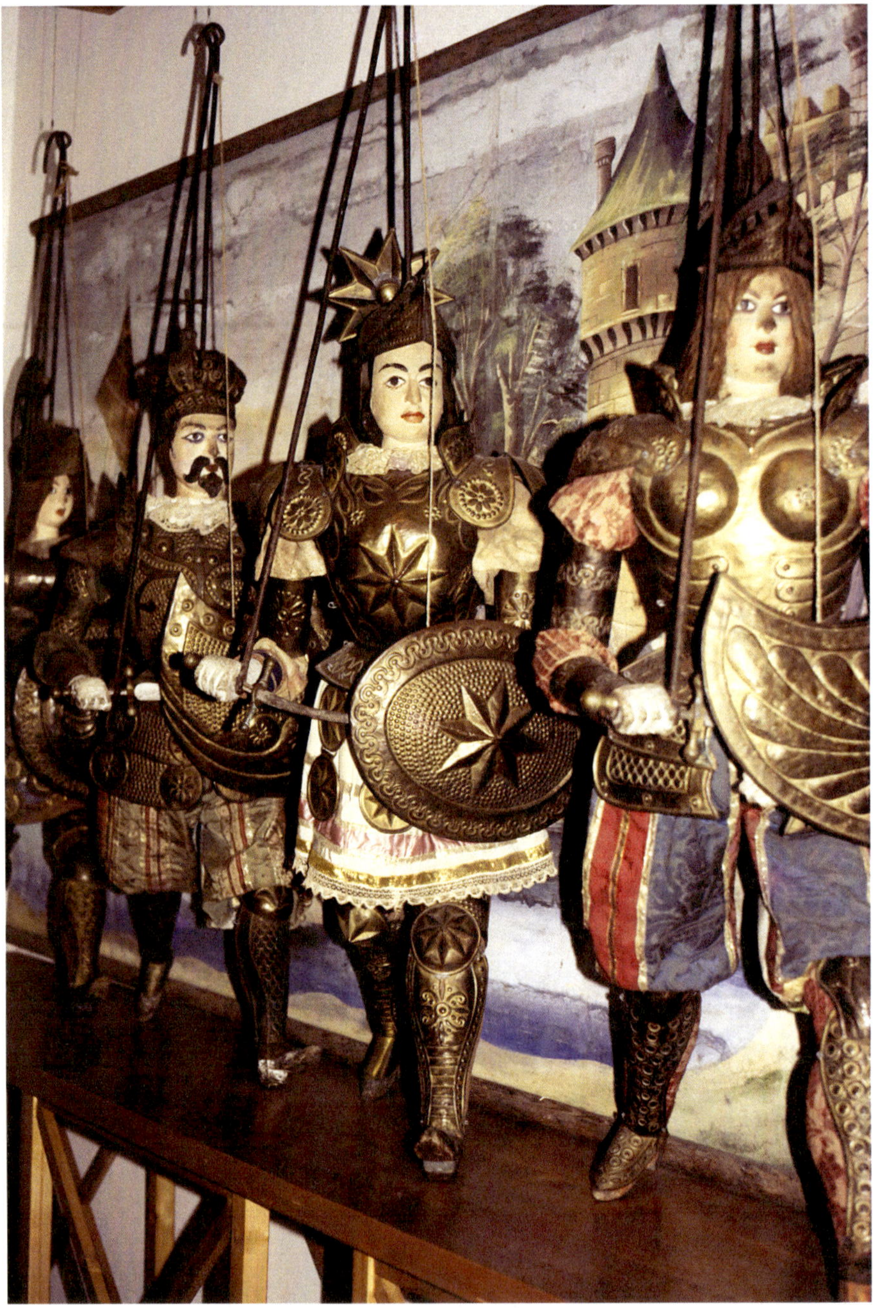

Catanese puppets of Christian knights; the one on the right is the female warrior Bradamante with special armor suited to the body of a woman (Pasqualino International Puppets Museum, Palermo).

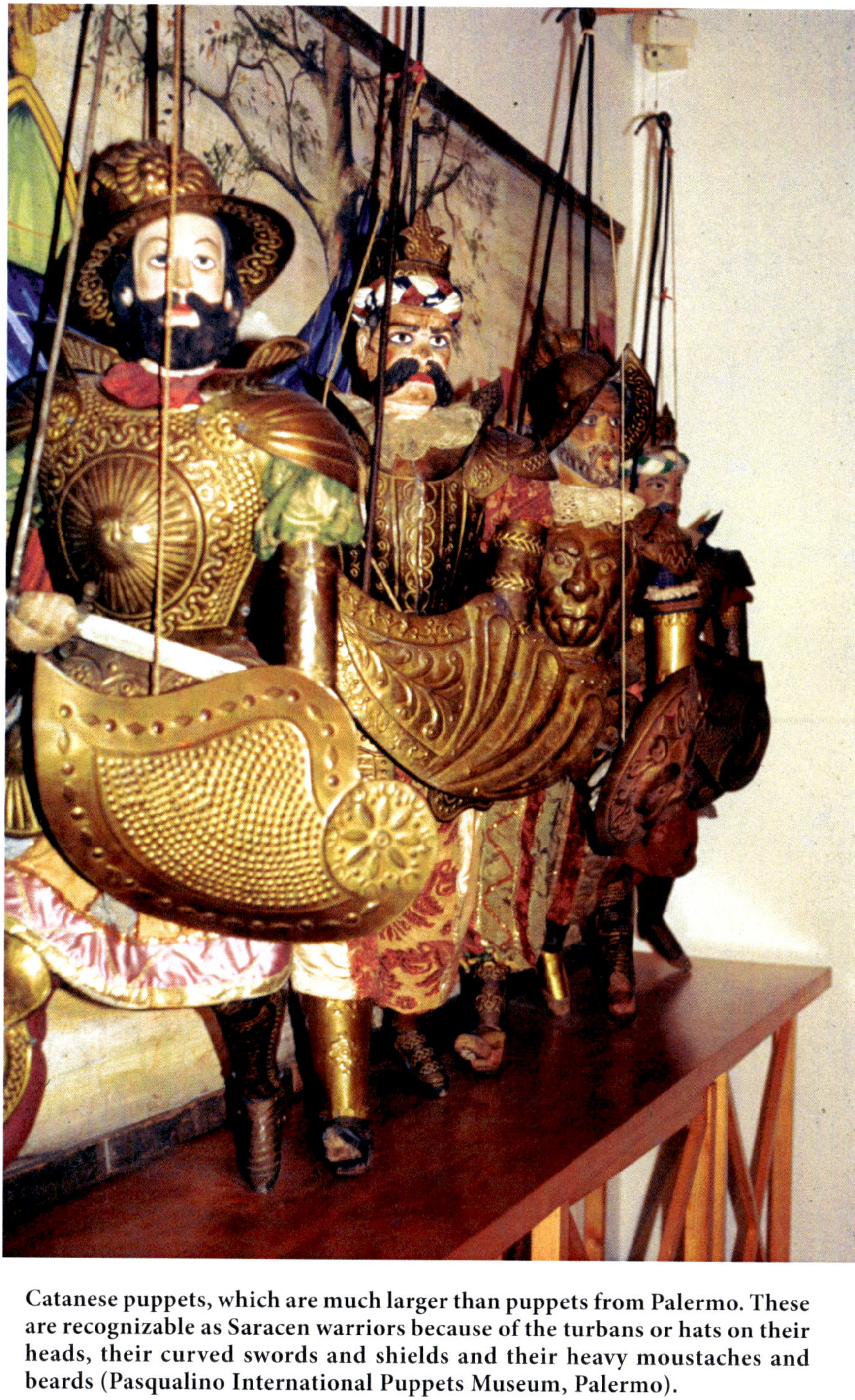

Catanese puppets, which are much larger than puppets from Palermo. These are recognizable as Saracen warriors because of the turbans or hats on their heads, their curved swords and shields and their heavy moustaches and beards (Pasqualino International Puppets Museum, Palermo).

C8

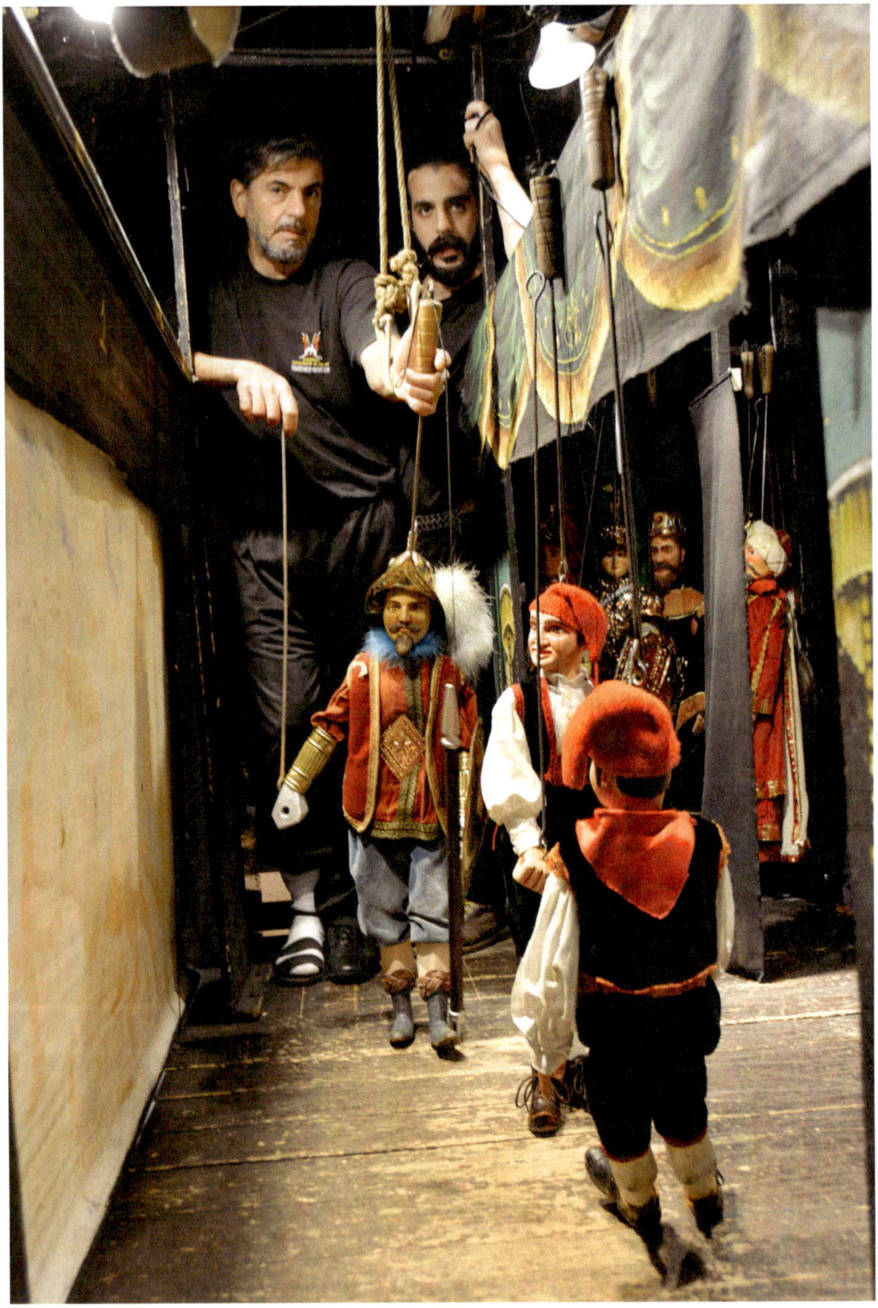

Franco Cuticchio (left) with his son Girolamo Jr. on the stage of their puppet theater. In their hands are the puppets of Nofriu and Virticchiu, the main characters of the farcical sketches (*farse*).

C9

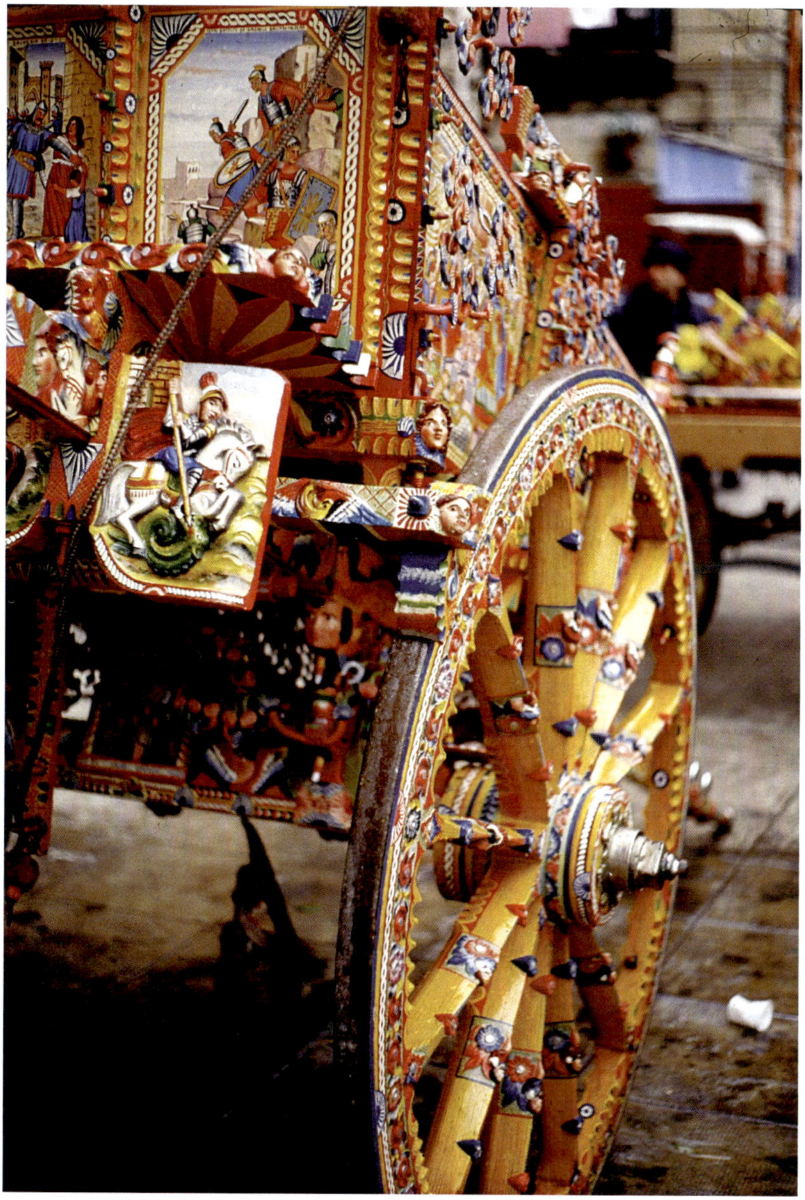

A painted cart from Palermo, as demonstrated by the predominance of yellow. The knight on the center left panel is St. George in the act of killing a dragon, a kind of fighting not very different from what had to be faced by the Paladins. A particularly interesting moment in the building of a cart was the "circling of the wheels." The iron rim was heated by placing it on burning coals arranged in a circle, then the metal was cooled off with water, clamped on the wheel and tightened with the aid of special pliers (*cagni*).

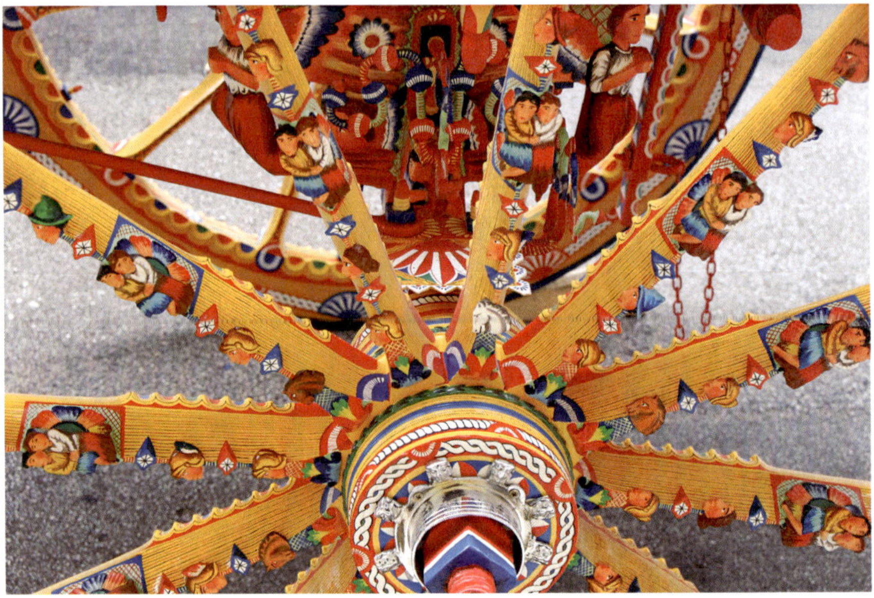

The sculpted wheel of a Palermitan cart.

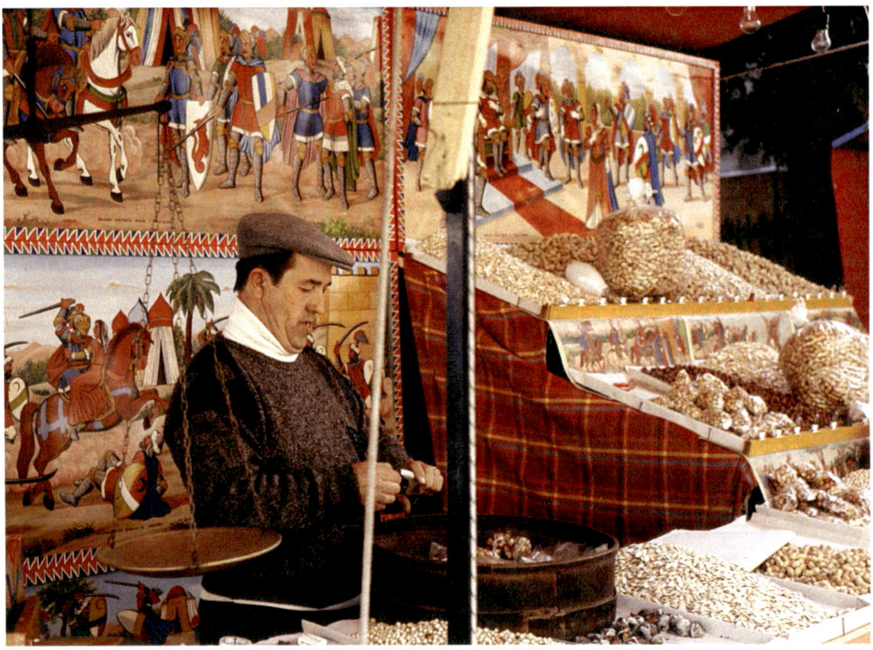

Many market stalls, like this seed vendor's (*semenzaru*), are painted with chivalric scenes.

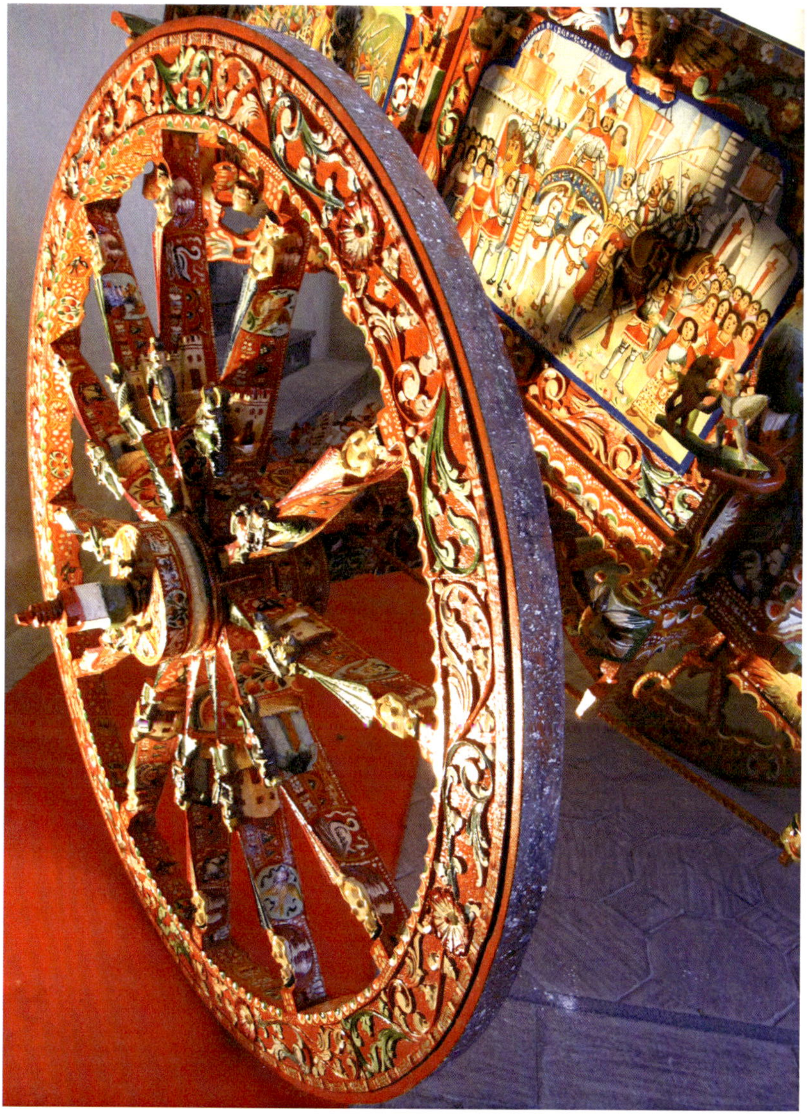

A cart from Eastern Sicily, painted by Nerina Chiarenza. In Eastern Sicily carts are generally smaller, the color red predominates, and the sides are rectangular rather than trapezoidal as in Western Sicily. As in most carts, the cylinder in the middle of each wheel hides a *boccole* (a thin piece of metal which "sings" as the wheel turns). This musical sound provided accompaniment to a cart driver's singing. The *boccole* were made of a bronze alloy frequently referred to as a *suono di campana* (with a bell sound). So important was the quality of the alloy that metal workers who could fashion the hubs to cart drivers' needs were highly sought after. These metal workers are now impossible to find, so the rings are recycled from cart to cart.

C12

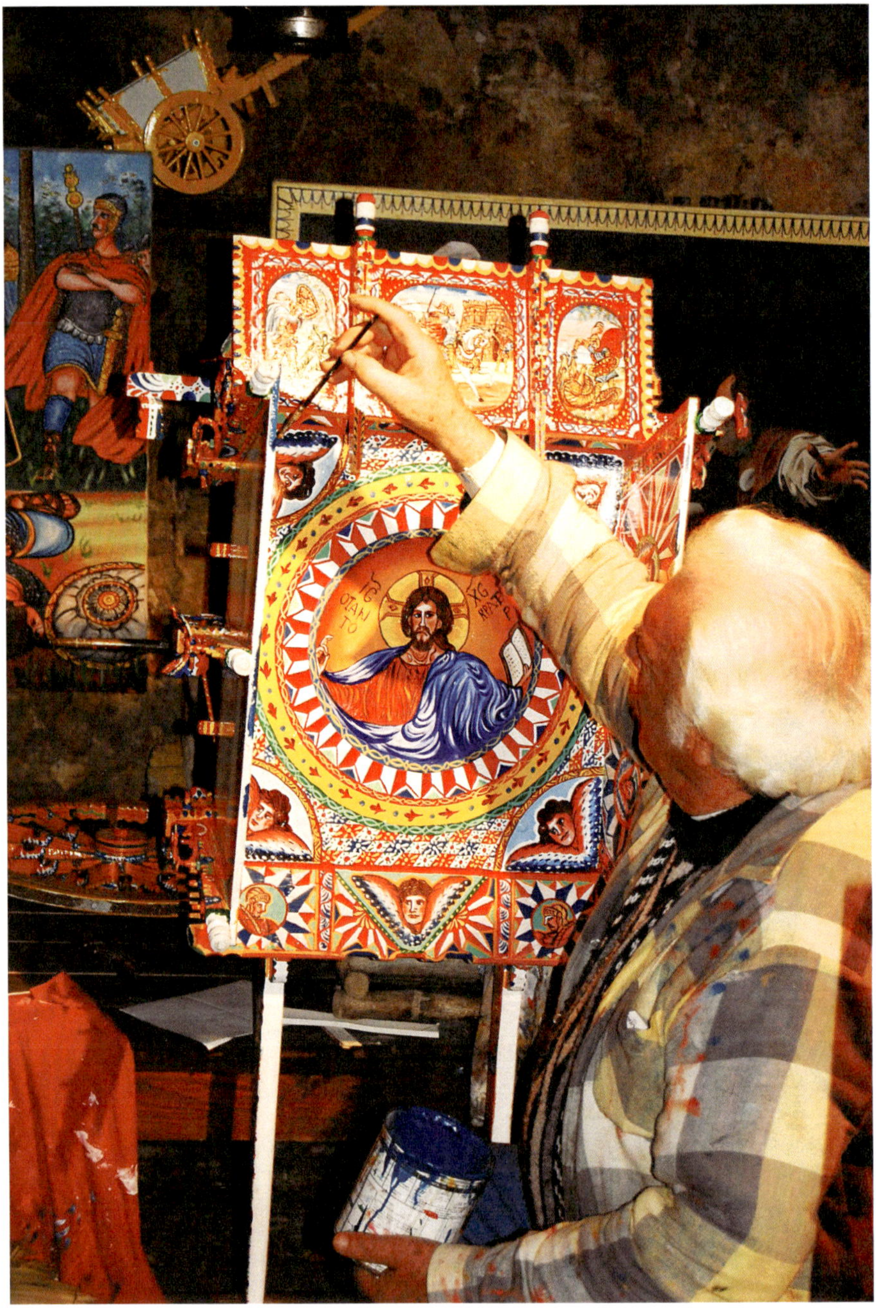

A painter at work on a small miniature cart decorated with a reproduction of the Christ Pantocrator (Almighty) of the Monreale Cathedral near Palermo, a magnificent church that is entirely covered with 13th-century mosaics.

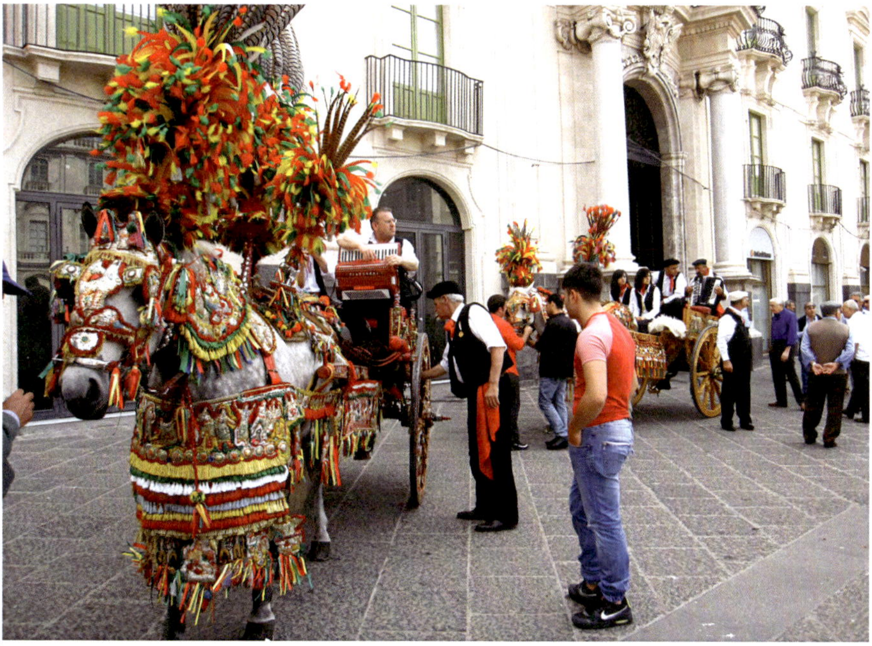

A horse fully decorated with feathers and trappings pulls a cart in the streets of Catania in 2009.

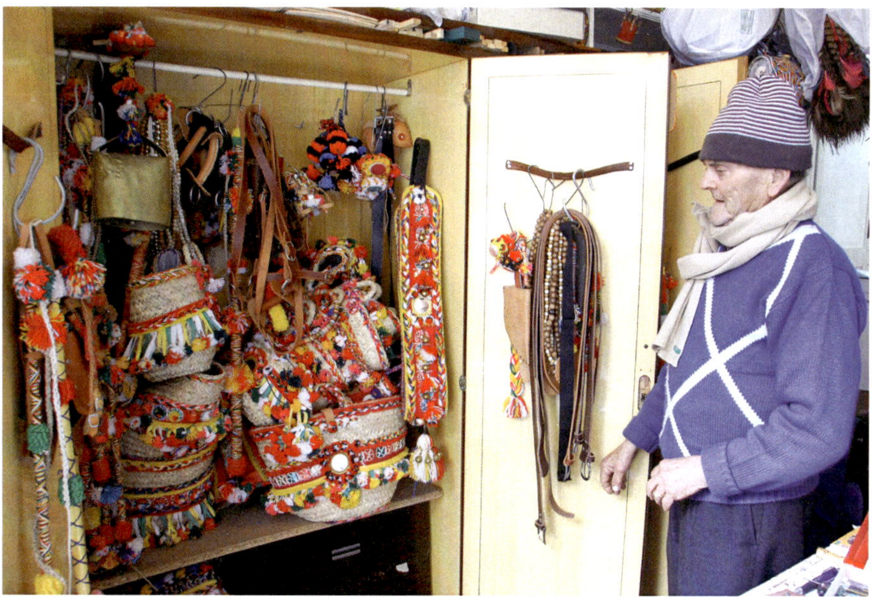

A maker of horse trappings, Michele Ajello, showing his products in 2008.

C14

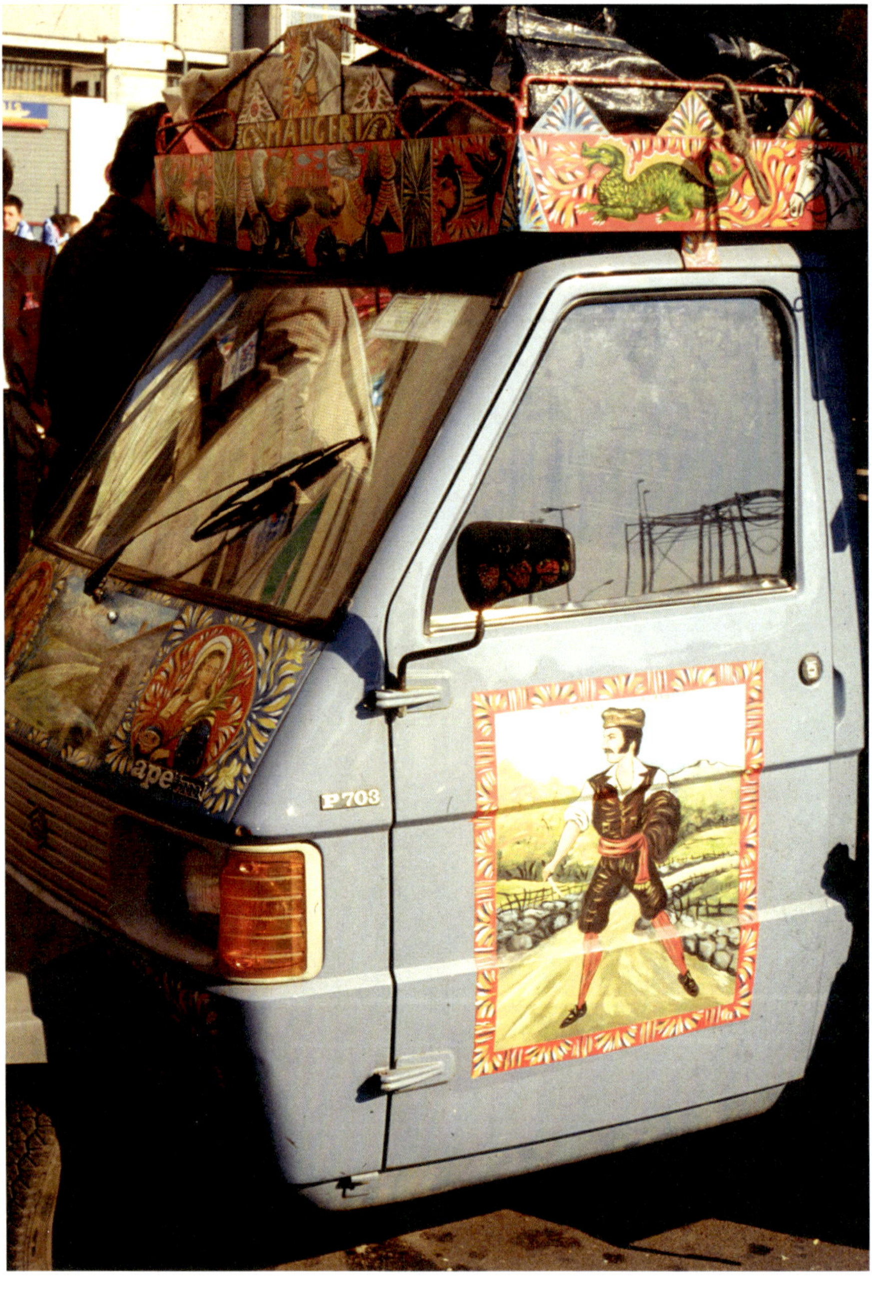

Ape motor truck painted in the fashion of a Sicilian cart. Turiddu, the main character of the opera *Cavalleria Rusticana* (Rustic Chivalry) by Mascagni, is painted on the door. The libretto was derived from a short story written by the Sicilian writer Giovanni Verga.

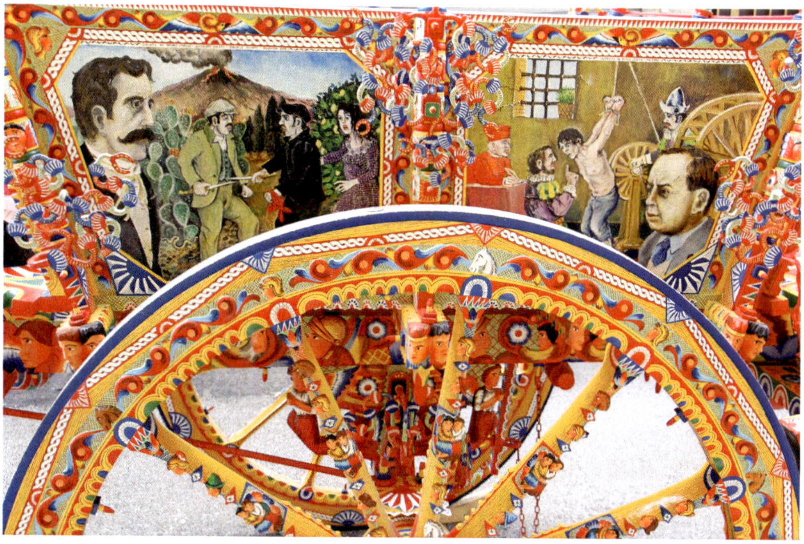

Giuseppe Ducato painted this cart except the main figures on the sides (*mas-ciddara*), which were painted by Bruno Caruso and depict some of the most important Sicilian writers: in this side panel, Giovanni Verga and his *Cav-alleria Rusticana* are on the left, while Leonardo Sciascia is on the right.

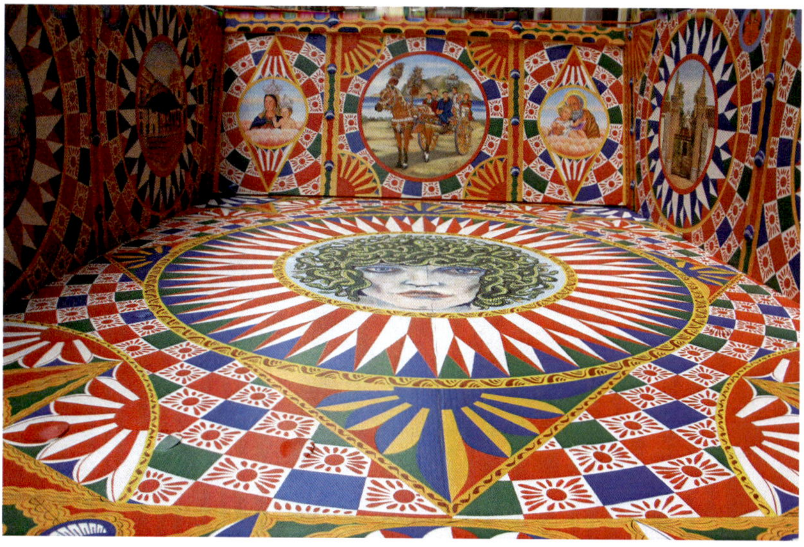

A large head of a Medusa, a mythological figure who has snakes instead of hair, is depicted in the bottom center of the cart box. This cart was decorated by both the brushes of Caruso and Ducato and is a symbol of their cooper-ation. In the background is a portrait of the Ajello family, owners of the cart, copied from a photograph taken from the 1950s.

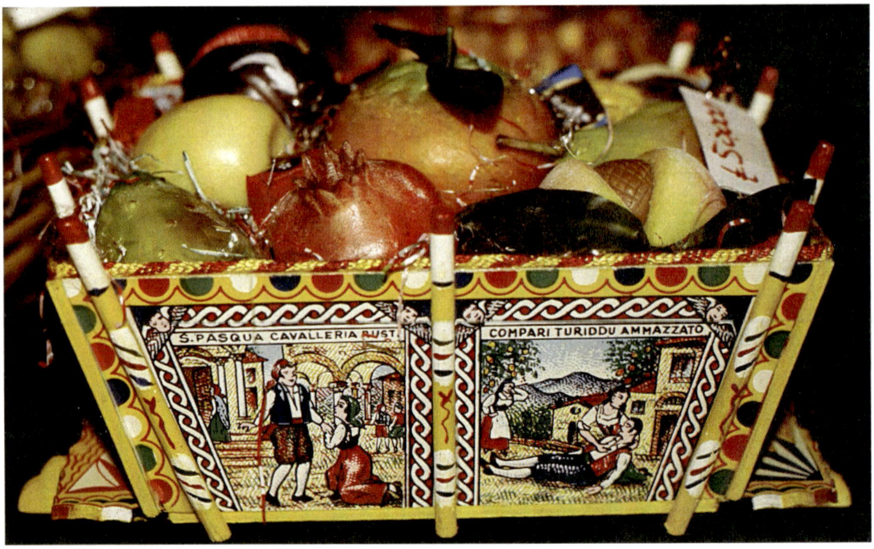

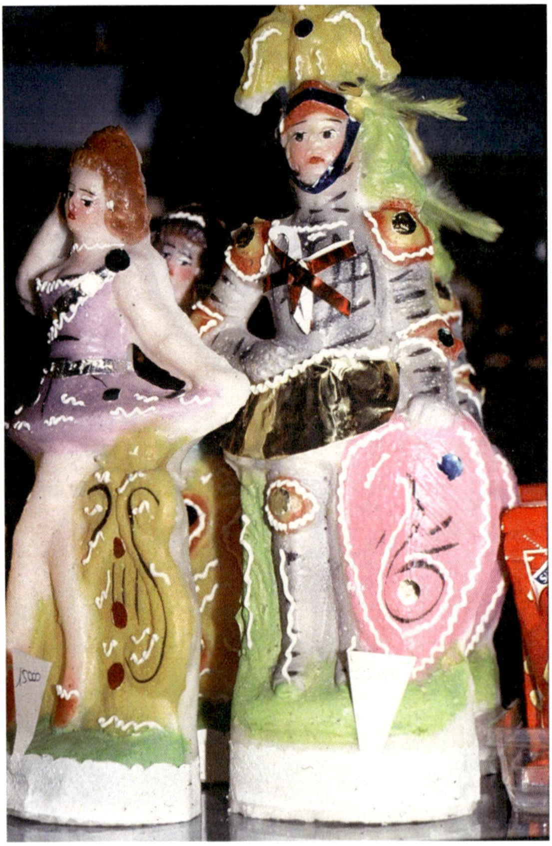

Above: Miniature cart filled with marzipan fruit for the All Souls festivity (November 2).

For the November 2 holiday (All Souls' Day), sugar figurines (significantly called *pupi a cena*—"puppets at dinner time") are molded with the human shape, and the Paladins are some of the most frequent characters represented.

• SIX •

The Playbills (*Cartelloni*) of the Puppet Theater

Definitions of Folk Art and Peculiar Characteristics of Sicilian Folk Art

In Italy academic interest in folk art started in a relatively recent time, and only towards the end of the 19th century did folk art start to be considered worth being studied by scholars. The Romantic poets of the beginning of the 19th century, who were raging about popular poetry, were giving no attention to folk art.

Even the concept of folk art itself was controversial up to very recent times. It seems appropriate to report some of the most authoritative opinions on this subject. Paolo Toschi applied to visual arts an analysis that is similar to what had been earlier accomplished by the Neapolitan philosopher and art critic Benedetto Croce in order to distinguish folk poetry from what he called great poetry or art poetry: "First of all folk art is different from great art for the psychological tone and the cultural background it derives from. Folk art is naïf, simple, elementary, ignorant, while great art comes from deep thoughts, vast concepts and deep knowledge, and it has a full mastery of expression even from a technical, and we should add professional, point of view. On the other hand, folk art can have and has the same absolute value of great art; it can reach, and it does reach, even if through hidden short cuts and secret paths and peaks of equal height."[1]

Toschi adds to Croce's statement that folk art is characterized by collectiveness (folk art as the "traditional patrimony of a community") and simplicity, interpreted not as a psychological feature as Croce had thought, but as a distinctive attribute of folk art in general. Without explaining further the term "ignorance," which rather disputably can be attributed to folk art, Toschi expresses his own definition: "We can recognize as folk art what, starting from a psychological and lyrical tone of simple and primitive quality, has become the expression of the taste of humble people. This kind of art satisfies the spiritual and practical needs of these people, and for this vital function it is transmitted through time, it is kept or modified or elaborated according to its own stylistic tradition, up until when people feel it and consider it as belonging to them."[2]

Toschi recognizes that Croce had had the very important role and merit of having clarified that the potential value of folk poetry and of folk art is not inferior to poetry and art of the leading social classes. Buttitta on the other hand, in the introduction of his book *La pittura su vetro in Sicilia* (Glass painting in Sicily), prefers using the term "elementary" rather than "simple," since we cannot, only because they belong to lower social classes, consider the psychology of certain artists not as complex as others, and he prefers to remove simplicity altogether from the list of the characteristics of folk art:

> We may call folk art elementary, a quality not to be confounded with simplicity. I don't intend elementary from the psychological point of view, as Croce considers it, which we don't really understand what it may mean, since the psychological mechanisms are identical in all healthy individuals. Folk art can be elementary since it uses elementary techniques and media as an answer to primary needs, which does not necessarily imply the result must be simple. Thinking that folk art is simple and naïf means ignoring, as if it were not part of the artistic phenomenon, the social conditions, sometimes dramatic, that constitute its background; it means disregarding the complex cultural history that it reflects.[3]

The techniques of folk art are sometimes simple, but not for this reason less important. In a certain way techniques are in fact identified with folk art itself, whose functionality is of basic importance. This makes folk art completely different from the art produced by bourgeois artists who consider the techniques of secondary importance and follow the ideal of "art for art's sake," totally devoid of any practical function: "The necessity of satisfying certain needs and of fulfilling precise functions results in stressing the importance of techniques in folk art, up to the point that the technical side is identified with the artistic one, and art and technique coincide. On the contrary, at least apparently, bourgeois art does not generally pursue any practical functions, which is in fact excluded by definition and by principle."[4]

The concept of "primitivism" in folk art is also quite controversial. As far as the relationships among folk art, primitive art and children's art, Toschi defines a series of characteristics that are common to these three types of artistic expressions and that can be useful to list. These characteristics are: (1) lyrical synthesis and emblematic value of images; (2) simplification of lines, colors, and volumes; (3) exaggeration, deformation and transfiguration of feelings and characters; (4) materialization of movements, sounds, sensations and ideas; (5) stylization; and (6) repetition of lines, colors and figures.[5]

Arnold Hauser has pointed out some fundamental sociological distinctions between folk art and primitive art which are particularly enlightening: "Primitive art is by no means a 'folk art' like the peasant art of today. At any rate, it is not a folk art so long as the differentiation of peasant societies into classes has not been completed—for 'folk art' only has one meaning, in contrast to the 'art of the ruling class': the art of a mass of people that has not yet divided into 'ruling and serving classes, high and fastidious and low and modest classes' cannot be described as 'folk art' for one reason, because there is no other kind of art at all."[6]

In folk art the individual artist sometimes does not really appear, in spite of the fame of some "masters," for example the famous painter of playbills, Nicola Faraone, whose excellence was highlighted by Pitrè, and whose real name was Giovan Battista Rinaldi, as Li Gotti had demonstrated.[7] These artists are recognized masters according to principles that are quite different from the ones applied to bourgeois art: "What counts in folk art and what builds up its value, are the technical skills and the capability of using them, and the degree of functionality of objects. This makes folk art different form naïf art, whose ingenuity and charm are due to single individuals who do not identify with the community."[8]

Within folk art novelties are introduced very slowly. This is even appropriate in a society like the Sicilian one, which in the past anthropologists have defined "cold" because it is founded (or we should rather say it used to be founded?) on repetition of the old and traditional, rather than on the introduction of the new.[9] The intentional repetitiousness and the deliberate adoption of certain traditional canons do not mean a lack of personal inventiveness altogether: "A skillful folk painter can easily introduce a new style or any other element of novelty. If this novelty is appreciated, it is automatically introduced in the social group and repeated in the works accomplished later by the same painter and his followers."[10]

"Especially in Sicily, many of these stimuli to the introduction of novelties come from the art of the ruling classes. The osmosis between folk art and the art of the ruling class is in a certain way comparable to the one between art poetry and folk poetry. In Sicily this process of osmosis has been particularly evident and we can trace the aristocratic origin of all aspects of Sicilian folk art."[11]

For example, as far as the subject of the present study is concerned, it is well known and generally acknowledged that the painting of the Sicilian carts was originally an imitation of litters and sedan chairs of the 18th century. Sicilian folk art, moreover, has shown a particularly strong tendency to receive and accept external influences, as a direct consequence of the numerous foreign dominations and conquests that the island has undergone. Another peculiar characteristic of Sicilian folk art is a very strong realism and, as a consequence, the refusal of any metaphysical attitudes.[12] We could think that this realism would contrast with the strong predilection for the chivalric repertory that is the object of our study, and which is so full with fantasy, the real reign of the heroic and of the wonderful. This contradiction actually exists only for us. What the painters of posters and of carts were painting was believed to have really happened in real life and at the same time it was idealized as an epic saga.

This identification of the real with the wonderful, which for us is often hard to grasp, was automatically and easily accomplished by the popular mind: "In brief for folk artists there is no difference between what is legendary in itself and what they, elaborating reality, transport into an enchanted atmosphere where every gesture, even the most common one, acquires an epic value. In this process of myth building the historical characters do not lose their nature of real beings. Just the opposite happens: the Paladins with their heroic deeds belong to a reality that is not mental but historical, and whose details we necessarily miss."[13]

Sicilian folk artists have been able to introduce this particular realism on topics and themes coming from social classes and artistic traditions that were foreign to them, with a result that is often rich of an extraordinary originality and has an outstanding aesthetic and artistic value.

Chivalric Subjects for Sicilian Folk Art

As already mentioned, the puppet theater afforded conditions for a thriving craft activity. The puppet shows were advertised by playbills (*cartelloni*) that were hand painted in tempera by the puppeteer himself and exhibited outside the theater showing the most important moments in each night's presentation in graphic book style. Other times the puppeteer would commission the paintings to other specialized artists.

Painters of backdrops and of the posters for the puppet theaters usually used the same stories from the legends of chivalry. Apparently cart painters who worked with oil paints felt that artists who used tempera paints for the puppet theater imagery, usually the puppeteers themselves, practiced a different trade, so the *cartelloni* were not created in cart painters' workshops. The *cartelloni* of the theaters of Palermo were painted in tempera on canvas cloths and were divided into various segments (*scacchi*), one for each evening's performance, on which the puppeteer moved the wording *Oggi* ("Today") from one day to the next. The posters of Catania were tempera paintings on heavy wrapping paper, which represented just one very large stage set (measuring around 150 × 200 cm), while eight or more were painted on a Palermo cloth. Each of the posters from Catania would illustrate with that single large scene the subject matter of each evening and referred only to the performance scheduled for the evening on which they were displayed. In Palermo posters were painted on canvas and rolled around a stick, while in Catania they were folded up and put one on the top of the other; since they were often kept in very humid places, they deteriorated quite rapidly.

In either case, the playbill posters were invariably exposed without any protection to the vagaries of the weather. Periodically, therefore, they had to be "restored" or thrown away. This lack of concern underlines once again the difference between the bourgeois and the popular artist: "The products of folk art are felt as communal objects, on which anyone, in order to insure their functionality, can freely operate. Contrary to what happens with learned art, for the popular artist the quality of being "one of a kind" is not necessarily a prized value."[14]

Lodico's book was illustrated by drawings that had great influence over the painters of playbills. According to one of the nonwritten rules of folk art, the concept of plagiarism did not exist for the popular painter, who was not hiding (and was not ashamed of) having copied from someone else. This did not mean lack of originality for the folk artist, who from many different sources was able to draw inspiration from an infinite number of subjects. It was rare he did not add anything to his source, and this made his art original: "The activity of the painters of playbills did not limit themselves to copying prints and illustrations. They would eliminate what seemed superfluous, they would add what they believed indispensable to increase the advertising effectiveness of the playbills, they would improve the stage effects, they would enhance the representation of an inner life leaning towards the dramatic and the amazing, and they would in one word re-elaborate in fantastic and popular tone the subjects they were working on."[15]

In spite of the intense use of fantastic and breathtaking elements that could better reach the popular imagination, the intention of the artists was realistic and the artist intended to portray the "real world" in the playbills, which were supposed to offer a representation of reality more faithful than the theater: "The scenes portrayed in the paintings are, like their models, illustrations of a setting imagined by the artist, not representations of stories set on the stage of the theater. In other words, we can say that in the paintings we see the characters in flesh and bones, not the marionettes."[16] "The playbills represent the "truth," not the theater. The theater is another medium to represent the same "truth," since for the traditional audience the puppets were not marionettes, but living characters of an exemplary story."[17]

In the backdrops, which were obviously much bigger in Catania, since the size of the theater was much bigger there, we notice a more remarkable imitation of the bourgeois art, in particular of the settings used in operas and in playhouses, which were the most important forms of theater of the ruling class in the 19th century. Giovanni Di Cristina, nicknamed Lo Scolimano, beside being a puppeteer and painter of playbills, worked also as stage designer in the Massimo opera house in Palermo.

The Rout of Roncevaux in Playbill Posters for the Puppet Shows

I am going to analyze the style and the characteristics of some playbills portraying the Rout of Roncevaux. I am going to call the posters A and B, both of which belong to the Pitrè Museum. A is the only one that is not entirely devoted to the Rout of Roncevaux, which certainly constitutes an exception. The episode of Roncevaux was so famous that its playbill was normally larger than the others and did not include other episodes. The subject of each evening show would normally be portrayed in three or four segments (*scacchi*). In the A playbill, however, there are eight *scacchi* in the upper part, which refer to other previous episodes. Each of these eight *scacchi* occupies half of the width of the playbill and carries a caption that refers to the episode portrayed in the segment immediately above. The last two *scacchi* in the lower part refer to the Rout of Roncevaux. They are larger than the others and occupy the entire width of the playbill; as a consequence they are "double" and in between there is a caption that refers to both ("La Rotta di Roncisvalle con la morte di Orlando," meaning "The Rout of Roncevaux with the death of Orlando"), followed by the initials of the painter Gaspare Canino ("C-G").

The upper segment is characterized by the intense movement of the battle. The two ranks of warriors are recognizable by the emblems on their shields: the Cross for the Christians and the half moon for the Saracens. Many shields with crosses can be noticed, which means the Saracens are about to win. The ranks of the enemies are very crowded and they are advancing towards the Christians, increasing the dramatic atmosphere of the battle, while the lower segment is static and mystical. Orlando is exhaling his last breath surrounded by the army accompanied by the Emperor Charlemagne, who is finally summoned by the sound of his horn. Charlemagne is helplessly witnessing the scene between the Archbishop Turpino and the traitor Gano di

Magonza. The latter's stature is lower than all the other characters; he is looking down and seems to foresee his approaching fate: his sadness has a different motivation than the other onlookers. On his chest an emblem is clearly visible: the initial letter M of his family name Magonza, which makes him clearly recognizable by everyone.

In the left side of this segment we can notice the naiveté of the painter who has put together in a small space three elements that remind the public the divine intervention to which the popular devotion attributed great importance: Durlindana, Orlando's sword, is stuck in the rock from which miraculous water is coming out; the sacred image of the Virgin with Baby Jesus in her arms, in a shrine that is undoubtedly very similar to the ones the painter could have seen at every street corner in Sicily; finally Orlando's soul, naked and young, who, surrounded by four angels, is going up to heaven enhanced by the Divine light. In these elements the painter shows his dependence from the devout images of the *ex-votos* and of the glass paintings. Here we can find the first among the characteristics of folk art listed by Toschi that have been previously quoted: "lyrical synthesis and emblematic value of images."

The painting of poster B is in much worse condition because it is much older than A. B was painted at the end of the 19th century by the painter Nicola Faraone, nicknamed "Rinaldo." This poster is divided into ten segments, all dedicated to Roncevaux, and has six horizontal lines. The third and the sixth segments are "double" and they span over the entire width of the poster. The episode is analyzed with great precision since the painter had a greater surface at his disposal; in the first two segments the poster includes two facts that happened before the battle (the angel giving back the weapons to Rinaldo, who had retired as a hermit in a cave and the secret meeting between Gano and the Spaniards), while in the last two segments two episodes following the battle are portrayed (quartering of Gano with four horses and Rinaldo's death). Each of these was the subject of an entire evening. While everybody showed up (and cried) on the evening Roncevaux was put on the stage and returned when Gano was executed in such a gruesome way (and enjoyed it thoroughly), very few people came to see Rinaldo's death: traditionally the episode was deserted en masse by the public who could not stand seeing the death of their favorite hero. The puppeteer expected it, but could not skip that episode in the long series of shows; he simply knew there would be less pasta on the table for the family that evening.

The B poster has only one caption ("La Rotta di Roncisvalle"), whose simplicity indicates it was such a well known subject it did not need further explanations. Beside the usual elements, the Divine intervention is symbolized by the devils who with a big fork in their hands are waiting to get hold of the soul of Gano, who is being quartered by the four horses. The gruesomeness of the battle, always full of movement, is made visible by the red blood that abundantly comes out of the wounds. The disloyal betrayal of the Saracens is shown by their hiding in caves. In the battle scene we can easily distinguish Orlando, who is riding a white horse and blowing his horn. The same horse is then shown in the eighth segment sadly lying next to Orlando while he is dying. The colors of the B poster are much darker than A; on the whole this poster can give us a fairly good idea of the way posters were painted in the 19th century.

I am going to call with the letters C through I some posters that belong to the International Puppet Museum. The first three have been painted by Francesco Rinaldi. C is in many respects unique and orig inal, for example in the way the segments are divided and in their shape. Instead of the usual rectangular shape, they are all square except for the first and the last segments. Moreover it has a sort of appendix, a real continuation of the story in another poster with only three segments, which is much smaller and must be exhibited next to the first one. The first segment, which is also unusual, is set in a hall of the castle of Montalbano, while the funeral ceremony for Rinaldo's wife Clarice is taking place. In the appendix poster there is also a segment that portrays the execution of Marsilio's brothers, Balugante and Falserone, who had been found guilty. They are being hung at that very same carob tree under which they had been planning the betrayal together with Gano. These are secondary episodes that have received very little attention by poster painters and they are normally not portrayed in Roncevaux posters. The scene of the betrayal with the Spaniards is present in all posters C, D and E, but in C it is made particularly dramatic because of the visualization of the divine signs: the thunderstorms, the lightning and the blood dripping from the tree. Both Orlando and Rinaldo are always recognizable by several emblematic signs: they have gilded armors, or they wear a characteristic band

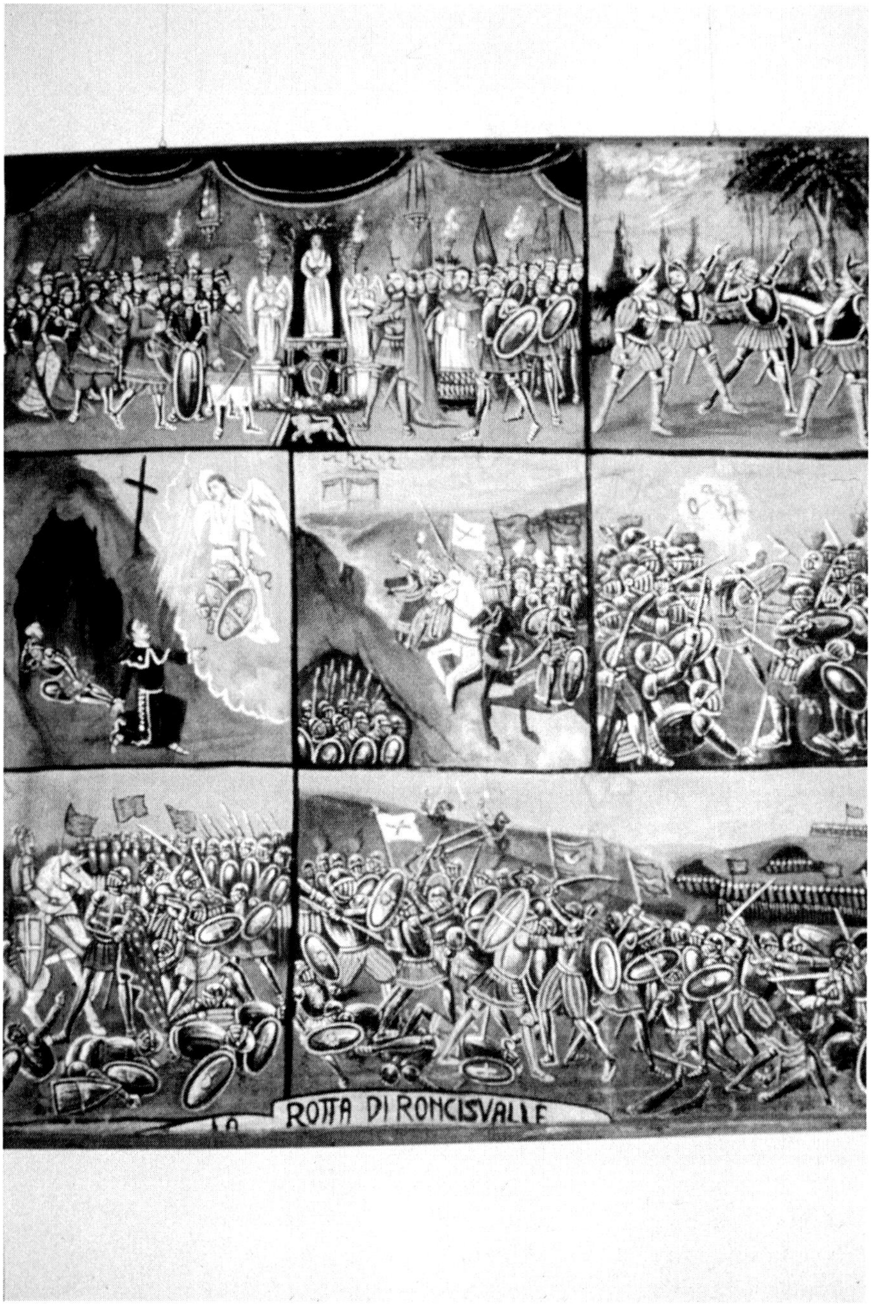

Palermitan playbill poster C portraying the Battle of Roncevaux (Pasqualino Puppet International Museum, Palermo).

crossing their chest, or Orlando is blowing his horn, and so on. The Magonzesi, relatives of the traitor Gano di Magonza, can be recognized by the short yellow skirt worn by all the members of their family. Oliviero can be recognized by the sun engraved on his armor, typical of the Austrian Royal family. As already mentioned, C is a very peculiar poster, so much so that Girolamo Cuticchio's sons, Carmelo and Giacomo, think that it cannot have been painted by Rinaldi, because its style is very different from the posters certainly painted by this artist.

C and E posters look very much alike. D is signed by Rinaldi's initials FR and carries a date (8–914, that is August 1914). Both D and E use the same division in segments and the same subjects of the paintings. E has an additional rectangular segment, which portrays other details of the battle. Moreover the E poster has a color that is darker and almost navy blue. According to the Cuticchios, this is due to the thick layer of linseed oil mixed with gasoline that was applied to the painting in order to preserve it for a longer time. In both posters the betrayal scene is less dramatic than in the C poster and it is made more realistic by some fragments of Saracen rural architecture that can be seen in the background and which stress the quality of the idyllic place where the conversation is taking place, according to the tradition of *locus amoenus* ("wonderful and tranquil place" in Latin), which is a very common *leit motif* of Medieval literature and art. In all three posters we can see the stage on which the false conversion of the Saracens should have taken place. It is portrayed in the first scene of the battle, while in the next segment we can see Rinaldo and his brother Ricciardetto who are at last intervening in the battle, even if in vain, in order to defend the Paladins. In the E poster we can see in the background the Danish knight Uggeri going away from the battle scene: he was the only Paladin who saved his life. In this poster there is another interesting detail: Orlando is not portrayed dying but is rather resurrecting, in order to give back the sword to the Emperor Charlemagne to whom it originally belonged. Orlando had appropriated the sword from Almonte, whom he had killed in order to avenge his father Milone's death, and he had promised to give it back to the Emperor at the moment of his death. Obviously only the eyes of the traditional public who knew the story in all its details could enjoy and appreciate all these nuances, which the occasional spectator would certainly miss, even when he or she found certainly appealing an art that was felt authentic and genuine.

The F and G posters are of the Palermitan type, coming from the Canino and Sclafani theaters, while H & I are of the Catanese type, one of which came from the Meli theater in Reggio Calabria. F is quite similar to the A poster already examined, but it includes all the episodes that normally preceded the scene of battle and followed the death of Orlando, and more precisely the betrayal of Gano: Rinaldo getting his weapons back when he decided to leave the cave where he was living as a hermit to go back to the fighting, the quartering of Gano with four horses once he had been found guilty of betrayal, and finally Rinaldo's death.

In the scene of Orlando's death in the F poster, Canino used extensively a technique quite fashionable among poster painters, the so-called "multiplication" of the army, which they imitated from popular prints that were produced in great number in the French town of Epinal at the end of the 19th century, which were widely available all over Italy, Sicily included. As Giuseppe Cocchiara noticed, the puppeteers managed to obtain the effect of a great number of soldiers by painting only the heads or the spears of the soldiers. The G poster on the other hand, painted by Salerno, has the peculiarity of having under each segment very detailed captions that, with their numerous spelling mistakes, reveal the genuinely popular vein of their author.

In the middle of the furious battle, the painter did not forget to remind the onlookers what the destiny of other knights like Agolaccio, Astolfo, Baldovino, Marsilio, Falserone and Oliviero had been. Baldovino, for example, is portrayed while he is getting rid of the famous blue mantle given to him by his father Gano, which was distinguishing and protecting him from a certain death without him knowing it. As a matter of fact, the Saracens had received instructions to save his life and when Orlando reveals the truth, he soon takes the mantle off in order to show his honesty, and for that reason he is immediately killed. Marsilio and Falserone, on the other hand, are portrayed on the stage while they are pierced by Rinaldo's and his brother Ricciardetto's swords.

As already mentioned, the posters from Catania were even more perishable than the ones from Palermo, since they were painted on wrapping paper instead of canvas. They are almost all fixed in the rear

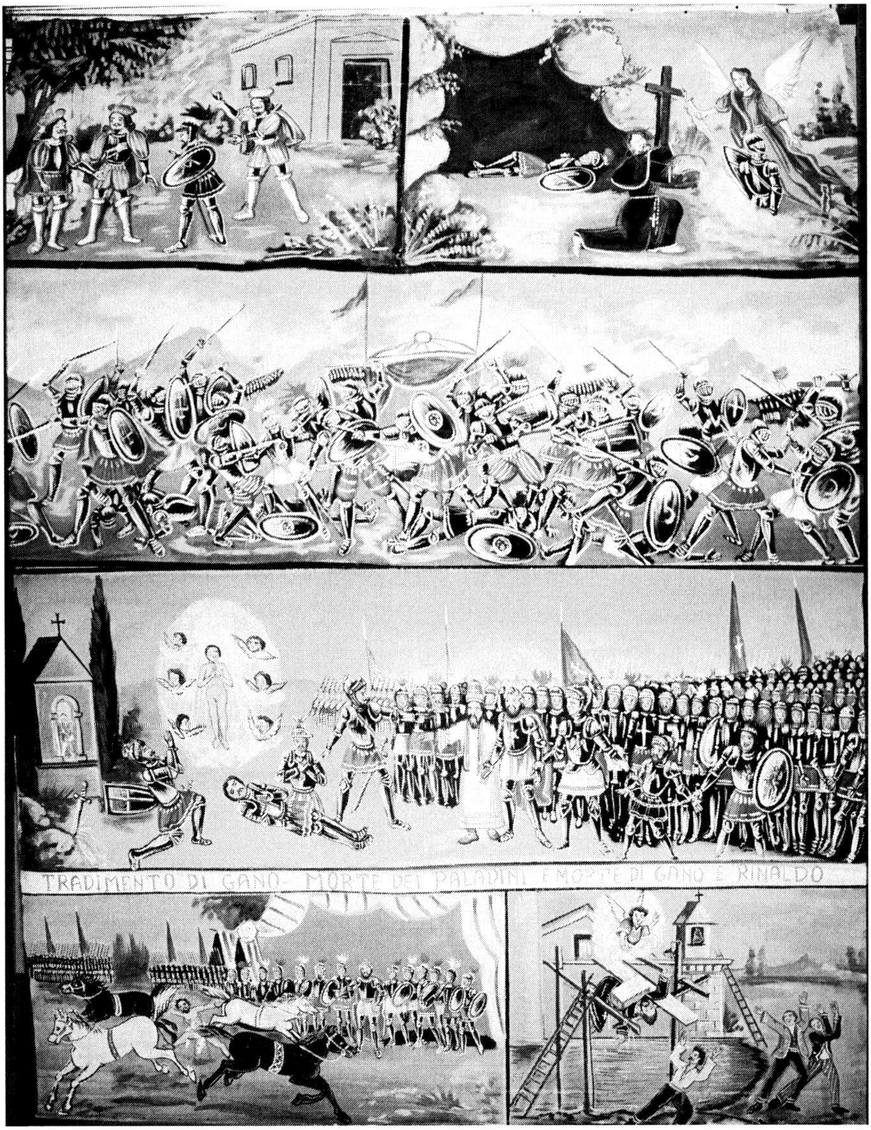

Palermitan playbill poster F portraying the Battle of Roncevaux (Pasqualino International Puppets Museum, Palermo).

side with very large scotch tape along the places where they used to be folded in order to be kept aside until their turn came to be exhibited outside the theater. These folds were one of the main causes of their deterioration, which did not happen in the posters from Palermo that were wrapped around the sticks glued to their upper and lower ends.

The posters from Catania normally carry their main subject written on the back, beside other notes written by the puppeteers, which are often quite noteworthy and interesting. In poster H these notes are lacking and the scotch tape is full of other notes, which surprisingly refer to other posters. There are very evident stains caused by the rain water they have been exposed to. The paper on which posters from Catania have been painted is light brown, which makes all colors rather dark on the whole, and white is never present. Main figures in the posters from Catania often occupy the entire space and they are obviously much bigger than in Palermo; also because puppets from Catania were much bigger, images were painted in order to be seen from a distance.

Poster H, portraying the battle of Roncevaux, has a Christian knight in the foreground, who is not distinguished by any particular insignia, and who is stabbed to death by the swords of two Saracens, one of which hits him in a particularly vulnerable spot: the throat. Moreover he is threatened by the sword of a third Saracen and he is hit by the stones thrown by a group of Saracens who are hiding behind the hill. These aggressions are performed from the Christian's back, a

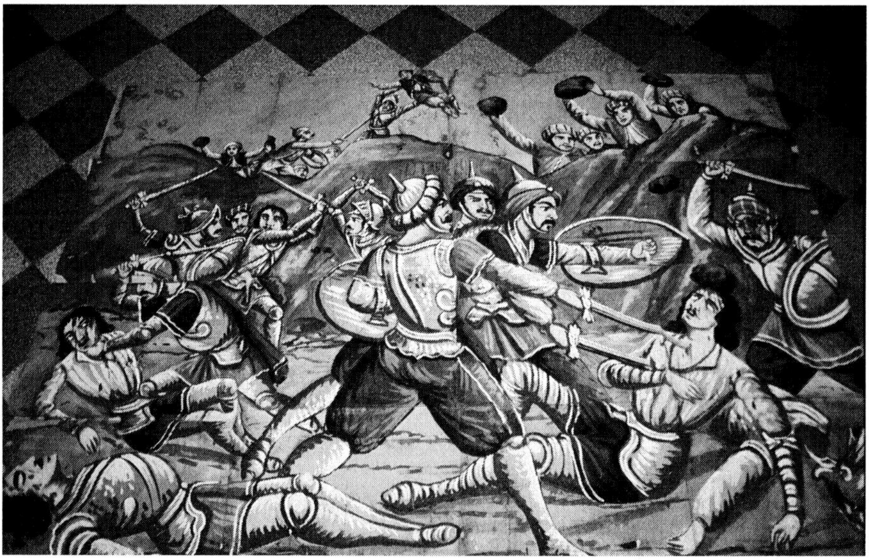

Catanese playbill poster H portraying the Battle of Roncevaux (Pasqualino International Puppets Museum, Palermo).

particularly coward act especially in the view of Sicilians, who traditionally have always shown a great appreciation for loyalty.

The launching of stones was a characteristic feature of the episode of the Rout of Roncevaux in Catania, consequently it was to be expected that the Roncevaux poster would show the same element. The sinister faces of the Saracens are characterized by big black moustaches and their threatening aspect is in sharp contrast to the eyes of the Christian, who is religiously looking at the sky and, already deprived of his armor and with his face flooded with blood, can remind us of Christ dying on the Cross. An oriental cap on the head and puffy trousers always distinguish the most notable Saracen warriors. This is precisely the way the Moor in the foreground is dressed; with his blatantly forward step, he occupies the entire visible space and he is the real focus of the scene. In the foreground on the left the body of a Christian is lying; behind him other secondary duels, whose outcomes are still uncertain, are taking place. The Saracens' pointed helmets are always indicating someone who is different in a negative way. The main function of the secondary characters is obviously to enhance the warriors in the foreground.

The posters from Catania, as stated in the book *Eroi di Sicilia* (Heroes from Sicily),[18] can often be divided into four parts: upper right, upper left, lower right and lower left. In the upper right part the character that embodies the maximum Good (or the maximum Evil) is often placed. In this case both upper parts of the poster are occupied by Saracens who from the hills are threatening and hitting the Christians with stones. In the I poster Orlando is offering the Emperor Charlemagne his sword whose name was Durlindana. Since he is portrayed in the standing posture it seems the poster is catching Orlando in the moment of his resurrection. The feathers that come out and hang from his helmet have some resemblance in shape with the fresh water that springs out of the rock behind him. Both water and blood usually represent life, even if in a different and sometimes opposite way: the water of the spring is the counterpart of the blood that is abundantly coming out of the dying horse's mouth in the lower right part of the poster. A woman, Alda la Bella (the Beautiful), is wearing clothes of the same color of those of the Emperor Charlemagne, who is next to her. This is a technique quite common in posters from Catania, used in order to indicate characters belonging to the same family.

Alda la Bella has her hand on her forehead to indicate her desperation in a very melodramatic attitude. As Pasqualino has noticed,[19] this exaggeration of feelings and the presence of a very wider background are among the characteristic features of posters from Catania compared to the ones from Palermo.

Both H and I posters have mountains in the background. But not all posters are set in the country: in another poster (called L), which portrays the quartering of Gano, the scene is set in a city. It's an anonymous and almost deserted city; the buildings look almost like the sides of a stage and with their symmetrical position become the backdrop of the main scene. In the far distance you can see a dome and a bell tower, which probably recall the Cathedral of Catania. It is significant that only two horses, instead of four as was normally the case, are quartering Gano, led by two characters who are probably the funny couple of Peppe and Nino. These two, like Nofriu and Virticchiu in Palermo (and Stan Laurel and Oliver Hardy in the U.S.), were always together, so much so that their names were usually fused into one: Peppenino. They belonged to the world of *farse* (comical sketches), which in this case, as so often happened in Catania, took part in the action on the stage next to the Paladins. This poster thus becomes proof of Pasqualino's hypothesis about the resemblance of Gano with the anti-heroes of the *farse:*

> A surprising resemblance exists between Gano, the super evil character, and the characters of the comical sketches (*farse*), who often mix to the serious ones carrying the role of servants of the heroes, as it happened with the so-called *maschere* ("masks," that is, comical characters) of the Commedia dell'Arte, from which they derive. Both Gano on one side and Peppenino and Virticchio on the other, are rather short, and move and talk in a ridiculous way. In the puppet shows in Rome and in Naples in the 19th century, the most common *maschera* was Pulcinella, who was always wearing white clothes. On a certain level the *maschere* who speak the local dialect represent the common people and every day life, the opposite of heroism. On a deeper level we can say that the outcome of the demons of the ancient ritual theater can be either a white or a black death: from one side Pulcinella, Peppenino, Virticchio, comical characters who are positive and help the heroes in their deeds; on the other side Gano, who puts obstacles in their way, causes their death, and rejoices for their killing.[20]

The scene of poster L is set in a city whose unreal atmosphere is stressed by the absence of the public around this execution. This poster

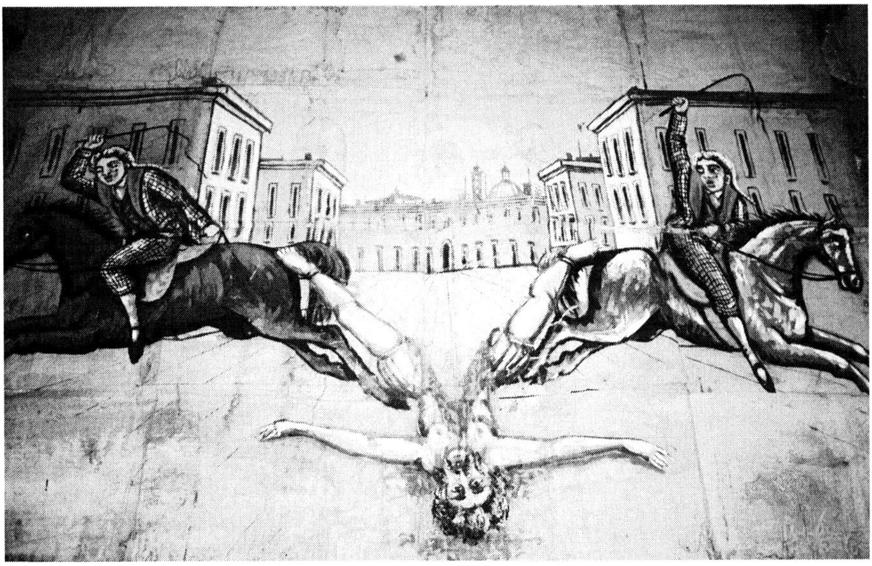

Catanese playbill poster L portraying the quartering of the traitor Gano di Magonza, who was personally responsible for the death of the Paladins at Roncevaux (Pasqualino International Puppets Museum, Palermo).

is not lacking a certain perspective though, contrary to most posters from Catania, who were under the influence of the lacking of depth in those theaters. Gano, who is portrayed with his head down and his body disintegrating in blood, stresses the main motif of this episode: through the annihilation of those who, fighting against the Good, turned the world upside down, natural order will be re-established, and the geometrical outline of this poster suggests that, too. Beside the usual four parts, a triangle can be seen, whose angles coincide with Gano's head and feet. It is important to recall that in Christian ideology Evil is often considered a channel for a more complete victory of the Good.

In the past the posters could offer a real "concentrate" of everything that happened in the chivalric stories and magically captured the attention of the passersby. The posters can still offer us vast information for studying folk art and for investigating what chivalric stories meant for Sicilian low social classes.

• Seven •

The Sicilian Painted Carts

The Sicilian Carts in a Nutshell

Chivalric motifs were painted on the sides of Sicilian carts that started to exist in their present form towards the middle of the 19th century when the Bourbon kings built the first carriage roads of modern times (Royal *trazzere*).

The Sicilian carts are the result of several kinds of extremely specialized skills, each of which requires the work of a different artisan. They have structural differences according to what area of the island they are from.

Sculptors carved several parts of the cart, including the wheels, the bars and *'u pizzu,* the center of the axle between the wheels, which has particular importance because it represents the image of the saint under whose protection the cart travelled. Early carts had blue religious motifs, but even when they started to have yellow and red chivalric and historical subjects, saints didn't abandon the cart, they were simply moved from the sides (called *masciddara*) to the *pizzu*, where we often find St. George, also a knight, on a horse while he is killing a dragon.

The blacksmith forged the *rabiscu* ("arabesque"), a particular iron frieze that together with the axle forms the *cascia 'i fusu*. In Palermo, the *rabiscu* represented almost exclusively vegetable elements, while in Eastern Sicily human and animal figures could also be found. It seems a bit strange that so much attention was paid to a part of the cart that is rather difficult to see. Nevertheless, it is necessary to remember that the breaking of the axle would have been very dangerous, if not fatal, for the cart driver who travelled on very uncomfortable and dangerous roads.

When the load was too big for a normal cart, for example a barrel, drays with two wheels (*traini*) or four (*strascini*) were used and they were usually painted in the same manner. In the past the same decorations could also be found on the stands for the sale of water in the streets or, even today, of seed vendors (*semenzai*).

The carriage was a real travelling book. The subjects were chosen according to personal tastes, as each cart was commissioned by a cart driver who chose the subjects for his cart from history books or prints so that the painter could faithfully copy them. Such subjects can be divided into extremely different types: the religious type preferred biblical subjects or lives of saints, the musical type could transform the cart into a promotional vehicle of the melodrama and the realistic type usually had hunting scenes. Scenes set in a castle or those of the story of Dante and Beatrice could be classified as fairy legendary.

The most common subjects were the chivalric ones, which in the second half of the 19th century invaded the sides of the cart, previously decorated with religious subjects. The great success of the puppet shows, like all fashions, could be easily exploited commercially. Chivalric subjects were soon followed by historical episodes to which they could be well assimilated, considering that historical characters were often represented as medieval knights, at the prime of their glory, while riding on a white horse.

Characters and episodes belong to all historical epochs, and historical characters were not usually connected to Sicilian history with some notable exceptions.

History of the Cart

The Sicilian landscape is almost entirely mountainous, and this has had an enormous effect on the local culture, making all communications and transportation tremendously difficult. Even now failing to take the modern motorways means hours and hours of extra driving. Many towns, even if today they are connected by paved roads, are still remote and difficult to reach. Sicily is a landscape, as Giuseppe Tomasi di Lampedusa says in his book *The Leopard,* which is never boring and which, we can add, winding endlessly through innumerable hills, offers a continuous change of scenery, like that of backdrops in the theater.

Telling the story of the Sicilian *carretto* can be either a very long or relatively short task. Long, if one begins with the earliest of wheeled vehicles; short, if the account is confined to the actual moment when the painted *carretto* is believed to have made its appearance in Sicily. To begin with the longest time frame, one could turn to Stuart Piggott. According to his history of wagons, chariots, and carts, from the Rhine to the Indus, unlike in the Americas, animal-drawn vehicles were known and in use by 3000 B.C. Usually oxen did the pulling and the wagons rolled on solid wooden wheels fashioned of three sections. The Greeks used two wheeled chariots pulled by horses and four wheeled wagons drawn by horses or mules.[1]

Through the examples of the Romans and Greeks the technology for building a vehicle on wheels was known to the Sicilians and those who ruled their island. Wagons were built for use in settlements and on farms, but cross-island transport was another matter. The rugged mountainous nature of Sicilian geography made travel and trade difficult. Roads were needed. The paths used for centuries were only suitable for animals and pedestrians as the terrain challenged anything on wheels.

Often cited in accounts of the antiquity of the *carretto* are the mosaic pavements in the Villa Casale at Piazza Armerina, dating to the 3rd and 4th centuries AD. In his home the wealthy owner of the villa admired pavements featuring heavy carts pulled by oxen, small chariots or horse-drawn quadrigas, and child-ridden carts tugged along by ostrich-power. Animal-drawn wooden vehicles were thus known to Sicilians, but whether they were in widespread use is unclear.

Among Sicily's early rulers, it was the Romans who were most eager and efficient as road builders. They built many roads, covering much of the island, especially in the interior. There were small hotels (*stationes* or *mansiones*) built at a distance that could be covered in one day's travel. Each stop offered the possibility of having a fresh horse, somewhat like the system of the Pony Express in nineteenth-century America. Roads were very well maintained, every irregularity in the surface was leveled, and bridges were built to cross streams and moats. Milestones marked distances and small votive shrines stood along the roads.[2] The Roman roads were not maintained by subsequent rulers. Lack of funds and lack of urgent need caused this neglect. Roads deteriorated into mule paths and the *trazzere* (tracks) used by shepherds and their flocks.

Unfortunately the paths often crossed the properties of absentee landlords who made no effort to maintain them. Until the arrival of the Bourbon monarchs in the eighteenth century, no large-scale road projects were undertaken. Thus, by the middle of the nineteenth century, tracks, not roads, remained. Bridges were also seriously lacking. One of the reasons given for the high wheels of the *carretto* was the need to cross streams or seasonal rivers where no bridges existed.[3]

Most transportation was on foot or muleback. A line of three to eight mules was called a *redina* and it was entrusted to a *vurdunaru* (or muleteer). Alexis de Tocqueville described travel in such a caravan in the 1820s. He rode on a horse; others in his party rode mules atop saddlebags, while their muleteers were in constant motion keeping men and beasts together on the path.[4] A *redina* was regularly used to carry wheat or sugar to the coast from the interior. Other cargo and people often travelled by sea, which was dangerous because of the possibility of pirates, but much easier than travelling by land. The sea could not entirely solve the problem though, as the interior of the island remained cut off.

The first road connecting Sicilian cities was the *Regia Strada* (the Royal Road) of 1830 from Palermo to Messina. Fifty years later, one visitor commented that roads were still not what she expected. Wrote Frances Elliot: "Poseidon is not king of Sicily for nothing. Roads in his island are constructed for fine weather; in bad weather you must stay at home."[5] Or one could emulate Poseidon and travel by sea as many visitors did.

But people did travel into the interior and the solution, according to Henry Tuckerman, the first American to write about Sicily, was the *lettiga* or litter. As he wrote of a trip to see the temple at Segesta, "Now and then they passed a *lettiga* with its complement of passengers and attendants. This is the national carriage of Sicily. It consists of a kind of box, like the body of a carriage, rudely painted with the effigies of saints and martyrs, and secured to two poles which are supported in front and behind upon the backs of two mules. The constant tinkling of the bells, and the uneasy motion of these animals, combined with the narrow dimensions of the vehicle, render it a comfortless conveyance."[6]

Tuckerman saw these painted litters in 1837 when he made his trip. Only four years earlier, another traveler had written one of the first descriptions of the *carretto.* The Baron Gonzalve de Nervo was traveling from Messina to Palermo in April of 1833. He and his companions were making the difficult trip on five mules, including one animal for their baggage and another for their guide. They were told that their party followed forty-two other foreigners who had already visited Sicily that year.

For four days, he wrote, they had only met mules, but outside of Bagheria they encountered *carretti*, that is, small carts, almost all painted blue. Images of the Virgin or of a saint were painted on the panels and their horses wore harnesses with plaques of copper or gilded nails. On their heads were colored plumes in the style of those in Rome.[7]

Litters and sedan chairs (*portantine*) were carrying people, but obviously *carretti* were transporting goods now that travel was becoming easier. Litters had been used for centuries in Sicily, although at first only for royalty. As Luigi Maria Majorca Mortillaro wrote, Queen Beatrice, the wife of Charles of Anjou, had entered Naples in 1266 in a litter and all Naples spoke with admiration of such a new and royal means of transportation. Twenty years later Queen Constance appeared in Palermo in a litter, undoubtedly causing similar astonishment.[8]

The litter, as Majorca Mortillaro described it, was elliptical in shape. It had doors and windows with curtains on both sides and was carried by poles attached to horses (in the city) or mules (in the country). The interior was usually upholstered and the exterior painted and gilded. Painters used the areas below the windows for garlands of flowers surrounding angels and biblical and mythical scenes. Sculptors created eagles, lions, and dragons to place along the litter's roofline. Horses and mules wore appropriately elegant trappings on their shoulders, heads, and backs.[9] Royal litters and those owned by important families were decorated in such sumptuous fashion while those that served a commercial purpose were far plainer.

A sedan chair carried one person, while a litter could be used by two or even six. Sedan chairs were also called "flying chairs" in Sicily and, in the historical center of Palermo, there is still a Street of Flying Chairs (*Via delle Sedie Volanti*) where they were once built.

The transition from litter to *carretto* is poignantly evoked in Giovanni Verga's story, "*Cos'è il Re*"[10] (published in 1883). In the story Cosimo, a litter owner, is hired to transport the Queen to Catania. He is very honored by the duty, but years later, reflects on its effect on his life. The King and Queen had come to Sicily in part to consider the problem of roads. When better roads were built, litter drivers became obsolete as *carretti* and coaches now carried people and goods. Verga, a very important Sicilian writer from Catania, wrote about cart drivers as well as those who escorted litters in his books and stories. For example, a character named Alfio is a cart driver in his novel *I Malavoglia* (*The House by the Medlar Tree,* published in 1881) and another Alfio, also a cart driver, appears in his short story *Cavalleria Rusticana (Rustic Chivalry)*, later used for the libretto for the famous opera by Pietro Mascagni.

Another visitor whose visual evidence on wheeled vehicles is important is the French artist Jean Houel. He was in Messina in 1780 where he did several watercolors of a major square. An ox drawn hay wagon with high sides is shown crossing the square in one of his watercolors.

By 1800 there were two precedents well established for the development of the *carretto.* Litters and coaches inspired its decoration, although the results were eventually quite different, while the expertise derived from building the numerous wheeled carts and wagons related to its construction. What cart builders built came in different sizes and configurations. Heights ranged from those of the small carts pulled by Sardinian donkeys to taller ones for mules or horses to pull. Photographers frequently posed a child next to the donkey cart to indicate how small both cart and animal actually were. There were flatbed, four-wheeled wagons for the heaviest ox-pulled loads (wine barrels, for example) and carts with removable back panels for extra lengthy cargo. Unlike litters, sedan chairs, and coaches, none came with roofs. Flatbed carts, known as *traini* (two wheels) or *strascini* (four wheels), usually lacked sides, but were still decorated on any possible surface.

Much of what is known about the history of the *carretto* begins with the work of Dr. Giuseppe Pitrè (1846–1916), Sicily's great ethnologist. Pitrè collected information about carts and examples of them.

In researching the history of the *carretto* he looked at what he termed *tavolette.* A cart driver's life was often endangered. Bandits frequented his route and tried to rob him; his horse or mule could stumble or fall, causing cart, passengers, and contents to fall as well. Cart drivers who survived such accidents gave thanks for their deliverance to the Virgin Mary or their patron saint. As evidence of that gratitude drivers commissioned small paintings, *tavolette* or more often known as *ex votos,* that showed the accident. The date and story of the event were usually given and the *ex voto* then hung in a local church.

By their very nature the *ex votos* were expected to be a realistic representation of an actual event. *Pincisanti* (or saint painters) usually painted *ex votos,* and generally carts could be expected to be shown accurately. What Pitrè noticed was that the development of cart painting could be traced visually, through the evidence of the *ex votos* which can still be viewed in the sanctuaries of churches at Altavilla Milicia or at Trecastagni. In fact, Pitrè wrote, fifteen percent of the *ex votos* he examined featured cart accidents.[11]

Pitrè discovered a dated *ex voto* that showed a cart painted only with lines on a yellow background. The cart shown was a tall-wheeled, square-paneled cart from Trapani with red and green lines framing each panel. In one of the cart panels was a large circle and in its center was the numeral 164, perhaps indicating the number from a town license. In black near the cart was the date "25 7bre 1829," indicating when the man fell under the cart, but was saved, thanks to St. Biagio (Blaise in English).[12] Thus it seems from Pitrè's research that at first *carretti* were given a simple coat of paint to protect the wood. A bit of decoration, like the lines framing the panel on the cart of the 1829 *ex voto,* came next. An 1855 *ex voto* from the church at Altavilla Milicia also shows this arrangement. The yellow cart has a simple red border on its panels while the decoration is limited to an eagle and the numeral 185 in a circle. The accident involved a mother and child who appear to have been run over by the cart.

The earliest *ex votos* showed simply painted carts. A solid color covered their side panels and the decoration consisted of a garland of flowers with a number in the center. The garland seems directly borrowed from painting on the side of a litter. Working carts probably never had much more decoration than that.

The next stage was figurative painting, religious in nature. On panels cart painters painted the Virgin Mary, the Holy Family, or a local patron saint, as Henry Tuckerman had seen painted on litters. As a change from religious history the up-to-date cart painter soon offered his clients something new: history, ancient or modern, or perhaps a combination. Thus, Giuseppe Tomasi di Lampedusa describes a trip made by a priest to his hometown in February 1861: "Getting there had meant a five-hour shaking in a cart with his feet dangling behind a horse's tail; but once he had overcome his nausea at the patriotic pictures newly painted on the cart panels, culminating in a rhetorical presentation of a flame-colored Garibaldi arm in arm with an aquamarine Santa Rosalia, they had been a pleasant five hours."[13]

With three notable exceptions cart painting was not usually used to record Sicilian history. The first example was the Sicilian Vespers of 1282, seen as a revolution by the Sicilian people against the French invaders; and second, the conquest of Arab Sicily in the eleventh century by Roger of Hauteville, the first of the Norman rulers. His son, Roger or Ruggiero II, is even more popular in cart painting. The third was the Risorgimento, shown in the battle scenes of Garibaldi. In the nineteenth century the Risorgimento, the struggle for the reunification of Italy, led to an idealized interpretation of all previous history. The Sicilian Vespers were then seen as a glorious rebellion against the French Anjou dynasty, and the Norman conquest was interpreted as a holy war against the infidels.

One of Garibaldi's men, Giuseppe Cesare Abba, wrote in his *Noterelle* (notebooks) that carts painted with religious scenes transported the artillery for the army in 1860. According to Abba, after the army left from Marsala, they headed for Palermo: "After we had gone a good way along the main road, we took to the open country along a difficult little path winding between the vineyards. Our guns followed with difficulty, mounted on carts painted with sacred scenes and drawn by spirited stallions, whose bells tinkled out merrily."[14]

The subjects of a cart's paintings have been classified into five types: history-chivalry, fables and legends, religious, music and realistic.[15] In the historical category a cart painter's repertoire could include subjects as old or as new as the customer wanted. Something Roman or Greek (perhaps, Alexander the Great), foreign (El Cid, Charles V, or Cortez), or relatively modern (Napoleon I or III) might all be of interest. The Napoleon III subjects related to the Franco-Prussian war and thus were nicknamed *prussiana.* A set of four *prussiana* images were a specialty of Michele Ducato of Bagheria and Francesco Armao of Santa Flavia. Often on the same cart episodes belonging to different epochs and distant places were painted side to side: Caesar crossing the Rubicon, the battle of Legnano, Christopher Columbus and the discovery of America, Garibaldi, the four Musketeers, Richard Lionheart, Frederick II, Francesco Ferrucci, Charles of Anjou, Geoffrey of Boulogne, Constantine the Great, Hannibal and the Crusades.

Cart paintings of contemporary history could present incongruous situations. When travelling near Erice after World War I, Louis Golding encountered a wedding party coming down the hill from the site of the temple of Venus. There were many painted carts carrying the bride, groom, family and friends, but one thing surprised the writer: "It was curious that, whereas elsewhere in Sicily, the only motives I had encountered on the painted panels of the carts were drawn from sacred story or the wars of the Christians and Saracens or from Othello, here in the cars jolting down from immemorial Eryx the motives were desperately up-to-date: torpedoes, attacks with liquid gas, tanks, airplanes."[16]

The subjects most commonly painted on the carts belonged to the chivalric repertory, very well known to Sicilians because, beginning in the 1840s, small theaters all over the island started to perform chivalric stories through the use of puppets. The chivalric stories painted on the carts were the same ones drawn upon for the plays of the puppet theater and the tales of the storytellers. Of all the categories these would be the most familiar to a Sicilian audience. They would recognize the adventures and the characters involved. These subjects would most often be painted also on market shop walls and, much later on, decorating the *motorlapa* or small trucks.

The fables and legends category included the stories of St. Geneviève of Brabant and of William Tell. Religious scenes were taken from both the Old and New Testaments. Cart painters painting musical panels found sources in operas popular in Sicily, such as *Carmen, Aïda, Otello,* and above all, *Cavalleria Rusticana,* since it was set in Sicily.

William Agnew Paton was fascinated by the subjects of carts when he viewed them on his visit to Palermo in 1897. He and his wife spent as much time as they could trying to decipher the subjects they saw on the "peripatetic picture gallery" of the streets. He wrote:

> Other series of four panels pictured the horrors of a dissecting-room, others dealt with the story of Jonah and the whale, Daniel and his lions, Noah and the ark, David and Goliath, the Four Evangelists; Popes, many; saints, innumerable; St. George and his dragon; "San Giuliano appearing to the Normans" to encourage them to renewed attacks upon the Saracens. There were fanciful portraits of beautiful women and handsome men; knights and ladies; enchanters, fairies, monsters, and angels; devils and monks. Many carts were adorned with scenes from Italian operas, and many more with designs of fruits and flowers or gaudy landscapes—Etna in eruption, for instance, and storms at sea. In the endless collection were portraits of Hannibal, Scipio Africanus, Julius Caesar, Dionysius of Syracuse, Charlemagne, Don John of Austria, Barbarossa the Pirate, Richard the Lionhearted, Giovanni da Procida, Napoleon I., Abraham Lincoln, Vittorio Emanuele, King Umberto; and more numerous than all, of Giuseppe Garibaldi.[17]

Usually all of the side panels displayed related imagery, but not always. Carts existed, much to the delight of onlookers, which mixed and matched times and places. Nor did the sculptor or metalworker feel obligated to carve or forge works that mirrored the subjects of the panel paintings.

In attempting to answer the question of why a cart might be painted, there are several reasons that have been proposed. One is the obvious necessity of protecting the wood. Next comes the argument of the presence of cart paintings as divine protection through the religious subject matter, used first on the side and back panels, later in the *chiave* and *pizzu* carvings. Painted carts were also advertising, both for the driver's business and for himself. Unlike painted wagons or carts elsewhere, however, a cart did not have the owner's name on it, a practice later more established with trucks. A beautiful *carretto* satisfied the driver's need for a status symbol. It became part of his persona, a sort of Ferrari automobile to exhibit with great pride. It was also an imitation of the vehicles owned or driven by the upper classes. Those who owned litters, sedan chairs, or carriages could parade around town in them, just as a driver could show off his *carretto* in the country.

From the studies of numerous scholars, beginning with Pitrè, it would seem that the painted cart first appeared in the early 1800s. Building of the carts became more widespread as the nineteenth century went on. The golden age of the cart may have been the 1920s. They were still very much in use through the Second World War, but by 1950 the small motorized truck provided too much competition. At that time the use of the painted *carretto* for most everyday commercial purposes ended and its role in festival and parade use took over. Mario Tschinke remembered that around 1960 small *carretti,* painted in somber colors of blue or gray, were used to make deliveries in Palermo. These were small carts, propelled by men, much in the way a rickshaw or peddler's cart is used.

A major source for any study of carts was written by Giuseppe Capitò, a professor of architecture at the University of Palermo. His study, *Il Carretto Siciliano,* was first published in 1923 as the last in a series of eight monographs on topics in the field of decorative arts. Twenty years later an English translation appeared, entitled *The Sicilian Cart,* which was printed for the U.S. Army then stationed in Sicily. *The Sicilian Cart* had no illustrations, making it at times a bit confusing. In 1979, Capitò's essay was published once more by the publisher Sellerio in a book that included excerpts from descriptions of carts written by some of the early foreign visitors to Sicily. "The *carretto siciliano,* so extensively used that in the city of Palermo there are 5,000 of them, may well be considered a specific regional element, for its form is found exclusively in Sicily.... It is a two-wheeled vehicle without springs, destined for the transport of light loads and made to be pulled, in general, by one animal which has the two-fold task of draught and of sustaining part of the weight upon its back. The weight, because of this, is ordinarily placed with a slight excess in the front of the cart.... It has no brakes of any kind."[18]

Capitò then declared that "it must be thought of as a mediocre product of the cartwright's art." The lack of brakes kept the cart from speeding but, continued the author, "Despite repeated municipal regulations, the narrow rim of the wheels has never been widened and it quickly ruins the surface of the roads. Moreover, it is a coefficient of weakness in the structure of the cart. On the whole, therefore, one might say that the cart is ill-designed, for although it has its good qualities, it does not overcome passive resistance."[19] Despite this criticism, he obviously felt that the cart was rather unique and deserved further analysis.

Documentation of Eastern Sicily's artisans had to await researchers such as Salvatore Lo Presti, whose book *Il Carretto* (The Cart) appeared in 1959.[20]

Makers of the Cart

The cart, whether small or large, is the work of five craft specialists: the carpenter who builds it, the sculptor who carves it, the wrought iron worker (*fabbro*) who creates the section placed over the axle, the two types of painters, and, for the horse, the harness and trappings maker. Without all of these artisans, the cart cannot be completed. Therein lies the current problem. The skill of creating wrought iron work is no longer being passed from masters of one generation to the next. Hence the complex arabesques in metal will either have to be omitted or recycled from existing, older pieces for future carts. In Sicily there are very few wrought iron workers. Carmelo Saccaro of Palermo is said to have been the last of this particular kind of *fabbro* artisans and he died some years ago.

Another master, this time of *armigghi* or horse trappings, also shares the craft spotlight with no one else. Rosario La Piana, a Palermitan like Saccaro, is in mid-career yet the skills he uses to create horse headgear, bridles, girths, collars, and saddle blankets under the bases for plumes are not being passed on to apprentices.

One of the first cart builders to be identified in print is Giuseppe Montalbano whom Pitrè commissioned to create the cart he exhibited in the 1881 Milan fair. Pitrè also mentioned Rosolino Castellano as the painter of the cart and Antonino Mangano as the maker of the horse trappings.

Some of the travel essayists who spent long periods in Sicily interviewed cart artisans recorded information on their techniques as well as mentioning their names. In 1896 French artist and travel writer Gaston Vuillier described the work of a painter named Mario Zizolfo who worked in the San Domenico neighborhood of Palermo and sketched him painting panels. He praised Zizolfo's work, saying that although he might never be an "official painter," his knights and bandits certainly gave more pleasure to those who saw them on the carts than did much of the boring and unskilled work usually termed "art."[21]

Cecilia Wærn was intrigued by the work of the wood carvers. The finest carts, she wrote, "are lavishly carved with a profusion of scrolls, detached rosettes, stars, whorls, grotesques of various kinds, and little human heads."[22] In talking to the carvers about the sources of their imagery, she learned that some motifs were based on book illustrations, some came from their own imagination, and some from the public garden. That was where one carver went when he needed to study details of Panormus, a symbolic statue representing the soul or mythical *genius loci* of Palermo.[23]

Giuseppe Capitò shared Mrs. Wærn's interest in the work of the wood carver. Capitò was impressed by a young man he met who worked in the atelier of Giuseppe and Paolo Sbacchi. In his carving the young sculptor used no models, nor did he copy any elements from other sources. He "drew" with his chisel, cutting away the excess with a blunt tool. He made no marks on the wood to locate objects or indicate spacing, but he seemed to plan his work from experience.[24]

Dorothy Leadbeater, writing in 1961, felt that sculptured ornament followed certain rules as to both location and design. What was carved on the cart shafts, on the *pizzu,* around the painted panels and elsewhere was determined by traditions that sculptors learned. She found that both in sculpture and painting there were parallels to the decoration of eighteenth-century coaches. Sculptured motifs, in the round or in relief, including seahorses, lions, *putti,* flowers, masks, and winged figures, appear on both coaches and carts. "The duplication," she wrote, "seems more than mere coincidence."[25]

Miss Leadbeater found that cart painters often used prints and postcards as the source for their panel paintings. She wrote that Francesco Paolo Cardinale, for example, "capably copied" Pietro da Cortona's "Meeting of Aeneas and Venus" for a cart panel.[26]

Horses, mules, donkeys, and oxen all pulled carts. A cart driver with a donkey often hoped to earn enough to buy a mule so that he could transport heavier goods, as Giovanni Verga wrote in *The House by the Medlar Tree* (1881). His character, Alfio Mosca, says, "when I've laid a little money aside, I'll buy a mule and set up as a real carter, like Cinghialenta."[27] Horses were more expensive, but today it is the horse, and perhaps even a white horse, said the Federicos of Partinico, that is requested when they rent carts for parades.

For those who came from abroad, or for Sicilian scholars, studying cart making and interviewing its artisans were made easier by the fact that most workshops could be found near each other. As Cecilia Wærn wrote: "These craftsmen's quarters merged into the region for the sale of country produce—as it still does. There is no better place for the study of the painted donkey carts than the old squares and *piazze* of this part of Palermo.... One of these squares, the Piazza di Sant'Anna, was in the eighteenth century still the corn market with huge warehouses for corn. The *bordonai* (muleteers) from the country had their church and we may be sure also their *funnaci* (inns—from Arabic *funduk*) here."[28]

Thus Mrs. Wærn and other writers headed for one neighborhood of Palermo to pose their questions. Few visiting writers spent time in Catania or any of the other towns where carts were built. According to Lo Presti, Catania's cart makers were to be found near the Castello Ursino and in the San Cristoforo quarter.[29] In addition, towns north of Catania had cartmakers' workshops of which the most famous, then and now, was Aci Sant'Antonio. For the cart artisans, working near each other made a great deal of sense since the cart needed to move from one atelier to the next for completion. Giuseppe Capitò would add that those interested should look on the roadway, because "a large part of the work, during the long summer months and during the beautiful days of the mild Sicilian winter, is done in the open."[30] Outside the shop was where carts were worked on, orders accepted and payments received. Carts were completed, one at a time, in a manner still followed.

Up to about twenty years ago, most of the remaining cartmakers in Palermo worked near the Corso dei Mille, the broad street on which Garibaldi and his army (called *I Mille*, "the Thousand," or *le camicie rosse* "The Red Shirts") entered the city and which was later named after them. A number on Corso dei Mille is frequently the address painted by both the builders and painters of carts above the side panels of their *carretti.*

The Cart Builder and the Sculptor

A commission for a cart began in the workshop of the cart builder. He would select three woods for the cart: walnut for the box, beams, and wheel rims; beech for the shafts; and ash for the spokes.

A particularly interesting moment in the building of the cart was the "circling of the wheels," when the metal rim was attached to the wooden wheel. First, the big iron rim was heated by placing it on burning coals arranged in a circle. At one time this operation used to happen near the sea or a river so that water could be used to cool the metal, but now, on the rare occasion of the building of a new cart, it occurs near the cart builder's workshop. Then the heated rim was clamped on the wheel and tightened with the aid of a special pliers (*cagni*).

Carts from Marsala and Mazara are easily recognizable because of several important details: they lack altogether both the richly decorated ironwork (*rabiscu*) and the sculpted wooden piece (*chiave*) between the wheels and have very large wheels that are not sculpted and richly painted and decorated as in the rest of Sicily. The reason for this is that carts from the Trapani province were often used for the transportation of salt and they were driven across the *Stagnone*, as the large lagoon area near the salt beds is called. For that function they needed the large wheels and the usual decoration is lacking in the part of the cart that was bound to be often in the water. The saltworks are still active in that area of Sicily. In Eastern Sicily carts are normally smaller and always had rectangular sides.

Cart names often indicated the intended cargo. The Palermitan carts can be of the *vinaruola* type, used for the transportation of grapes or wine barrels, hence the "*vino*" in its name, and its sides (*masciddara*, that is, "jaws") were more open than the *frumentaru* type, used for the transportation of straw and grain in its more closed box (*frumento* means wheat in Italian). The *tirraloru* carried things of the earth (*terra*) such as sand, gravel or dirt.

In addition to the different wheel sizes, the shape and number of panels differed, according to regional preference. In Eastern Sicily panels are square while in Western Sicily they are trapezoidal in shape. Two panels are found on each side of a cart, with three panels along the back with the notable exception of Marsala and Campobello di Mazara in the Trapani province, where the panels were rectangular, divided into three sections instead of the normal two, and the three panels of each side are surmounted by a bar along the top.

To identify parts of the Sicilian cart there are special terms, in both Sicilian and Italian. The cart is called *carretto* in Italian (or sometimes, *carro* or, if it is small, *carrettino*). *Carretta* is the word in Spanish and *charette* in French. The box of a cart is the *cassa* (Sic. *cascia*); there are two wheels (*ruote*) connected by an iron axle (Sic. *fusu*). At the hub where the axle meets each wheel are *boccole* (thin metal pieces that "sing" due to the friction as the wheel turns). On the sides of the cart are panels (*sponde*), painted on both inside and outside the cart; these side panels are called *fiancate laterali*. Along the back the smaller panels form the *portello*. Panels are separated from each other by carved and painted dividers (the *pioli;* Sic. *barruni*).

Other parts of the cart, all painted and carved, have individual names, but in most cases I have used their English equivalents, such as shafts, spokes, and supports.

A sculptor carves all of the details of the cart's parts: the sides of the shafts, the areas around the panels, the dividers that separate the panels, the spokes of the wheels, and, underneath the cart, the hidden gallery where both his and the metalworker's finest efforts dwell. Underneath the box, attached to the axle, is the *cascia 'i fusu* assemblage, which included the wrought iron work known as arabesque (Sic. *rabiscu*), and, in the center, a small carved wooden square (Sic. *pizzu*), which was normally dedicated to a sacred image.

Often blocking this from view and stretching horizontally from underneath one side of the cart box to the other are the two sections called *chiavi* ("key"). One is placed above the axle and below the metal frieze (Sic. *rabiscu*) and forms the *cascia 'i fusu* section. The term indicates its location below the box (Sic. *cascia*) and above the axle linking the wheels (Sic. *fusu*). This is the smaller of the two *chiavi,* or *chiave anteriore.* On its narrow surface carvers often repeated motifs of daisies or acanthus leaves.

In the center of the *chiave anteriore* is yet another carved work, the square *pizzu.* Here, the carver and cart builder thought, was the most vulnerable area of the cart. A broken axle was a calamity and the subject matter of the *pizzu* emphasized that axles needed to be protected. Thus the *pizzu* carving was almost always religious in nature. Two among the most common figures occupying the *pizzu* are the Holy Family and St. George killing the Dragon. The latter portrays a kind of fighting not very different from what had to be faced by the Paladins, who were often fighting against dragons, monsters and demons. The growing nationalism subsequent to the unification of Italy (1861), and especially during the fascist Period (1921–43), deeply fascinated the cart painters, and led cart sculptors to portray Italy as a statuesque woman in the *pizzu* of several carts. One of the oldest *pizzu* carvings known, dated to 1850 by Antonio Daneu, shows St.

George riding a large-eyed horse while attacking the enemy beast. The eye may distantly be related to the eye still painted near a boat prow as a protective symbol in many parts of the world. While this practice was also certainly common among ancient Mediterranean peoples, it has not been observed in Sicily for at least half a century. Other choices were scenes from the New Testament: the Flight into Egypt, the Annunciation, or the Holy Family.

The second *chiave,* or *chiave posteriore,* as shown in an exhibition catalogue, is the large, heavily sculptured piece, best seen when the cart is tipped forward and its underneath sections are visible.[31] This *chiave* received more attention than the *pizzu* because it is more visible. The same word (*chiave)* is used, but its shape is not identical in both parts of Sicily. Carvers in Palermo preferred a rectangular shape, while those in the east chose a half moon. In each case the *chiave* ends in carved elements with heads, animals, or perhaps entire figures repeated as pairs. Below the *chiave,* in eastern Sicily, carvers added the title of the scene, a practice not followed in the west.

The scene on the *chiave* could be religious or secular, drawn from all the same genres as the paintings on the cart panels, but not necessarily related to them. On a cart with painted panels showing the deeds of Columbus, the carver of the *chiave* below might contribute something distant in time and place, a scene from an opera, or even the inauguration of the cart, or just the cart itself with its cart driver. The back panel of a cart features Columbus in chains, being returned to Spain as a prisoner. Below the paintings is the carved *chiave* with its biblical scene of *The Triumph of King David.* In the area of Palermo the patron saint of the city Saint Rosalia is often portrayed. What is seldom possible to determine is how a *chiave,* once it was separated from its cart, might fit into the original decorative scheme.

The *barruni,* or dividers between panels, may terminate in carved heads, often featuring the somewhat quizzical faces of Paladins. Paladins are also carved on the spokes of wheels, although not all wheels have decorations. In the corners above the panels a Palermo carver may place large faces, while a sculptor in Catania may carve a border of rosettes. The long narrow shafts have long been seen as appropriate locations for snakes, mermaids, dolphins, cupids, acanthus leaves and vines. On one shaft a small figure called *scarpuzza* ("little shoe" in Sicilian) is carved. The driver could rest his foot on it and insert the reins through its small hole, if the horse becomes restive. Once the carving is completed and the metalwork attached, the cart can be delivered to the painter. On occasion, said Carmelo Saccaro, a cart will be left unpainted, but varnished. The sculpture is easier to see on this cart called *in frasca* and, he said, these carts are often intended for exhibition.

The Metal Worker

The metalworker, the *fabbro,* unlike the cart painter or builder, is basically responsible for one major element of the cart: the wrought iron section located above the axle. Intricate and complex though it is, this portion of the cart can only be appreciated when the cart is tipped, shafts pointed down, and the undercarriage of the cart is visible. Its name, *rabiscu* or arabesque, suggests a relationship to Islamic sources, as do the abstract, vegetal sources in the composition. Carmelo Saccaro described the basic form as a line that turned and twisted, but held no recognizable shapes. The turns and twists suggest leaves and vines but were not intended as such in Palermo-style work. The design also suggests a relationship to the floral forms favored by Palermo Art Nouveau architects and designers, practitioners of the Liberty style.

The *rabiscu* is painted. On Palermo carts solid paint areas contrast with cross-hatched portions, often in red or blue and white. With the aid of a simple air blower the metalworker feeds his fire so that his iron bars become incandescent. These, beaten on the anvil, are widened to create the discs characteristic of Palermo work. Some carts also display a bouquet of spiraling metalwork over the nails of the *barruni,* or dividers.

The Pitrè museum in Palermo owns a beautiful series of *casce 'i fusu* from Eastern Sicily, which have characteristics that are quite different from those of the western part of the island. The wooden centre called *pizzu* is often lacking; when it's present, it is usually rectangular instead of square; in one case instead of the usual sacred image, it has two people with knives in their hands. Even the iron work is different; while in western Sicily it has several metal discs without figures, in eastern Sicily we can see several metal leaves that are mixed with a

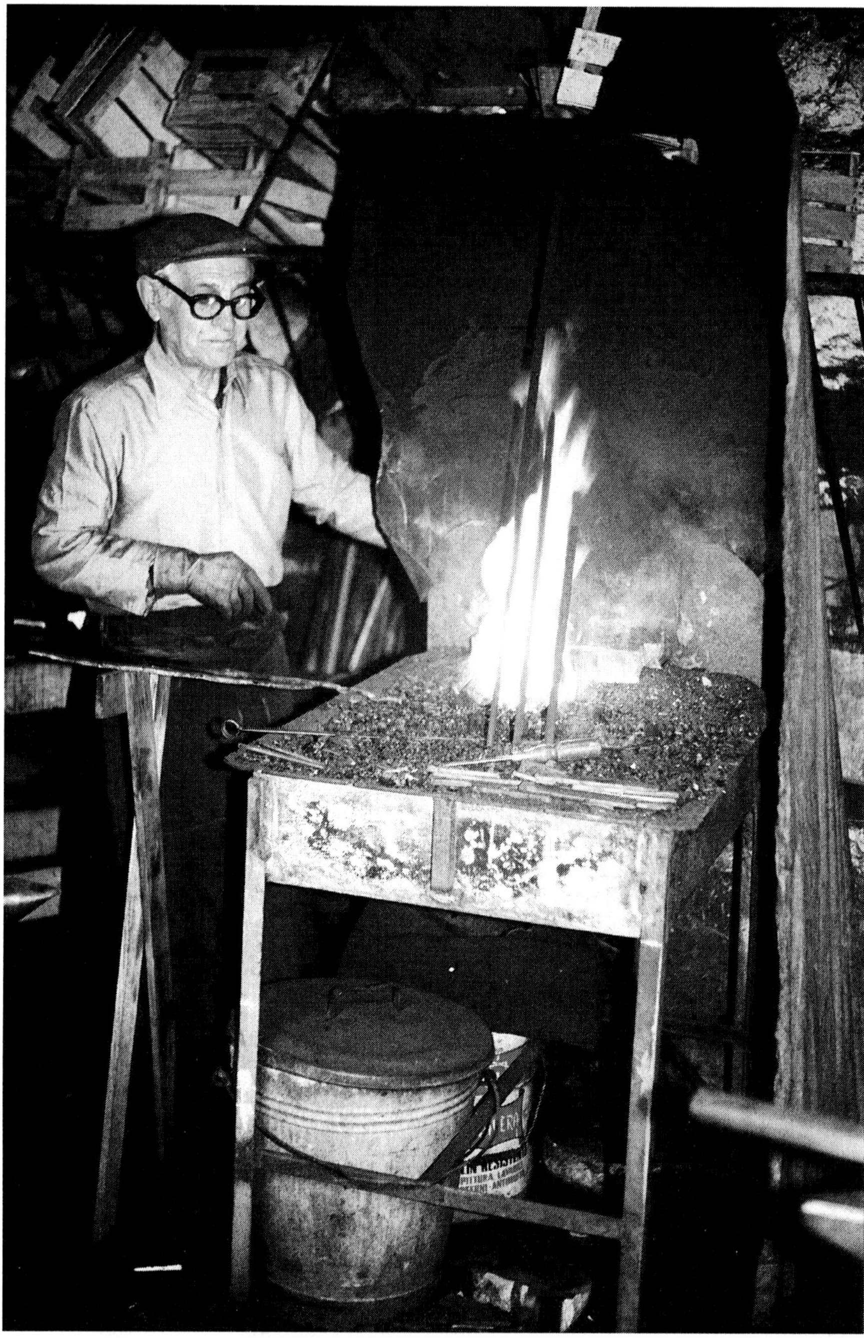

The iron worker Carmelo Saccaro at work in his workshop in 2002.

"baroque" crowd of small flowers, birds, wings, and heads of Christian warriors. In another cart two of these leaves are dedicated to the sea world and another to the country world. There may be a link between these *casce 'i fusu* and other craftsmanship objects produced by Sicilian ironworkers who used to be very prolific working out garden gates, beds, and balconies. Many decorations belonging to the repertory of manneristic and baroque art became popular with lower classes.

The Catania-area metalworker introduces people, horses, equestrian knights and much more, which are soldered to his *rabiscu* designs. Small figures may be inside the basic composition or protrude so horsemen seem to gallop away from their backdrop. Dancers and musicians in the *rabiscu* of the Pillitteri cart were said to refer to the family of the original owner. Joseph Pillitteri commissioned the cart in Sicily in 1949. When he moved to Canada in 1962 he brought the cart along. It later became part of the collections of the Canadian Museum of Civilization. Its panel paintings show Angelica at Charlemagne's court, Charlemagne entering Paris, the death of Oliver, and Orlando's ghost handing the legendary Durendal (in Italian, *Durlindana*) sword to Charlemagne.

The weight of the *cascia 'i fusu* (the *rabiscu* and the *chiave* assemblage) has a very practical function. It altered the center of gravity of the cart, thereby making it more stable. It also makes it easier to lift the shafts of the cart, even with one hand.

Since the art of metalworking for carts is no longer learned, old pieces are often salvaged, refurbished, and reattached to carts. This is especially true for *boccole*, the bronze elements in the middle of the wheels, once made by special artisans who have long since disappeared. An occasional *rabiscu* or *cascia 'i fusu* also became a table or a chandelier.

The Painter

Probably more has been written about the painters and their workshops than about any of the other cart artisans. Often their work has been identified and information about workshops in the Palermo and Catania provinces has been published. There were several artists' workshops in Bagheria (the Ficano and Ducato families), Palermo (the

Picciurro and Carrozza families) and Partinico.[32] Some of them are still active.

Among the especially well-known names of painters are those of Bagheria, beginning with Filippo Ficano in the late nineteenth century. Michele Ducato opened his own workshop as a teenager in 1895. Ducato's sons—Onofrio, Domenico, Ernesto, Giovanni, and Giuseppe—continued the family occupation, each developing his own specialty. Giuseppe Ducato, who died a few years ago, used to show visitors with pride a painting, hanging on a workshop wall, of Renato Guttuso, the famous Sicilian painter who was from Bagheria and was a friend of the cart painters. The Ducatos have reproduced on a panel Guttuso's first painting of the Garibaldi battle at the bridge of the Ammiraglio.

Such family traditions were once common among cart artisans, but a painter from eastern Sicily is certainly unique. Nerina Chiarenza (class of 1933) is the granddaughter, daughter and sister of men who built horse carriages, sculpted puppet heads and created *carretto* art, but she is apparently the only woman to have a career in the field. She has recently been included by the Sicilian Region in the list of Living Treasures of the Sicilian Heritage. Her hometown, Aci Sant'Antonio, has long been well-known for cart artists. As a child she watched her father Sebastiano, who was a cart maker, and in his workshop as a child she had the role of throwing water upon the wheels that had just been applied a metal rim. She did not begin painting until the 1970s, after marriage and children. Her first works were wooden statues of Carabinieri that were apparently very popular with American army and navy soldiers stationed in NATO basis in Italy like Sigonella, Brindisi, Aviano and Bagnoli, and she later devoted herself to *carretto* painting. Her husband was supportive of her career and often brought her old panels to repaint. Like Domenico Di Mauro, another painter from the region, who died in the 1980s, she has exhibited widely and given numerous interviews.

Usually a painter began his career as an apprentice in the workshop owned by a family member. As an apprentice he would be allowed to paint the undercoats on the cart. First white, then yellow in Palermo or red in Catania. Then, depending on age and skill, he would graduate to painting the carved details of the cart. More experience led to painting the inside of the box with its scenes, faces, and geometric designs. Painters could use cut patterns for the triangular shapes of the interior box. Reserved for the master painter were the outsides of the side and back panels with their complex imagery, known as the *masciddara* or "jaws" of the cart. Now, however, the few remaining cart painters are forced to do all of the work themselves.

Painters kept on hand a supply of lithographs and illustrations from which to create cartoons or drawings for their work. Drawings were done on very thin paper by the master painter who marked each area with the letter indicating the proper paint color to use. These drawings, the *viline,* were kept in a box ready to show cart clients. Carlo Levi referred to the *viline* in the Ducato studio as "precious designs handed down from father to son, of which there was a big chest full, in one corner."[33] It was a valuable collection, seldom lent or shared. Giuseppe Ducato told of one request to borrow a *vilina* that was honored with pleasure. The borrower was the above mentioned artist Renato Guttuso.

The painter imitates the contour lines of the figures from lithographs or book illustrations and copies the scene on *vilina* paper with the aid of a pantograph or by free hand. This copy becomes his original, and it is carefully preserved for re-use later. Instead of the *vilina,* Giuseppe Ducato used a photocopy, on whose reverse side he spread some red soil. He then placed this copy on the wood and traced the design. A very weak trace remained on the wood. He avoided using carbon copies because they would leave indelible traces on the wood and would alter the colors. The surface of the wood was then washed, so that the trace lines are even fainter and, when covered with a thick color, became absolutely invisible. Facial features were not copied and their colors were normally different from the ones of the original print. The Ducato family donated a number of their *viline* to the planned Bagheria cart museum.

Probably every painting studio had a collection of these patterns, but few have survived. *Viline* could be made from several source materials, which included many illustrations by Scarpelli and Fabbi from books published by the Nerbini publishing house, calendars, school textbooks and, of course, the already mentioned *I Reali di Francia,* Giusto Lodico's encyclopedia of the world of Charlemagne. Other sources were eighteenth- and nineteenth-century French lithographs of both historic and religious subjects as well as German prints of operas such as *Othello, Aida,* and *Faust.*

Carmen was an especially popular choice for cart paintings. When Guy de Maupassant visited Palermo in 1885 he wrote that people seemed to adore the score. In the streets, from morning to night, the "Toreador Song" could be heard.[34] Thus cart owners with scenes from *Carmen* on their carts were certainly aware of the latest fashion.

René Bazin interviewed a cart painter whose workshop was near the central station in Palermo. He was shown five or six "bad lithographs" that the painter had used, but which only represented a part of the artist's repertoire. Awaiting his brush were cart panels to be painted with scenes from operas and the life of Columbus. The price at that time (1891) was 70 to 80 Francs for the painting and 250 Francs for the completed cart.[35]

Puppeteers and cart painters used mainly, but not exclusively, chivalric stories for their repertory. Assimilating historical and legendary episodes that could vary far apart in chronological time and/or in political and social motivations, an incredible variety of topics could be interpreted in chivalric fashion.

Saints, brigands, heroes of the melodrama, and ancient Roman and Greek historical characters could all end up on a cart, and cart painters were not as linked to the puppets' repertory as the playbill poster painters who were often the puppeteers themselves. Even their iconographical sources were much more miscellaneous, including a great variety of prints, elementary school textbooks, and various other publications. They were then free to include episodes never present on the stage of the puppet theaters, like the Napoleonic wars, Cavalleria Rusticana, the Crusades, the Sicilian Vespers, and so on. The painters often obeyed a nonwritten law that ordered a sort of unity for the subjects of the main four scenes of the cart sides. This "law" was not universally accepted and it is not rare to see on the same cart paintings belonging to completely different stories, which the syncretism typical of lower classes felt and interpreted as similar. Antonio Daneu saw the breaking of this "law" as a sign of decadence of these traditions,[36] and he was probably right. The most common topics of the Sicilian cart paintings can be divided into five fundamental genres: (1) historical and chivalric; (2) legendary and fairytale; (3) devout (Biblical stories or stories of Saints); (4) musical; and (5) realistic (hunting scenes).

Just to give example of the variety of subjects, the carts belonging to the Pitrè museum in Palermo feature hunting scenes in the countryside, the so-called "Pompeian" scenes with lyre and flute players among classical temples or among the palm trees of enchanted Oriental gardens, court scenes set at Medieval castles, operatic scenes, even legends of the stories of St. Geneviève, who was a saint quite popular among puppeteers who dedicated to her a short cycle of the puppet shows that were also attended by women. All these subjects do not show any direct relation with the chivalric repertory, even if we can notice a common predilection for sumptuous furniture and interiors and the fabulous and fairytale atmosphere of many scenes. Among the historical scenes, Caesar is often shown passing the Rubicon river.

Subject matter of the panel paintings, divided into genres, has already been discussed. But which genre came first and when? Pitrè based his opinion on the chronology on two sorts of evidence: visual and written. The written descriptions came from the accounts of foreign visitors, which he compiled and annotated.[37] Those who visited Sicily when carts were everywhere always mentioned them; those who came earlier did not discuss carts at all. Patrick Brydone (1773) and J. W. Goethe (1786–88) said nothing about painted carts. Since they complained about the roads in Sicily, it would seem logical for them to mention carts as part of their travel memories. The reason they didn't, as Antonio Daneu pointed out, was simply that such carts did not exist before the early 1800s.[38] The first major road, the *Regia Strada,* connected Palermo, Catania, and Messina in 1830, passing through the mountains near Enna. It was a road filled with holes, difficult in winter and dusty in summer. It was perfectly suited for the seemingly fragile *carretto* with its high wheels; since there was not a road, there was no need for carts.

In 1835 the first written description of painted carts appeared in the travel memoirs of the Baron Gonzalve de Nervo. This French visitor wrote that, while traveling along the northern coast of Sicily, he often had to enter the ocean to avoid the many sharp rocks along the shore. He met only muleteers and their animals until, between Termini Imerese and Bagheria, carts appeared. The carts, he wrote, were painted blue with images of the Virgin and various saints. Horses wearing plumes on their heads pulled the carts.

Later cart painters would refer to religious paintings as either "Holy Bible or holy history."[39] In the biblical panels painters stressed magnificent décor while their works of holy history appeared to be more devout.

The first cart painters had a wealth of religious source material to use as models, but they probably often turned to the simple style of paintings on glass and prints, both of which were already very popular. In Sicilian homes, wrote the critical Mrs. Alec-Tweedie, "walls were covered with sacred pictures, all more or less hideous–generally oleographs, in horrible frames...."[40] The Holy Family and the Saints, hanging on the wall, protected the woman's sphere while the same figures painted on carts protected her husband's world.

A reporter for an American magazine described seeing such carts on the road to Monreale in 1880:

> Now a string of the high carts, so peculiar to Sicily, painted with bright yellow ground, covered with arabesques of pictures of the most primitive drawing but in the most brilliant colors. On one would be seen the history of the achievements of Orlando, or of Tancred, on another some holy subject: a Madonna, a martyrdom, or a miracle. Very wonderful are these quaint Sicilian carts, with perhaps a dozen peasant men and women—not counting children and an occasional priest, tucked away in the corners—the whole drawn by a mite of a pony or a very small donkey, fairly gorgeous in harness of extreme brilliancy. Sometimes these astonishing vehicles travel along soberly enough, but the chances are that they will pass you at a frantic gallop, which the diminutive beasts seem to enjoy quite as much as their drivers.[41]

Carts with religious images were what Eliseo Réclus noticed when he visited the Catania province in 1865. Réclus, a French geologist, had come to witness an eruption of Mt. Etna. On the roads near the volcano he passed carts whose panels were mostly painted with religious scenes: Jesus Christ, the Virgin Mary and Sicily's patron saints, Sts. John the Baptist, Rosalia, and Agatha, as well as Geneviève de Brabant.[42]

Religious scenes, the legends of chivalry, and episodes drawn from history were apparently the most popular themes for cart painters before 1900. The two carts that Pitrè arranged to send to exhibits were both painted with historical scenes: Roger II for the 1881 fair and Christopher Columbus for the 1892 Palermo exposition.

In discussing the 1881 exhibit, Pitrè commented that fifty out of one hundred carts he saw would have scenes showing Tancredi from Torquato Tasso's *Gerusalemme liberata,* but the second most popular choice was the life of Roger (or Ruggero) II, the first Norman king of

Sicily. Those scenes showed Roger fighting the Saracens, receiving the keys to the city from the Palermitan senate, at the Archbishop's palace, and at his Coronation.[43]

Later, both Columbus and Cortés became favored subjects for American cart buyers. William Agnew Paton, who visited Palermo in the 1890s, thought the Columbus panels he saw were very similar to those painted for the Chicago World's Fair of 1893. In a Corleone house Paton saw two colored lithographs featuring the "submission of America" and the triumph of Cortés. "Thus, in another form, we beheld examples of the handiwork of the artists who decorate the carts at Palermo; and the lithographs testified to the universal craving of Sicilians for illustrations of mythological or heroic subjects."[44]

The four subjects on a Columbus cart usually were the landing of Columbus, his return to Spain, his appearance at the council in Salamanca, and, at a dinner in Spain following the first voyage, his proof that an egg could stand. In Italian, the saying "It's Columbus' egg" means something is obvious. Each of the scenes included many individual figures and the arrangement of them, at least in one case, was based upon a particular set of German lithographs. Michele Ducato had purchased the set in 1920 from a Palermo dealer and from them drew *viline* for his painters to use.[45]

Often historical scenes, especially of contemporary events, appeared in the lithographs known as *images d'Epinal.* These widely circulated lithographs were originally printed in black and white, but later hand stenciling made these large sheets available in full color. The best known of the printers was the firm of Jean-Charles Pellerin of Épinal (which opened in 1796), although other firms in northeastern France also were involved. In these prints cart painters would find scenes from the Franco-Prussian war (often known as "*prussiana*"), Napoleon I's Italian campaign, or the Russo-Japanese war, and still other events of the later nineteenth century, to inspire their *viline* and paintings. According to Antonio Daneu, these were the most popular episodes derived from the *images d'Epinal,* all repeated in many cart paintings from the 1870s until about 1925. The *prussiana* set of four subjects was often supplied with titles in French: "En batterie, Bataille du Mans, Bataille de Bapaume, Charge." As Daneu noted, the French soldiers are surrounded by decoratively drawn clouds of smoke on their tidy battlefield; the Emperor appears on a white horse as every hero, even a losing one, should, and Victory flies overhead waving a laurel wreath.[46] The *prussiana* scenes with their smiling mustachioed soldiers were also painted on a *tavulidda* (or small table) purchased by a Minnesota collector, Carolyn Christian.

The most popular images were derived from the chivalric legends, the sagas involving Charlemagne and his Paladins, as his knights were called, whose stories had been performed on the stage of the puppet theaters since the 1840s. Today paintings showing knights are seen so often that they are recognized as "traditional" *carretto* art yet they really represent only one of the genres used by the *carretto* painters.

Cart painters developed various conventions for decorating the *carretto,* both inside and out. On the outside of the cart side panels were the illustrated historical scenes, often surrounded by a chain motif called the *catenella,* which was also seen on pottery.[47] The rear three panels usually had a single figure on the central removable panel–the Virgin Mary, for example–flanked by a pair of soldiers, knights, or flying angels. That was the basic plan for the outside.

A traditional design used on the wheels are narrow lines in red, blue, and green, known as the profiles (Sic. *priffili*). Giuseppe Ducato used a particular narrow brush called a *scarpidduzzu* (*scalpellino* in Italian, that is, "small chisel") to paint these lines. Ducato told me he used to prepare his own paints by mixing powered colors with linseed oil, as he believed ready-made colors do not cover the wood as well, being "too transparent."

Inside the box of the cart were other surfaces that required painting even though this was where both cargo and passengers would ride. How elaborate this decoration became depended on the customer. The simplest scheme involved large stars, diamonds or rays painted in red, blue, black, and white. This work was once assigned to apprentice painters while the master of the workshop worked on the outside panels.

Another arrangement involved a checkerboard pattern known as the *maruneddra a tri culura* (the three colored bricks) as an overall background. Large circles or roses were placed in the center of each panel and on the base of the cart box. Inside these circles could be landscapes, portraits of kings or Paladins, or symbolic designs such as open-mouthed masks or sun and moon figures. On many carts the symbol of Sicily appears. This is the *Trinacria* or *Triskeles,* a figure

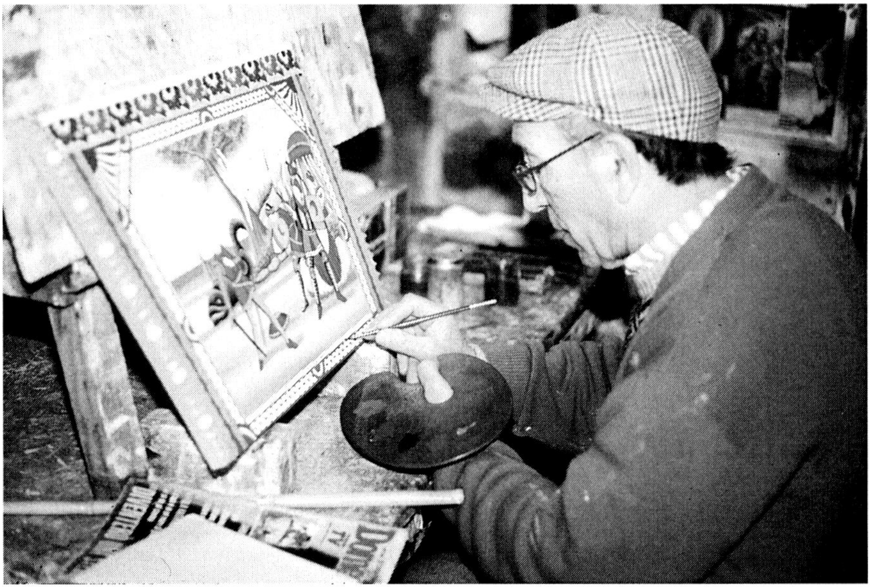

The painter Giuseppe Ducato at work in his Bagheria workshop in 2008.

with three running legs attached to a face, sometimes with wings, of Medusa. The *Trinacria,* which at a much later date became the symbol of the Sicilian Region, probably derived from ancient Oriental symbols such as the swastika, meaning the ever turning wheel of life and found already on Greek plates, which was later associated with three cornered Sicily and was briefly used as the name of the island in the fourteenth century. The bottom center of the cart box is often the location for a painted *Trinacria* symbol, usually set in a circle, and sometimes wearing "collars" of stars (Sic. *stidde*).

On the inside panels of the 1881 cart sent to Milan, Pitrè wrote that the painter selected landscapes appropriate to Palermo: Monte Pellegrino, the mountain which surmounts the city, and its shrine of Santa Rosalia.[48]

Some carts from eastern Sicily show a quite different background pattern set behind elongated diamonds enclosing portraits. An ornamental grape leaf pattern folds and unfolds in the background on inside panels and on the base of the cart's box.

Wood carvers, painters, and carpenters were mostly found in Palermo or in the town of Bagheria. They created new carts and repaired old ones. Because carpenters and painters were apt to sign their work, more is known of their identities and skills than about any other cart artisans. Since the nineteenth century, cart builders' names have been painted above a left-hand panel on a cart while cart painters' names appeared on the adjoining right hand panel. Each name was often followed by a street address. Below, cart painters helpfully painted the title of the scene.

Chivalric Subjects Painted on the Carts Belonging to the Pitrè Museum in Palermo and to the Palazzo d'Aumale Museum in Terrasini

I am going to examine in more detail a cart portraying the Sicilian Vespers and another one dedicated to Napoleon, both belonging to the Pitrè Museum in Palermo.

Napoleon occupies a central position in the side and back panels of cart 2017. His famous hat is similar to the ones worn by other soldiers of his army, but no doubt can exist about the identity of the leader who, like the Paladins, is marked by particular signs: his uniform is more elegant and his horse, which is painted with remarkable skill in a very dynamic posture, is white.

Among the four main panels, two are portraying battles, with the captions Napoleone in Boradino and in Metz respectively, while the third, with the caption *Napoleon ferito al piede* (Napoleon wounded in his foot), is showing a moment of difficulty for the hero, which may have been chosen for its close similarity with an episode of the life of an extremely popular hero, Garibaldi, who was wounded in his leg during the Aspromonte battle, and which was thus suitable to raise the emotional participation of the public. The fourth panel, with the caption *Napoleone riceve la Regina di Prussia* (Napoleon receives the Queen of Prussia), shows a scene at court where Napoleon, putting aside his sword and taking off his hat, gives honor to a foreign queen. His hat seems to hold a particularly emblematic value: while it's always on Napoleon's head during a battle scene, it is in the hands of the lieutenant who frowns worryingly looking at Napoleon wounded in his foot. There may be a correspondence with the helmet of Medieval knights. The painter shows Napoleon in his full glory, with particularly young features. In the Metz scene, though, his coat is giving him a more mature aspect, and in the scene with the Queen of Prussia his low stature is stressed, which does not diminish his authority.

As had frequently happened in the posters of the puppet theater, the painter uses the already mentioned technique of French prints of Epinal, obtaining the "multiplication" of the army with a few important features, in this case the rifles of the soldiers. It was a very common procedure for a subject that had great success on the carts and which derived directly from the French prints: the Franco-Prussian war.

Only three colors were used in the entire cart and they are rather dark: white is not brilliant, and red and navy blue are mixed to black. On the contrary, carts from Western Sicily are always characterized by very bright colors, red and yellow being the most common ones. The panels of most Sicilian carts are framed by a chain motif (*catenella*), which is very similar to the one used in many Sicilian ceramic artifacts. All around the chain motif there is often a second frame that is sculpted in bas relief and painted with flower motif. All these elements contribute to stress the link between the decoration of the Sicilian carts and the Baroque style, which had had great diffusion in Sicily in the 17th and 18th centuries. In the Napoleon cart, on the other hand, there is a sculpted band only in the upper part of the panels, and the chain motif is reduced to a line of small crosses.

Cart 2019 was painted at the end of the 19th century by Santi Marino. It is entirely devoted to the revolution of the Sicilian Vespers of 1282, which were seen and interpreted as a glorious act of revenge of the Sicilian people against the French domination of the Anjous. The publication in 1886 of the book by Michele Amari, *La Guerra del Vespro Siciliano* (The war of the Sicilian Vespers), had awaken the memory of this event among the people who considered it a real Sicilian triumph. Here is how Buttitta expresses this type of interpretation of the historical events:

> The panels with a historical and legendary subject derive their inspiration from the Romantic atmosphere of the Risorgimento, which in Sicily had assumed clear trends towards movements which demanded political autonomy for the island. From this derived the emphasis the cart painters gave to the Norman conquest of Sicily in the 12th century, to the revolution of the Sicilian Vespers, even to Garibaldi's arrival in Sicily in

> 1860, which several aristocratic and bourgeois people had understood and approved as a struggle against the central government. On the other hand, if the Sicilian people had had the courage to oppose the official historiography, they would have had many other events to commemorate, for example the peasant revolt of the *Fasci Siciliani* in 1893.[49]

Several sociological and anthropological conclusions can be derived from the process of selection and interpretation of historical events. In this particular cart the painter has chosen the episodes that stimulated the people's fantasy and love for the epic stories. One of the panels on the cart's left side, generically titled *Vespro Siciliano o La cacciata dei Francesi* (The Sicilian Vespers or The expulsion of the French from Sicily), the episode that ignited the revolt, is portrayed: in the cemetery of Santo Spirito in Palermo a French soldier is being disrespectful towards a Sicilian woman. We can see the woman who is about to faint, while another woman is hugging her husband in whose eyes the outburst of rebellion is shining. The broken chain is next to the symbol of Sicily, the three-legged Trinacria, and it is quite meaningful: the Sicilian slavery to the French is being broken. Next to this one we can read a very dramatic caption in the next section of the panel: *Massacro dei prigionieri—gli furono date grandi coppe di vino che bevvero mischiato con il sangue* (Slaughter of the prisoners—they were given large cups of wine which they drank mixed with blood). In the painting we can see the captives who, with their hands tied behind their backs, and surrounded by soldiers holding long spears, are waiting for their destiny to be complete and, like souls in Purgatory, seem to be asking for mercy. We can admire in this, as in other sections of this cart, the great skill of the painter who was able to give a very beautiful expression to the prisoners' faces and to distribute shapes and figures with a good balance so that the final result does not give the impression of a confused mess; on the contrary, it has a quite orderly setting.

On the other side of the cart over the caption *L'infante Giacomo andava in ogni luogo onorato come un re e ricevuto con grande affetto* (The infant Giacomo [James] was in every place honored like a king and received with great affection), we can see the interior of a city within which two wings of people, where several children can be seen, are opening to give way to the steed, white once more, on which Giacomo, brother of Peter, King of Aragon, is riding. Giacomo's face is

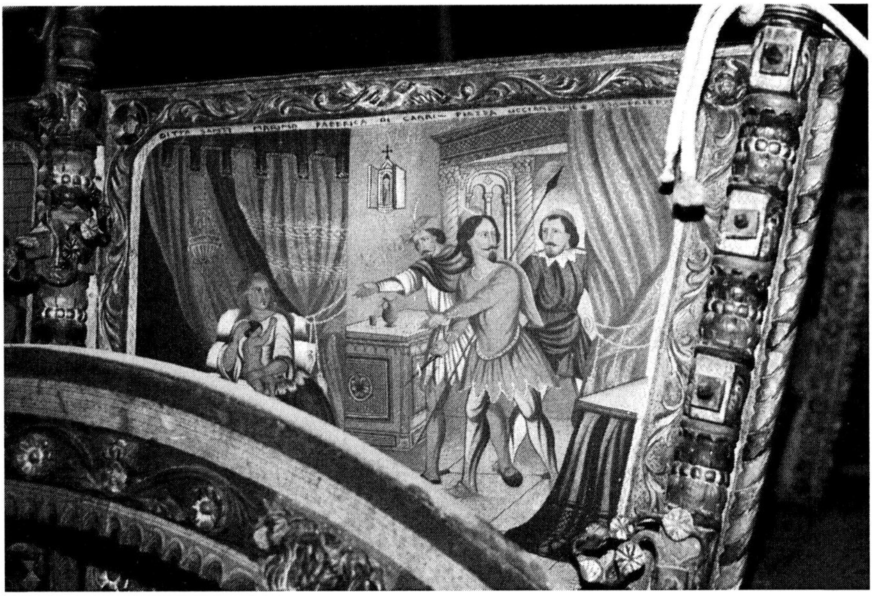

The revolutionaries of the Sicilian Vespers are entering a bedroom where a French mother is holding her child trying to defend him. Painted side of a Palermitan cart (detail) with the caption "The people will exterminate all of you, and will look for your children to kill them even in their mothers' wombs" (Pitrè Museum, Palermo).

beardless and calm, and he looks somewhat like a saint. Below the fourth section of the cart panel we can read another melodramatic caption: *Il popolo sterminerà tutti voi, e cercherà i vostri figli per ucciderli fin nel ventre delle madri* (The people will exterminate all of you, and will look for your children to kill them even in their mothers' wombs). It expresses the tremendous atrocities committed in 1282 against the French, thousands of whom were killed on the spot as soon as they were recognized as such. Pitrè refers to a popular poem that tells how the mob killed all those people who were not able to pronounce correctly the Sicilian word for chickpeas *ceciri* (che-chi-ri) without mispronouncing it as se-si-ri as most French would do.[50] Here is the English translation of the poem:

> Don't dare to come to Sicily
> Because they swore to kill you all
> And each time you come to Sicily
> The funeral bells will toll for you in France

Today those who say chichiri in Sicily
Are being cut in their throats for one's own glory
And when we'll say: here is Sicily
The memory of France will be cancelled

In this section of the cart panel, we can see a mother who hugs her child while the revolutionaries enter her bedroom. All the elements that are more likely to raise emotions are present: the woman, with long blonde hair, is caught in the most intimate part of her house while she is holding close what is most precious for her, her child. In Sicilian society where home and children represent one's most valued belongings, the revolution of the Vespers is narrated in its terrifying reality with deep participation to the grief and tragedy of both sides of the struggle. In the sumptuous furniture of the house, which satisfied the popular fascination with luxury and lavishness, a small niche with a sacred image is also present, to remind everyone that the victims of the revolution were also Christians. There are also vases and glasses on the table, stressing the sudden outburst of the tragedy, which like a real natural catastrophe did not allow anybody any time to prevent it or avoid it.

It should be noted that the wooden sculpted *chiave* of the Napoleon cart is unrelated to its side panels and portrays Ruggero liberating Angelica, while in the Palermitan cart of the Sicilian Vespers the *chiave* does refer to the main subject of the cart and shows a group of Sicilians who are plotting against the French around the table, with the engraved caption *I Vespri Siciliani—la congiura* (The Sicilian Vespers—the plot).

The Palazzo d'Aumale, built in the 19th century near the seashore of the town of Terrasini, about 30 km from Palermo, was one of the numerous properties of the Duke Henry d'Orleans, son of King Louis Philip of France; its large storage space was used to stock up grapes and wine, products of the extensive vineyards the Duke owned in his nearby fief of Zucco. This magnificent building now belongs to the city of Terrasini. It has been beautifully restored and today it houses the Regional Museum of Natural History and wonderful collections of traditional boats models and Sicilian carts.

In the paintings of the numerous carts exhibited in the museum, we can observe the same matching of characters and events belonging to very different historical periods, which we already noticed elsewhere, so that Dante and Beatrice, King Saul, a Neapolitan Tarantella dance, and even a Roman triumph are all on the same cart. There are several nonchivalric subjects: everyday life scenes like the grape harvest, religious ones like the *Ultima Cena* (Last Supper) and the *Madonna degli Angeli* (Holy Virgin among the Angels), or neoclassical ones like the *Aurora* (Dawn) seen as a Goddess bringing light to the world. In some carts the Paladins are next to the Longobards (Germanic tribes rulers of Northern Italy in the Middle Ages) and to Beatrice Cenci (Roman noble woman of the 16th century), Julius Caesar is coupled with Tancred (Medieval King of Sicily), the Biblical King Saul with the ancient Greek general Phyrrus, and the Carthaginian leader Hannibal with the Crusades. This last subject was extremely popular since the historical period of the Crusades coincided with the Paladins and they were fought against the Saracens.

Among the historical characters interpreted in a "chivalric" fashion, we can notice Christopher Columbus, the Three Musketeers, the Norman King of England Richard Lionheart, the French King of Sicily Charles d'Anjou, the Roman Emperor Constantine the Great, the Florentine hero Francesco Ferrucci, and the Swabian Emperor Frederick II. The Carthaginian leader Hannibal is portrayed during his famous passage of the Alps with the elephants, which represented the invincible tanks of the time: in the background of this painting we can notice the Alpine fir trees and, with the lack of proportions that is typical of folk art, the elephant is actually not taller than people: the painter knew it was a big animal but he had obviously never seen an elephant in his entire life. In the background of another cart painting we see the tall minarets of the Arabic mosques of Jerusalem besieged by the Crusaders.

The obvious iconographic sources of chivalric subjects were the puppet shows and their posters and the illustrations of the chivalric books like Lodico's, which provided a more genuinely popular inspiration compared to books and prints used for the historical characters. In a cart painted by the Ducato brothers from Bagheria in 1982, the cart sides are painted with a chivalric subject, but the interior of the cart shows a reproduction of the Christ Pantocrator (Almighty), the enormous image of the main apse in the Monreale Cathedral near Palermo, a magnificent church that is entirely covered with 13th century mosaics. It is clear that this cart, whose interior also shows the coats of arms of the cities of Palermo, Monreale and Bagheria, and an image of Sicily surrounded by some of its most common products, oranges and lemons, was little or never used in real life, as is demonstrated by the perfect condition of the painting, of the brakes, and of the metal rim around its wheels. All this demonstrates that this cart was commissioned and executed by people whose cultural background was not really popular. The Christ of Monreale has become a relatively common decoration for miniature carts.

On the other hand some historical characters were portrayed exactly like the chivalric ones; for example the Norman King Roger, in a cart painted in 1953, is caught in four battles (fighting against the Saracens in Sicily and in Piazza Kalsa in Palermo, during the attack to the city of Cefalù and during the furious battle of Misilmeri), which all take place outside the walls of a city just like the battles painted in the posters for the theaters of the puppet shows. If it were not for the great Cross that is present on Roger's chest, we could not really distinguish him from the Paladins of the court of Charlemagne. We can then conclude that the chivalric tradition is central to the inspiration of Sicilian cart paintings even when, as is quite common, the chosen subjects are not directly referring to the stories of the Paladins of France.

The Maker of Horse Trappings

Outfitting his horse, mule or donkey was the final necessity for the cart owner. Beyond the basic everyday needs of bridle, reins, and girth straps there were lots of possibilities. A collar around the animal's neck could be simple or complex, hanging low and heavy, enveloping him just as the padded covering does on a picador's horse in the Spanish corrida. In this pectoral ornament the harness maker can insert photographs, printed images of saints, mirrors, tassels, pom-poms and bells. Pom-poms and tassels are handmade, usually of wool, said Rosario La Piana, since that lasts longer.

Bells were what Emily Jackson noticed when she visited Sicily in the 1920s. Mrs. Jackson, who was interested in fiber arts and crafts, wrote of this element: "Above all, or rather as the leading motive in Palermo's industrial symphony, is the tinkle of the *carretto* bells: their original use as scarer away of evil spirits seems to be forgotten. They are sewn in dozens on the harness of the mules who pull the lorries.... Rows on rows of jangling bells adorn the *carretti* and combine with the tassels of gaily coloured wool, brass nail-studded woodwork, pieces of looking-glass, and the gaudiest painting to make these characteristically Sicilian vehicles a delight to the eye."[51]

Bells were also placed on the backs of the litter-carrying mules. They served to alert the world that a litter was approaching. The woolen tassels, Mrs. Jackson noted, were similar to silk ones attached to other examples of woven and embroidered work created in Sicily. Another element of horse gear that caught her approving eye was the tall ornament placed on the animal's head or back. "In Syracuse a feather, ostrich or pheasant, half a yard high, fits into a brass holder between the ears of the animal and stands erect. In Catania there is an upright wool and horn covered erection, a yard high, on the back of the animal, with a great bunch of scarlet, green and yellow feathers at the top.... A great bunch of feathers also decorates the horse's head: they are in nowise put there to ward off flies or for any other useful purpose, but simply for show and glory in the colour and decoration."[52]

Today the feathers are placed in a holder that is set upon a painted wooden stand, which in turn sits upon a small pom-pom-edged pillow (the *sellino,* that is "small saddle") on the animal's shoulders. In order to make the pom-poms for such a pillow, Rosario La Piana explained, he has the regular task, before beginning this assemblage, to measure the animal's shoulders with a special wooden device to establish the dimensions for the holder and pillow. Like other cart makers La Piana learned his craft from a relative, through observing at the workshop of his father Giuseppe.

While the feathers themselves can be extremely tall, another elaboration of the entire construction can be a platform attached to the wooden support piece just below the receptacle for the feathers. In examples seen in Partinico, these platforms held silver horses or urns, in pairs.

With the horse trappings, as with the carved, painted and wrought elements of the cart, there is the sense that every space must be decorated. Sicilians have a love for extremely rich decoration, a *horror vacui* ("fear of the emptiness"), which is perhaps a legacy of Islamic influence in Sicilian culture, but which also shows evident links with the baroque art that decorates churches and palaces all over the island.

For the cart buyer a pertinent concern was that every bit of such decoration had to be complete with nothing missing.

The World of the Cart Drivers

From the time when roads first made travel easier across Sicily, the world of the cart drivers (*carrettieri*) began to develop. Each *carrettiere* usually owned his cart and operated it for freelance services for the delivery of raw materials such as salt, sulphur, and cement to cities, as well as wine in barrels. Carts also brought fruits and vegetables to market and on occasion carried people anywhere in between.

Just how many carts or cart drivers once traveled the roadways of Sicily may be impossible to establish. Pitrè gives the surprisingly precise number of 4,758 carts that "delighted the eye" in Palermo in 1913. A decade later Giuseppe Capitò wrote that 5,000 carts were to be found in Palermo.[53]

While the Capitò number seems more of an approximation, Pitrè's total is so definite that it suggests an official city statistic. Old photographs do show town names and numbers that may well have been evidence of a license fee payment.

There were quite early attempts to regulate carts in Sicilian cities. In the fifteenth century, wrote Henri Bresc, there were efforts made to control heavily loaded carts or drays. Because of the damage their narrow wheels did to the pavement, cart drivers were asked to be driven close to the walls along the streets. In the case of extra-long loads (heating wood or sugar cane) they had to have a small boy walk ahead of the cart much as American trucks are often required to suspend a red warning flag.[54]

Several years after Giuseppe Capitò had written his criticisms of the cart's lack of brakes and of the damage caused to pavements, the government took legal measures to correct both problems.[55]

Cart drivers rode on a slightly raised shelf at the front of their carts, called the *tavulazzu*. The same term was used for the wooden table on which prison inmates slept, which was also slightly raised for a head rest. According to the painter Giuseppe Ducato from Bagheria, the similarity in the shape suggested the use of the same word in both cases.

Underneath the *tavulazzu,* a cart driver hung a net bag in which he carried a brush, curry comb, water basin for the animal, and sometimes a bottle of wine for himself,[56] and where his dog often traveled. Lanterns were hung from one of the posts, while a straw bag carried food for the horse or mule. These straw bags (Sic. *coffe*), usually decorated with mirrors and ribbons, became popular as purses for teenage upper middle class Sicilian girls in the 1960s, an example of how folk art could, even in those times, become trendy.

When the cart was fully loaded, the drivers walked alongside the mule or horse. It was a slow form of travel so the drivers expected to stop for the night at very basic inns, called *funnachi,* a word derived from the Arabic *funduk* (hotel). There they slept all together, sharing the same big room with their animals, much the same way as camel drivers used to do when stopping at caravanserais while crossing deserts. There they entertained each other at night exchanging road stories, telling of old adventures and singing. Songs were composed and remembered on the road, then often sung in competition. The singing frequently ended in an "aaah" sound at the end of a verse, which while traveling was said to encourage the horse.

While at night a driver might occasionally be accompanied by a mouth organ or percussion instruments, on the road his sound of music was provided by the noise of the metal rings inserted in the hub (the *boccole*) working against the iron washers. The *boccole* was made of a bronze alloy frequently referred to as a *suono di campana* ("with a bell sound")—78 parts of copper and 22 of tin. This created a thinner, more fragile metal, which gave, however, a better sound.[57] So important was the quality of the alloy that cart drivers sought out metal workers who could fashion the hubs to their needs. Men who could forge the *boccole* are now impossible to find so these rings are also recycled.

Pride continuously pressed cart drivers to compete among themselves also in other kinds of exhibitions. "Pulling" competitions were organized, during which the animals were urged to considerable efforts. In the most common type of competition, carts were tied together (*fusu cu fusu*) and the horses then pulled in opposite directions. In other cases horses were obliged to pull extremely heavy loads or to extract themselves from deep mud or sand. A series of codified rules applied to these competitions, which otherwise could end up being quite dangerous for the horse and economically disastrous for the cart driver and his family. In order to avoid these consequences, a horse that exhibited the faintest sign of superiority was often declared the winner. But, many people say, there were also cart drivers so stubborn as to be unwilling to concede defeat until the very end. The traditionally proud temperament of cart drivers can also be observed in Mascagni's opera *Cavalleria Rusticana.* One of the main characters, Alfio, is a cart driver and his wife's betrayal cannot be washed but in blood.

Cart drivers selected artisans to fashion carts of their dreams and for their businesses. The cart built to their order was a testimony to their taste and success. It was both an advertisement for their livelihood and an acknowledgment of their status. When the cart was not in use for deliveries, a cart driver would install benches for his family and friends to use as they rode for a day in the country or for a saint day's parade. In the proud and continuous celebration of their vehicles, several cart drivers had sculptured parts (*chiavi*) carved with secular scenes showing the dedication of a new cart, or the cart itself in use.

A cart was an expensive investment and this column written by Elio Vittorini captures both the driver's care for his cart and the arduous nature of his work:

> In Sicily people travel a lot. They have to cover great distances in order to work. The man who has a cart to travel in is more fortunate than others. But he accepts work farther afield. And the donkey, which is pulling the cart, is no longer a quick-footed beast. He becomes slow. The journey becomes endless. The man's life becomes endless, sleeping on the road, through night and solitude, day and solitude, with the creaking of the cart in his ears like a cicada singing in the solitude. He leaves home at three in the morning and doesn't return until nine at night. Then he unhitches in the empty lot at the edge of town, loads his sacks onto the donkey, unscrews the wheel-hubs, and takes the wheel-hubs and the donkey home with him, to the one-roomed house he lives in. If the cart has decorated sides, he removes those, too, and takes them home with him as well. The carts remain in the open air, their shafts tilting skywards. But the man sleeps, heavily, with the song of their creaking still in his ears.[58]

Owning and driving a cart was not an easy life. A retired cart driver told writer Gavin Maxwell that, in addition to the accidents that could easily befall both cart and animals, there were holdups and robberies perpetrated by Sicilian bandits. It was vitally important, according to Don Nicola, to remain on good terms with the *amici*, giving these bandits whatever they wanted.[59]

Nineteenth-century travelers often reported seeing cart drivers drive their carts close to mail coaches since they knew that armed guards protected the mail. Despite these efforts at protection and self-preservation there were accidents and incidents. Those that did not end tragically were often remembered on the painted *ex votos* hung in churches and chapels.

In 1926 Emily Jackson wrote about a large procession she encountered near Alcamo. First she heard the cart bells even before she saw the cart. Then she described the driver.

> ... the driver wears a hooded Sicilian cloak of blue frieze cloth, for it is cold on these mountain heights; he sits hunched up; his cart is piled with the little barrels called trentino, holding 5½ gallons. This small size is generally used for transport of the wine whose highly prized flavour is only obtained from grapes grown on the terraces high up on the mountain side.... Behind comes a procession of five great red lorries, drawn by wild-eyed, wide-horned oxen; they bear the immense barrels at a slow and stately pace, while the men walk beside encouraging, threatening, or coaxing with strange sounds which were in use at Dante's time and before.[60]

Mrs. Jackson's lorries are the strong, sideless *trainu* mentioned earlier. Her description of the cart driver's dress seems close to the one Gaston Vuillier had sketched on a driver from Carini, when he visited Sicily in the early 1890s and added it to his list of books about islands. Although other writers described visits to cart makers' workshops, Vuillier was fascinated by the completed carts and their owners. A number of illustrations in his book show cart drivers posing with their carts and horses, showing off the elegance of the horse trappings. In one case he sketched a horse whose red trappings, bells, and shiny mirrors guaranteed protection against the *jettatura* or evil eye. In Catania he sketched cart owners bringing carts and horses to the port late in the afternoon.[61]

Sicilian writer Giovanni Verga (1840–1922) wrote about cart drivers in several stories and novels. As already mentioned, one of his stories was the basis for the libretto of Pietro Mascagni's *Cavalleria Rusticana*, first performed in Rome in 1890. When cart painters began to use scenes from operas for their painted panels, the sad story of Turiddu and Alfio who both love Lola was often chosen by cart drivers, especially in the Catania province where *Cavalleria Rusticana* takes place. The close connection of Verga with the world of cart drivers is stressed in a pair of postage stamps issued by Italy in 1972 for the fiftieth anniversary of his death. On each stamp a photograph of the writer is seen on the left and a painted cart appears on the right.

While the peasants quite willingly changed their jobs and moved to the cities, the cart drivers for the most part only substituted vehicles and, instead of a cart, they now use an Ape (*Bee*) truck, popularly called *lapa,* in order to sell or transport their goods. Especially in the Catania province it is not rare to see trucks decorated with small and big scenes of chivalric subjects, which are meant to remind the driver of his old cart. Sometimes it is only a small detail, such as a knight painted on the back of a mirror, that suggests the past.

In Palermo, in the area near Corso dei Mille, there are still a few workshops and carts and drays (*strascini*) kept in garages and storage areas. There are even people who keep a cart at home, in one case located between the refrigerator and the washing machine. These carts belong to former cart drivers, by now quite old, who in their spare time remember their lives on the road.

Giuseppe Capitò quoted several songs that spoke of that former life. For instance,

> How beautiful is the road to Monreale,
> Lined with stately poplars, row on row!
> Four fountains mark the halfway point, and give
> Refreshment to those who come and go.[62]

The relatively strong concentration, up to not long ago, of artisans' workshops in this area of Palermo, which is close to the former Virga flour mill, and on the surrounding roads leading out of the city, is explained by the one-time need for carts to carry flour to the Palermo bakeries and to supply the city with foodstuffs coming from the nearby villages.

The Feast of St. Joseph in Bagheria

St. Joseph's day (San Giuseppe) is March 19. He is the patron saint of many Sicilian towns, each of which organizes the celebrations around that date. Several towns prepare wonderful altars in his honor, very artistically decorated with bread shaped by hand in the most extravagant and beautiful forms, a custom that goes back to pagan times and which is continued today also by Sicilian Americans in New Orleans and in many other Sicilian communities in the United States.

Bagheria's celebrations for the patron St. Joseph are centered around the local traditions of carts, and the festa has long ago been moved to the summer. It used to be June just after the lemon harvest (Bagheria's traditional source of income), when people had enough money to pay for the high expenses involved. Nowadays it is the first or second weekend in August, when all the Bagheresi residing abroad have had time to come for their vacations and they too can enjoy the festivities.

As part of the 2011 Festa of San Giuseppe in Bagheria, several events were planned, including the singing of traditional cartdrivers' songs and the magnificent final cart parade, which featured fifteen decorated carts of different sizes and a couple of *strascini* (drays). The concert of cart drivers' songs was held in a small public garden next to the city hall, during which eleven singers (three of them quite young and one just a boy) had been invited to perform.

As it has always been customary among cart drivers, each of them "called" the next one, inviting and challenging him to do better. There is no musical accompaniment and the tune is always the same in cart drivers' songs. In order to make their voice resound better, drivers always sing with one or both hands cupped behind their ears. At this August concert, most of them belonged to the Testa family, who has recently been included by the Sicilian Region on the list of Living Treasures of the Sicilian Heritage. The audience was filled with old friends and former cart drivers and few tourists were present. The atmosphere was quite authentic, mainly thanks to this audience, who knew very well and continuously interacted and supported the singers, most of whom were related to each other. For those not fluent in the Sicilian language and not familiar with the repertory, the words, mostly related to love and the daily life of the cart drivers, were impossible to understand. Undoubtedly some of the traditional sexual double-entendres were missed.

In the spectacular final parade, two among the carts present were completely and very richly sculpted instead of painted, a work done by the artist Sparacio, who is not active anymore. On the carts we saw again all the singers and many of the audience of the previous musical performance. The entire population of Bagheria was in the main street watching the parade, an event, as it always happens in important celebrations, that has a powerful unifying meaning for the town community.

The Cart as a Sicilian Symbol

The year 1881 marked the international debut of the Sicilian *carretto* at the Esposizione Nationale in Milan as a well-designed example of popular art. The *carretto* was part of an exhibit of Sicilian art assembled by Dr. Giuseppe Pitrè. From that moment on it represented Sicily to the world, perhaps even more than the *Trinacria,* the three-legged icon that has long symbolized the three-cornered island of Sicily.

Every visitor, and certainly every guidebook writer or travel essayist, captured a *carretto* on film. Whether the shot was taken by a writer's own camera or was stock footage purchased from a Palermo photographer such as Interguglielmi, Dante Cappelani, or the Florentine firm Fratelli Alinari, a *carretto* view was always among a book's list of illustrations.

A *carretto* view was also a typical photograph for a travel lecturer to use. As a form of educational and escapist entertainment, a slide lecture was really a latter day equivalent of the canvas panorama show that once unrolled its vistas of faraway worlds by candlelight in round panorama halls.

One such travel lecturer was Branson DeCou, who visited Italy on several trips after World War I and through the Great Depression. DeCou showed his hand-tinted lantern slides as part of his travelogue presentations. Naturally there were views of festive *carretti* on the road, filled with people, among his Italian subjects. The DeCou Archive of over 10,000 lantern slides was given by his widow to the library at the University of Santa Cruz, California.

There are two principal ways in which the *carretto's* significance as symbol can be seen. First is the image of the cart itself. Usually artists and photographers show the cart in festival garb. The horse or mule is thoroughly covered with every bit of embroidered and feather-bedecked finery possible. The cart is filled with smiling people, dressed in their best. Cart and passengers pose along a road with either Mt. Pellegrino or Mt. Etna in the distance. This is the typical view used for postcards, poster stamps, photographs, lithographs, and in package design. It is printed on handkerchiefs, scarves, table linens, posters, tambourines and small wine barrels or kegs.

Three-dimensional miniature carts with passengers are made in every conceivable size. When England's Queen Mary visited Palermo in 1925 she purchased one of these model carts, called a *carrettino.*[63] Cart-decorated plaques can be found, as well as tiles, plates, bowls, and matchbook covers. Covers for collections of Sicilian music on tapes, records or disks add singers and musicians to the jaunty crew in the festival cart. The decorative panels of the *carretto* have also been adapted to adorn miniature scissors and knife-grinding carts.

The second way in which the cart lives on is through its elements. Although carts were sold to tourists, most souvenir seekers probably bought parts of carts: the carved *pizzi* and *chiavi,* the painted panels, and the wrought ironwork. The *rabiscu* (ironwork) has been hung as hefty chandeliers or, with glass on top, transformed into coffee tables. Sicilian shops display all of these remnants from old carts for sale as well as new copies of them in a trade that has been carried on for many years. Members of the Daneu family often traveled into the countryside in search of worn out or abandoned carts from which parts could be salvaged. From the number of parts in collections, others long emulated this practice.

In *Sea and Sardinia,* D. H. Lawrence mentioned the carts he saw at Palermo in 1921. The Lawrences left Sicily (they had been living in Taormina) soon after his trip to Sardinia and with them went a cart panel. In a letter to his mother-in-law he mentions the panel whose scenes were based on the life of Marco Visconte.[64]

It is the painted panels of the *carretto* that are linked to a further survival of the *carretto* as symbol in Sicilian culture. Although every part of the *carretto* was painted, it is the inner and outer sides of the cart's box that exhibit the painted scenes, making it a vehicle of illustrated history.

The sides of most carts are divided into two panels (except in the Trapani region where taller carts often had three panels on each side), while the rear has three. Panels are separated by wood strips that terminate in small heads. Ropes tied around the heads secured cargo.

Above and below the panels painters left space for the titles of the scenes (below) and the names of the cart's creators, builder and painter (above). Sometimes even a street address was given (Corso dei Mille in Palermo, for example) as a subtle bit of advertising.

Framing the scene is a decorative border, either carved and painted or simply painted. Within that border appear repeated motifs of flowers, leaves, chains, or shells with *putti* or other small figures filling any extra spaces. Colors used on carts were the primary shades of red, blue, yellow, and green.

The subject matter for cart panels, as previously noted, can be religious, operatic, literary, mythical, or historic. It is, however, the adventures of Charlemagne and his knights, the Paladins, that most often represent the transfer of cart painting to other media.

Scenes from the legends of the knights appear on ceramic plates and jars, on boxes to hold candies or marzipan, on bicycle-powered food carts, on market-place stalls, and on automobiles. A *National Geographic* photographer found in Palermo a two-door car whose entire side was devoted to a battle between Paladins.[65] A Fiat automobile had even more elaborate *carretto* art.

Perhaps one of the most interesting transfers of subject matter is to the *lapa,* the small three-wheeled truck seen all over Sicily. Not only is the truck the modern replacement for the cart and was often first driven by former cart drivers, but the painting of the *lapa* was undertaken by cart painters.

The first of these small trucks was shipped to Sicily from the Piaggio factory in Genoa in June 1947. Salvatore Pappalardo studied the decoration and history of these trucks in the Catania region where they became especially popular. In an article about the *lapa* he published several photographs of trucks decorated in *carretto*-style. The doors, hood, sides of the cargo area, and the back of the cabin, which is protected by a ladder-like arrangement of metal bars, are all painted. Sculpture and metalwork can also be incorporated into the composition.[66]

An interesting little book, entirely devoted to *lape,* has been written by Francesco La Cecla with photographs by Melo Minnella, in order to explain their complex anthropological meanings in present Sicilian society.[67]

According to Pappalardo, the specialists in *lapa* painting worked in Aci Sant'Antonio, north of Catania. They were Domenico Di Mauro, Raimondo Russo, and "above all," Antonio Torrisi. To this list should be added a mother-son team from the same town: Nerina Chiarenza and her son Giuseppe Lanzafame. The son was responsible for sculptured elements and his mother did the decorating of some incredible trucks, illustrated in the 1978 edition of Giuseppe Capitò's book.[68] Mrs. Chiarenza continues her work as a cart painter, a specialty in which she followed her father, Sebastiano.

Pappalardo also noted that, in addition to the paintings on *lapas*, many trucks carried names or slogans painted above the windshields. The words probably have no connection to the legends of the Paladins, but they reflect opinions or relationships of the *lapa* drivers. In this there is a direct comparison to the words found on motor vehicles throughout the world. The area above a windshield or on a bumper is a favored spot for writing on a Haitian tap-tap, a Colombian chiva, or a Mexican truck. In a sense the use of chivalric motifs on trucks can be compared to the use of flames on American vehicles. First used on hot rods of the 1930s to suggest speed, flames migrated over the years to trucks, motorcycles, and even to other models of cars.

The subject matter of the panels and the geometric patterns have been used on other objects. The small tables carried by itinerant water sellers in the market were imitated in side tables or *tavulidde* sold to tourists. The idea was Antonio Daneu's. A table of this kind once stood in the family's antique store. The paintings on its four sides were of Charlemagne and his knights.

Just as Sicilian writers described travel by cart and the lives of cart drivers, Sicilian painters depicted that world in their art. Two important artists found *carretto* subject matter for their paintings. Pippo Rizzo (1897–1964) is usually linked to the Futurist group of writers and artists. The point of departure for this group was the world of tomorrow: its scientific inventions, technology, and above all, speed. Futurist sculpture, such as that of Umberto Boccioni, seems driven by hurricane-force winds in its rush to meet the dawn of the new. In painting, Futurist canvases seem fragmented as if forms are splintering and fragmenting away at warp-speed. Some of the Futurists became strong nationalists and supporters of Mussolini's Fascist government. Sicilian Futurists often painted Sicilian subjects and several of Rizzo's paintings involve people watching puppet plays. At least two of his canvases show carts, both belong to private collections and both were painted in 1928. One, titled *Ritorno*, shows a cart returning through almost cubist-shaped fields of grain, while *Il carretto* has a brilliantly painted cart.

Rizzo was briefly a teacher for an even better known artist, Renato Guttuso (1911–1987). Guttuso was born in Bagheria where, as a child, he first learned about art by visiting the workshops of cart painters Emilio Murdolo and Michele Ducato. He later developed a realistic expressionistic style, based on strong colors and contour lines. Several of his finest history paintings include carts. There are two versions of the Battle of the Ammiraglio Bridge (1951–52 and 1955), a famous episode that happened near Palermo in 1860, during the Risorgimento, the struggle for the reunification of the country. In both Garibaldi leads his red-shirted men against the blue uniforms of the Bourbon soldiers. In the first and smaller work, the panels of a painted cart can be glimpsed next to the bridge, collapsing under the falling bodies of the living and the dead. In the second painting the cart and its horse are gone, hidden by more men and a flag. Horses expiring with a cart's shafts and wheels rising behind them in the mass of people are shown in Guttuso's painting of the First of May Massacre at Portella della Ginestra (painted in 1953) where the gang of the bandit Salvatore Giuliano shot eleven and wounded many more peasants as they were picnicking and rejoicing for the Labor Day festivity in 1947 near Piana degli Albanesi.

In another painting, a vastly more somber scene is of people walking out into the country to occupy empty lands (1949–50). A crowd of people, mostly on foot, carrying their tools and a flag, heads toward the fields they hope to claim. Two mule-drawn carts are in their midst. All of these paintings come from the same period in the early 1950s. A decade later Guttuso turned to more autobiographical works such as *Il Pittore di carretti* (The cart painter), circa 1966. The painter, certainly Guttuso himself, is at work on a panel. He sits outside painting a panel under a bright blue sky, but he has no head, suggesting that his hands and the panel deserve a viewer's focused attention.

Carts or cart parts have long been a perfect gift for the people of Sicily to offer. After the end of World War II American funds were sent to aid in the reconstruction of Sicily. That program became known as the Marshall Plan after a concept proposed in a speech at Harvard

University in 1947 by Secretary of State George C. Marshall. In gratitude for this help the government of Sicily gave him a *carretto* in 1951. On accepting the gift, Marshall said he had seen some like it when he visited Palermo in 1910 but had never dreamed that he would own one.[69]

The Marshall cart used images appropriate to the circumstances of the gift. One panel shows Marshall speaking at Harvard University, flanked by circular portraits of President Harry Truman and Marshall. A row of identical new graduates in their caps and gowns faces the speaker. The cart was painted by Francesco Paolo Cardinale of Palermo. This cart is now located at the Smithsonian National Museum of American History in Washington, D.C.

In 1943 a cart was painted for and given to General George S. Patton Jr., who commanded the U.S. Seventh Army during the Sicilian invasion. The cart is now part of the collection of the Patton Museum of Cavalry and Armor at the U.S. Army Armor Center at Fort Knox, Kentucky. One panel of the cart shows American troops attacking German soldiers and a green dragon on the beach.

Many other important visitors have probably received carts or cart panels. Going to Rome to present a gift was an incredible thrill for members of a church group from Aci Sant'Antonio. Two busloads of friends and neighbors accompanied Nerina Chiarenza and Don Vincenzo Torrisi to an audience with the Holy Father John Paul II on October 16, 2002. Mrs. Chiarenza's panel's depicted episodes from the life of St. Anthony Abbot, her town's patron saint. More recently she has donated a panel to the president of the Italian Republic, Giorgio Napolitano.

Lights and Shadows on the Sicilian Carts

Foreign tourists do not look only for cheap souvenirs in Sicily, among them there are also connoisseurs: about fifteen years ago a Sicilian American commissioned a full size Sicilian cart for each of his grandsons from the workshop of the cart painter Giuseppe Ducato, recently deceased. Looking at the long series of carts waiting to be painted, Giuseppe would say: "My clients have to light a candle to the

Virgin Mary, so that I can finish all of them." He was lucky, since his son Michele (it is still quite customary in Sicily for children to be named after their grandparents) was working next to him. Fortunately, Michele's degree in architecture did not hinder his decision to collaborate with his father when he was still alive, and he still paints and also sculpts carts in his workshop. Many other artisans have died without transmitting their skills to anyone, or are still working in bitter loneliness. For instance, as already mentioned, no one is able to produce the elaborate ironwork typical of the decoration of the cart.

Today the tradition of the Sicilian cart is agonizing. Giuseppe was the last one still living among the four Ducato brothers, all of them traditional cart painters. "I was born in 1972," says today Giuseppe's son Michele, "when my parents after 16 years of marriage had almost given up all hope of having a child. As a young man, I was lucky enough to absorb a tradition that was waning but was already being missed. I decided to hang my degree on the wall and work with my father. My cousins, who are much older than me, were very young in the dark 70s when everybody was trying to forget as soon as possible all about traditions and the tremendously harsh cart drivers' life, and they all did something different."

The last sculptor of that generation was Giovanni Raja, who had a workshop in Corso dei Mille where he worked until he was 90 years old. Near there, in a very primitive workshop, which looked like the cave of Vulcan, the Roman God of Fire, Carmelo Saccaro worked. As mentioned, he was the last *fabbro* able to forge a *rabiscu* (ironwork decoration) in the old style, but he died about ten years ago.

Not far form the Ducatos' workshop in Bagheria used to live Michele Ajello, *u' siddunaru* (the saddle maker). In a little courtyard he had a cupboard full of *armiggi* (horse trappings and other decorations), straw bags, saddles, mirrors, bells, even frames for portraits of the Holy Virgin and other saints. "I closed my workshop because they told us they would give us some space in the Guttuso Museum in Villa Cattolica, but the mayor changed. That was twenty years ago, and that's what happened to my stuff," he told me.

"Without the artisans it is very difficult to produce new carts, as the ironwork, the sculptures and the bronze elements in the middle of the wheels can only be recycled," Giuseppe Ducato used to say. Especially in Eastern Sicily some carts are now decorated with decals

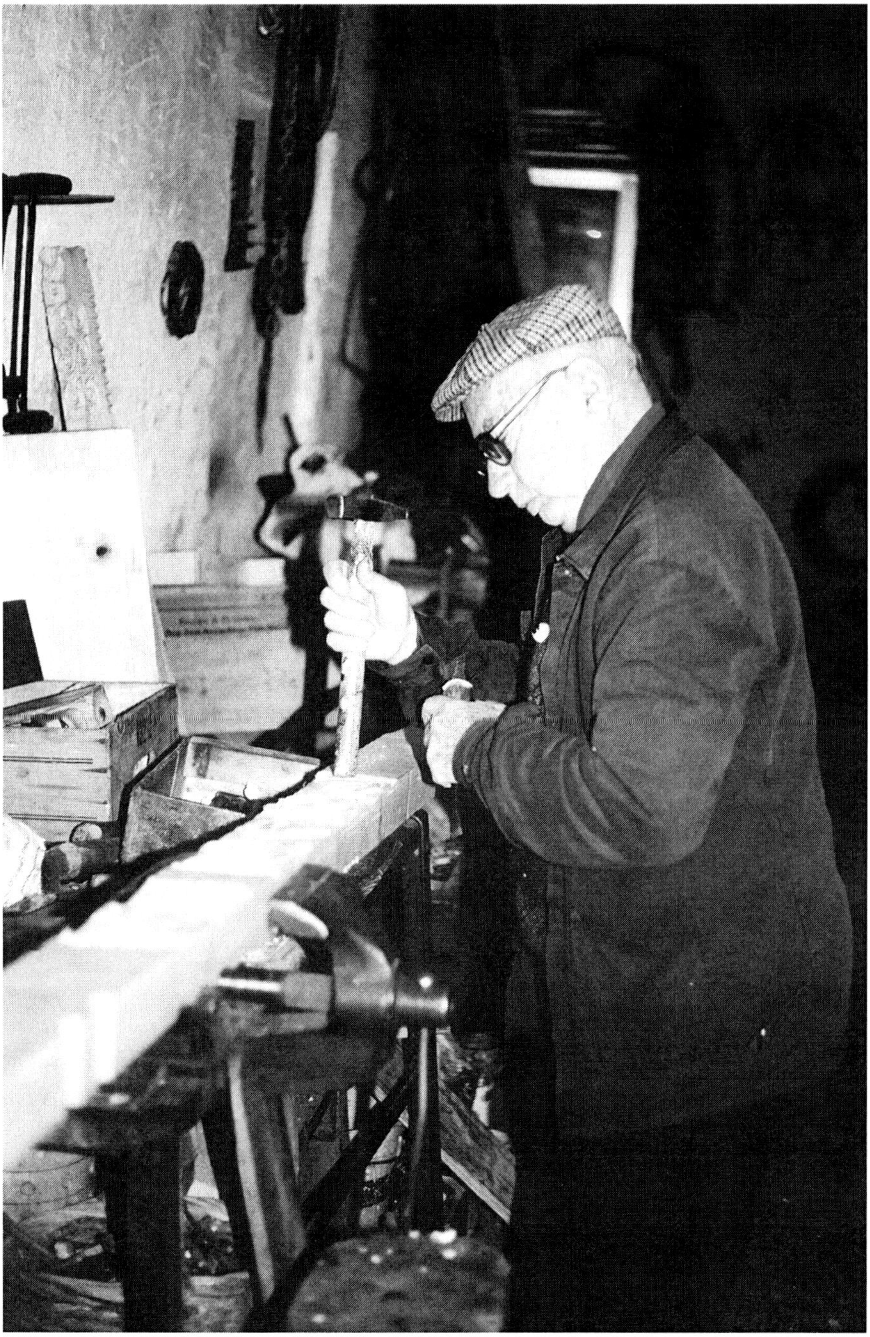

The sculptor Giovanni Raja at work in his workshop in 2002.

instead of paintings or are drawn by horses with machine-made trappings and an overabundance of plastic feathers.

Even if the artisans die, the cart culture somehow survives. There are carts locked in garages in towns once thriving with workshops like Aci Sant'Antonio in Eastern Sicily and Partinico and Bagheria on the western part of the island. They belong to collectors or to former cart drivers who in their free time "review" the chivalric stories painted on their sides, or rent the carts for special occasions or parades.

One particular cart is worth a special mention and it is the product of the collaboration of two painters very different from each other: Giuseppe Ducato and Bruno Caruso, representatives of folk art and learned art respectively.

"I met the Ducatos and appreciated their work in the 1950s," says Caruso, "and 50 years ago I edited the book *Arte popolare siciliana* (Sicilian Folk Art), published in Palermo by Sergio Flaccovio. I think the *carretto* is the quintessence of the Sicilian soul, but I had never thought of painting one. I was enthused by the proposal."

The idea of Caruso's collaboration is due to Giuseppe Ajello, owner of a well-known printing press in Bagheria, who commissioned the cart and owns it. With the new cart Ajello wanted to give homage to his own family whose male members had been cart drivers for several generations; a family portrait with a cart, copied from a photograph taken of the 50s, is now painted on the new cart. "The cart driver's blood is still flowing in my veins," says Ajello, and we can see that from the pride and the skill with which he is taking the cart out of the garage to let us admire and photograph it.

It took ten years to finish the costly project; once the cart was built, the sides have been taken apart and taken to Caruso's studio in Rome, where the master painted them in about one year. "I would have liked to repeat the experience for other subjects, for example fruit and Sicilian sweets. I also suggested that Ajello take the cart on a tour with actors reciting passages written by the authors portrayed on the cart or to take it to America in order to publicize our island, or even to make another cart over there. I would be ready to go, but in the end nobody did anything about it and nothing happened." Caruso adds that he is now in his 80s and it is difficult for him to have another similar chance, but his voice is firm, and his excitement is that of a young person.

I asked both Ducato and Caruso how they divided their work: Ducato painted the entire cart except the main figures on the sides (*masciddara*) and on the back, and Caruso decorated it with some of the most important Sicilian writers, Luigi Pirandello and his play *Six Characters in Search of an Author,* Giovanni Verga and his *Cavalleria Rusticana,* and then Quasimodo, Vittorini, Brancati, Sciascia, and Tomasi di Lampedusa. A large head of a Medusa, a mythological figure who has snakes instead of hair, sticks out in the bottom center of the cart box; it is due to both brushes and a symbol of their cooperation. Caruso remembers the unusual choice: "I had the idea of transforming into a Medusa the large sun which, according to the tradition, Ducato had destined to that part of the cart. The Medusa is also at the origin of the *Trinacria* or *Triskeles,* a figure with three running legs attached to a face, which has long symbolized the three-cornered island of Sicily."[70]

Folk art and learned art were never completely apart. As already mentioned, the Sicilian painter Renato Guttuso, also from Bagheria, as a young boy was fascinated by the Murdolo cart-painting workshop. When he had already become famous, he wanted to sign the reproduction of one of his paintings copied by the Ducatos upon a cart now belonging to the Galioto collection. Ajello's new cart is Ducato and Caruso's masterpiece, it is the first example of a real collaboration, but also the last wonderful singing of a swan: extinction is now threatening the Sicilian cart. And the extinction of a cultural phenomenon or product is irreversible, exactly like the extinction of an animal or of a vegetal species.

Other Objects for Chivalric Subjects and Revival in Today's Folk Art

Besides the objects already examined, Sicilian folk art has represented the Paladins of France in many other different media and occasions. Salvatore Salomone Marino at the end of the 19th century referred to shepherds who were inmates in the prison on the small island of Favignana and who were killing time by painting and sculpting chivalric subjects, some of which, and in particular those done in 1844 by Giuseppe Sciarrino from the town of Borgetto, were shown in the National Exhibition held in Palermo in 1891–92.[71]

Antonino Uccello, in his book *Civiltà del Legno in Sicilia* (The Culture of Wood in Sicily), mentioned that the folk artist Don Santo Lombardo, born in the town of Canicattini Bagni near Syracuse in 1897, carved figures of Paladins in the trunk of trees and used to say that he had started his career in 1910 drawing Paladins on the walls of his house with carbon sticks.[72]

There are no Sicilian mosaics with chivalric subjects like those seen in the cathedrals of the cities of Otranto and Brindisi in the region of Apulia in the southeastern part of the Italian peninsula. Sicilian ceramists, on the other hand, often use figures of Paladins and Moors in their products. In the volume written by Paolo Toschi, *Arte Popolare Italiana* (Italian Folk Art), there are photographs of large Sicilian flower pots (*graste*) in polychrome ceramics with chivalric characters. Even today the artists of the De Simone family often choose the Paladins for their well-known ceramics.

On the Eve of the 2 of November (All Souls' Day), which is a very important celebration in Sicily, there is the very old tradition of hiding gifts in the house for the children, in order to let them find the toys the next morning and tell them they came from deceased relatives. On the same days and for the same festivity, pastry shops sell fruit made of marzipan and special sugar figurines (significantly called *pupi a cena*—"puppets at dinner time") molded with the human shape, the Paladins being among the most frequent characters represented.

The fashion for the Paladins' repertory was extended to a plethora of objects of extremely diversified everyday use: prows of boats, desks of water sellers, stalls of toasted seed vendors (*siminzari*), tricycles of ice cream vendors, wheelbarrows of knife sharpeners (*arrotini*), even furniture have been decorated with knights and chivalric subjects. Even today it is not too difficult to see the already mentioned small trucks (*Ape* or "Bee") painted in the same way.

Chivalric tradition in Sicily is in crisis today. Most young Sicilians do not know the chivalric stories anymore and never went to regularly see the puppet shows. This cultural patrimony is getting lost, and the characters with whom people identify are quite different.

On the other hand there is a folk revival nowadays and in Sicily, like everywhere in the world, we can notice a trend of the "official" culture towards the re-appropriation of themes and images traditionally belonging to the art and culture of the lower social classes. Many famous Sicilian painters of the 2nd half of the 20th century took some of their subjects and got inspiration from the chivalric tradition; Pippo Rizzo, Renato Guttuso and Bruno Caruso have already been mentioned in this book. We should also mention Salvatore Fiume, who ordered posters and puppets precisely with this purpose, as remembered by Mrs. Italia Chiesa Napoli, wife and mother of the most important puppeteers' family, who is still active in Catania.

Graphics and "minor" arts follow this trend, so much so that before the political elections of 1987, one of the local Palermitan newspapers, *L'Ora*, published a sketch where the two political leaders of the time (Ciriaco De Mita for the Christian Democrats and Alessandro Natta for the Communists, both parties not existing any longer) are represented as two Paladins engaging in a duel. In recent years *Il Giornale di Sicilia,* which is the most important local newspaper, has published in its Sunday issues inserts with cartoons of chivalric stories. Advertisements have selected images of the Sicilian puppets to attract new customers, with Orlando conquering the Kit Kat chocolates in order to offer them to her beloved Angelica.

Conclusions

As it always happens with revivals, new situations, emotions and media are profoundly different from those of the time past. Still this trend reveals the desire to resume a cultural identity that may otherwise be definitely lost. Under the storming of the anonymous and undistinguished cultural patterns that are promoted by the mass media, Sicilian people try to return to their cultural background and to reestablish a contact with their cultural heritage.

Unfortunately this does not necessarily mean a real return to the "time of the fireflies," as the Italian writer and filmmaker Pier Paolo Pasolini poetically referred to the irretrievable past when in the Italian countryside, still unpolluted by industries, one could see those sparkling insects.

In an impressive article Pasolini wrote, published by *Corriere della Sera* in 1975, he described the "terrible anthropological and cultural degradation" of the Italian people who, as a result of the economic boom of the 1960s, had enthusiastically embraced everything new and modern and swiftly abandoned their cultural heritage, which was now identified with poverty, hunger and harsh life:

> As everybody knows, we are no longer in front of "new times"; rather we are experiencing a new epoch in human history: a change that usually takes the span of a millennium to get accomplished. It was impossible for the Italians to react in a worse way to such a historical trauma. In only a few years they have become (especially in the central and southern parts of the country) a degenerate, ridiculous, monstrous, even criminal population.[1]

> But of course in order to understand the changes people are going through, you must love them. And unfortunately I did love these Italians, I loved them beyond the patterns dictated by the Establishment (and actually against it), and I loved them beyond common or humanitarian patterns. It was a real love, deeply rooted in my being. Then I witnessed "with all my senses" that their behavior, forced by the powers of the consumer society, was being re-created and the conscience of the Italian people was being deformed, up to an irreversible degradation.
>
> In any case, speaking for myself (if that is of any interest for the reader), let me simply state: however multinational it may be, I would give up the whole Montedison industry for one single firefly.[2]

The last words of the article sound like a tombstone upon the past which, even when it is very close to us, cannot come back. We can only hope that the poetical fireflies are not completely extinct and that, in the particular case examined, the chivalric tradition can go on and survive, even with unavoidable changes, as a symbol of the Sicilian identity.

Appendix: The Puppets and Their Stories

How to Recognize a Puppet: Twelve of the Most Famous and Popular Characters Revealed

Orlando (Roland)

Born in a grotto like Jesus, Orlando had lived in Sutri near Rome until the age of seven. His French name, Roland, is supposed to derive from a legend: when he was very young, he had fallen from his mother Berta's arms to the ground with a play on words with *rotolare* (rolling), which in Italian also means to fall precipitously.

First Paladin of France, he is always faithful to the Emperor Charlemagne. He can be recognized from his several insignia: the cross divided into four parts, which occupies all the space on his shield and on his armor, the eagle on his helmet, and the green color of the feathers on his helmet. He is especially distinctive because he is cross-eyed, a detail that is present only in Sicily. It seems that Sicilians wanted to humanize a character who was otherwise too perfect. Orlando's straightforwardness is such that he postpones consummating his marriage until he conquers all of Spain. He is not very lucky with women and, at least in the Sicilians' eyes, not very smart. Not only his armor is magically protected, but also his famous sword Durlindana (Durendal in English), which he had taken from the Saracen king Almonte. Like Achilles, he is invincible, and his weak spot is behind his heel.

In Roncevaux he is a prisoner of his *hybris,* the exasperated pride that encourages him to wait too long before calling for Charlemagne's help with his horn Olifant, whose name is an old alternate spelling of the word elephant: it was the name applied in the Middle Ages to ivory hunting horns made from elephants' tusks. When he finally blows it, it is too late, and he dies because the veins of his breast burst. When the angel comes to ask him if he wants to live or to die, he chooses to die in order not to survive the slaughter of the Paladins of France. The public compared these scenes to the death of Jesus Christ, but they went to see en masse this episode, always with great emotion, accepting to pay double price in order not to miss it.

Rinaldo di Montalbano (Renaut de Montauban)

Second Paladin of France, cousin of Orlando, both of them belonged to the family of Chiaramonte (Clairmont). Because of his wedding with Clarice he had acquired the property of the Montalbano fief from the Emperor Charlemagne. He can be recognized by his insignia, a band with a lion worn across his breast, and by the red color of the feathers on his helmet and of the short skirt, called *foroncina.* He is a great womanizer, very brave, always ready to joke, and gifted with great slyness, which is considered a highly positive characteristic by Italians in general (and even more so by Sicilians) and which he often uses during fighting with enemies, for example against Dama Rovenza.

Both Orlando and Rinaldo fall in love with the beautiful Angelica: because of her they fight against each other in a famous duel during which they shout a series of colorful insults at each other. At a certain point he had retired as a hermit in a cave, but after the angel informs him about what is happening at Roncevaux, he takes up his weapons again but he arrives too late. He is a rebel but always for a just cause: that is why he always enjoyed great success with the Sicilian public, who loved him dearly and could not stand seeing him die. The night Rinaldo was going to lose his life falling from the scaffolding that some envious workers, during the building of a cathedral, had artfully damaged, few people would go and watch the show.

Angelica

Princess from Catai, which does not mean China in this context, but a faraway non–Christian land, she arrives at the court of Charlemagne with the pretext of finding a spouse, but in reality, with the aid of the magical spear of her brother Argalia, she intends to imprison, or even better to kill, all the Paladins. She is dressed in Oriental garb, with trousers that cover up her knees and a vest that is short in front and long in the back. She is very beautiful and sly, and she also detains magic powers because she had stolen the books that belonged to the sorcerer Malagigi. Orlando loses his wits when she falls in love with the humble Medoro, who was a simple soldier in the army of King Dardanello. Even the Saracen warrior Ferraù falls in love with her and kills all her suitors, Medoro included, but she kills herself in order not to marry him.

Gano di Magonza (Ganelon de Mayance)

He can be recognized by the black color of the feathers on his helmet, by his low stature and from the initial M on his shield and on his armor. He is Charlemagne's brother-in-law, since he married his sister Berta, who was Milone's widow. He is a dreadful traitor since he instructed the Saracens on how to attack the Christians at Roncevaux; as a consequence he is personally responsible for their defeat and for the death of the best Paladins of France. He is always ready to give bad advice and he is always next to Charlemagne, who is not able to distinguish the good from the bad. He is finally found guilty and he is sentenced to die by being quartered by four horses in the public square, a gruesome scene that attracted a swarming crowd, who were anxious to witness with their own eyes the physical annihilation of the Paladins' worst enemy. Many anecdotes comment about the hatred of the public towards this character—the real quintessence of Evil, almost a Shakespearean villain.

Carlo Magno (Charlemagne)

He can be recognized by his crown and his insignia of the lily of France on his shield and chest. He can be either with or without his sword. His father, King Pipino, had two other illegitimate sons: Lanfroi

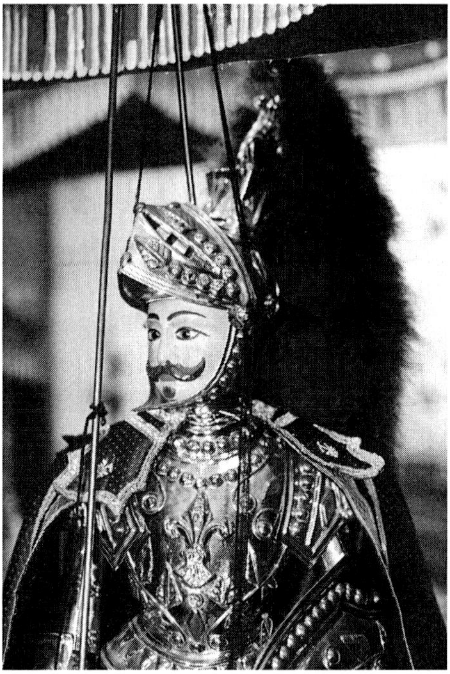

The French Emperor Charlemagne, recognizable by the lily of France on his chest, Palermitan puppet of the Franco Cuticchio theater (photograph by Andrea Matranga).

and Olderigi, who were the result of the traitors of the Mayance family, who had for many years substituted the true queen with Elisetta. After Pipino had been killed by his half brothers, Charlemagne took refuge in Spain and was working incognito as a servant at the table of King Galafio, waiting to return to the throne of France. He is rich and stingy, and he is not loved because he is not able to distinguish the loyal warriors from traitors.

Ferraù

Strong Saracen warrior, Falserone's son and nephew of Galerana, Charlemagne's wife. Like all other Saracens, he wears large knickerbocker trousers oriental style and boots carved in wood, and he has a half moon molded on his shield. He is a mixture of a giant and a normal person, and he can be recognized by his unusually large head. He has a face that is typically "Spanish," with a big moustache and pointed beard. He is the only character who has a face with a mysterious expression on the visor of his helmet. He is very violent and his weak point is his navel, which is protected by seven layers of steel. During the duel with Orlando, they both swear to reveal to each other their own weak points in a chivalric and loyal way, but Orlando's is behind the heel and it is too difficult to hit, while Orlando is able to kill Ferraù after breaking one after the other all the steel layers and his weapons, which the puppeteer had forged in a way suited for the purpose beforehand.

Malagigi and Nacalone

Malagigi is a cousin of Orlando's and of Rinaldo's. He was called Onofrio before being saved and brought up by the wizard Merlino after his nanny had been killed. His twin brother Bernardo on the other hand had become a Paladin with the name of Viviano del Bastone. Malagigi is the good wizard; he is dressed in red, and he always holds in his hand the magic wand that used to belong to the wizard Merlino. He had become the most powerful wizard after having obtained books that had belonged to the Saracen wizard Tuttofuoco ("All fire"), with whom he will engage the famous *Lotta infernale tra Malagigi and Tuttofuoco* (Infernal duel between Malagigi and Tuttofuoco), one of the most spectacular and famous episodes of the Sicilian puppet shows. Nacalone is one of the several devils at Malagigi's service, and he has his skin a little burnt by the fire of hell. Nacalone's horns are similar to a ram's and make him look somewhat like the God Pan of the ancient Greeks; even his legs, which are going the opposite way with respect to the rest of his body, are those of a goat.

Milone d'Anglante

He had married Berta, Charlemagne's sister, who fell in love and eloped with him. He is Orlando's father and, like him, wears his insignia of the eagle, and the feathers on top of his helmet are green. On his armor and on his shield he has a transversal cross that allows him to be recognized. With a few changes his marionette may become Baldovino (Baldwin), who is Gano di Magonza's son. After having risked being executed naked in the public square of Biserta in Northern Africa, he was finally killed in the mountains of Aspromonte in Calabria by Almonte, who has broken his sword and his weapons, which the puppeteers had prepared beforehand for this purpose. Orlando, who has escaped from the seminary—that is, the knights' training school—arrives in Aspromonte. After having learned about his father's death, he gets hold of Almonte's magical weapons, among which is the famous magical sword Durlindana.

Many puppeteers had their debut on the stage with the episode of the death of Milone's death, which required particular skill.

Bradamante and Dama Rovenza

Both of them, like all female warriors, had special armors with the shape of their breasts molded on them. Bradamante is Christian and she is Rinaldo di Montalbano's sister. She can be recognized by the lion, insignia of her family, by her long blonde hair, which comes out of her helmet, and the pink feathers on top of her helmet. Nobody ever succeeded in defeating her. She loves Ruggero, but she was promised as a spouse to the Prince Leone, son of the Emperor Constantine: after a series of adventures Ruggero and Bradamante will succeed to get married. Many puppeteers simulated a real party on the stage for their wedding and offered the traditional sugar-covered almonds (called *confetti* in Italian) to the audience.

Dama Rovenza is a Saracen warrior, daughter of the Gran Baldassore of the Mountain. He wears a Saracen curved sword, but when she fights against the Paladins he uses a steel hammer. During a duel he hits Rinaldo and she stuns him, but Bradamante arrives to rescue her brother. Her weak spot is behind her knees. Rinaldo, having being informed about this detail and about all the other magic tricks operated by the wizard Tuttofuoco ("all fire"), will finally succeed in killing her. Changing the half moon on her shield with an eagle, her marionette may become Marfisa, Ruggero's sister.

The Stories: Main Plots Put on Stage by the Franco Cuticchio Figlio d'Arte Company

Among the most famous and characteristic stories, four have been chosen. They are not the real *copioni*, which, as has been already mentioned, are the outlines of the shows that the puppeteers used to write by hand on notebooks and pass on from father to son. In any case the *copioni* did not carry the exact words that would have been pronounced and they would have been quite difficult to read because of their particular language. The following four stories, which have been selected among hundreds that exist, have been rewritten by Giacomo Cuticchio. He has tried to keep as much as possible the typical mixture of learned and popular expressions that would characterize them. Grammar and syntax in the Italian version of this book have been intentionally kept rather approximately.

The Siege of Paris

This episode, which is a re-elaboration of the history of the Paladins of France done by Giacomo Cuticchio, presents the most important characters in the war between Christians and Saracens, and the duel between Orlando and Rinaldo for the love of the beautiful Angelica. This episode is the *pezzo forte* of the Teatro Arte Company, which has presented it during highly successful tours of many different countries of the world.

THE ROYAL PALACE IN PARIS

Charlemagne and his Paladins are receiving the ambassador of the Saracen army who, under command from King Miriante, is putting the city of Paris under siege. Charlemagne is sending Ruggero to Rome in order to get help from Pope Leone and hopefully convince him to send an army to defend the city.

SARACEN ENCAMPMENT

King Miriante and his subjects learn from the ambassador about the refusal of Charlemagne to surrender and immediately go to the attack.

PARIS DEFENDING WALLS

Ruggero is fighting against the Saracens and he is obliging Miriante to retreat.

WOOD

Rinaldo is looking for the king but he is assaulted by a terrible snake.

GARDEN

The necromancer Malagigi hears from the devil Nacalone that his two cousins, Orlando and Rinaldo, are going to engage in a duel for the love of the beautiful Angelica. So he flies there with Nacalone in order to convince them to make peace.

SEA VIEW

Orlando and Angelica are at the harbor and they are going to set sail for India. Rinaldo arrives and they start fighting. While Angelica is running away, the sorcerer Malagigi succeeds in setting apart the two Paladins and in convincing them to make peace. They immediately run to Paris in order to save the city from the enemies.

Room in Paris

Charlemagne is worried because Rinaldo has not yet come back to Paris with the army. The two Paladins arrive and Orlando promises to set the Saracen encampment on fire as soon as possible.

Walls of a Castle

Ruggero is on his way to Rome; because night is about to come and a terrible storm is approaching, he asks for hospitality in a castle.

Hall in a Castle

The owner of the castle is Pinamonte, who is a subject of the Saracen King Miriante; he pretends to offer Ruggero hospitality but, because he is his enemy, he decides to poison him treacherously.

Bedroom of the Castle

Ruggero feels strong pain in his stomach during the night. Pinamonte arrives and, after revealing he is a Saracen, he gives Ruggero the fatal blow.

Hall in the Castle

Pinamonte is very happy about having eliminated an enemy and decides to throw a big party in the castle in order to celebrate the event.

Saracen Encampment

Orlando succeeds in entering the Saracen encampment in order to destroy their army. He orders that it be set on fire.

Angelica Goes Back to the Kingdom of Catai

Landscape in the Countryside

Medoro and Angelica, after getting married, are on their way to reach the faraway kingdom of Catai. Ferraù is arriving from Spain and, since he is madly in love with Angelica, he kills Medoro. Angelica asks for help and Sacripante, who is also in love with her, engages in a duel with him. During the duel Angelica runs away, and Ferraù runs after her.

ROYAL CASTLE IN CATAI

The old king Galafro is complaining and narrating how his two children, Angelica and Argalia, had left his kingdom many years before, in order to imprison the Paladins of Charlemagne, but they had not given any news to their father for a long time. All of a sudden Angelica arrives, but she immediately runs away because Ferraù is entering the scene with an arrogant attitude. Galafro is asking for explanations and Ferraù reveals to him his love for his daughter and asks her hand to Galafro.

Galafro is very happy about it and enters Angelica's room.

BEDROOM IN THE ROYAL PALACE

Angelica is worried. Galafro comes in and, hearing from his daughter that Ferraù has killed both Angelica's spouse Medoro and her brother Argalia, orders his knights to arrest him.

ROYAL PALACE IN CATAI

Ferraù is fighting against the knights that wanted to arrest him.

Galafro, seeing his formidable courage and worried that his life might be in danger, forgives Ferraù and grants him his daughter's hand.

BEDROOM

Angelica has heard everything. In order not to marry the Spaniard she kills herself. Overcome with terrible grief, Ferraù considers killing himself too, but then he thinks it over and abandons the idea of taking his life for a woman who has always despised him, and he then decides to go back to his lands in Spain.

ROYAL PALACE IN SARAGOZA

The king of Spain, Marsilio, is under siege from Charlemagne because he refused to be his subject and tributary. In Saragoza he receives his nephew Ferraù who, promising to defeat Orlando in a duel, advises his uncle to be ready with the Spanish army in order to surprise the enemy.

King Marsilio accepts and they both go and get ready.

French Encampment

While Charlemagne is holding counsel with his knights, they hear the challenge to fight. Orlando goes to face Ferraù's assault.

Fearing a betrayal, Charlemagne orders Rinaldo to prepare the army and be ready to intervene in the battle.

Walls Around the City of Saragoza

During the duel between Orlando and Ferraù, their blows do not succeed in breaking their weapons. Ferraù and Orlando reveal to each other the weak spots of their magical weapons.

Orlando succeeds in defeating Ferraù and goes back victorious to the French encampment.

The Arrival of Charlemagne in Italy

This is one of the most moving episodes of the entire epic and chivalric repertory. It requires great ability both in the manipulating of the puppets, since the weapons must get cracked piece after piece, and in the particular kind of acting, with great emotional involvement stressed and caused by the intense vibration of the puppeteer's voice.

It recounts the tragic death of Milone, Orlando's father, and how Orlando becomes a knight.

Royal Palace in Paris

Emperor Charlemagne and his Paladins are to arrive in Italy because a Saracen army is marching in order to conquer the Christian territory. He receives his nephew Orlando, who would like to become a knight and join the war. Charlemagne does not accept because he is still very young and orders his brother-in-law Milone to get the army ready for the war.

Bedroom in Paris

Berta is in grief because her spouse Milone is about to leave France. Milone arrives and reassures her that he will soon come back victorious.

Royal Palace in Rome

Pope Leone has learned that the Saracen army has conquered Sicily and Calabria and it is now marching to conquer Rome.

Emperor Charlemagne arrives and he promises the Pope that he will defeat the enemies. The Pope, before the French army leaves for Calabria, is giving them his Holy Blessing.

Countryside in the Aspromonte Mountains in Calabria

King Almonte from Asia hears from a soldier that the French army is arriving and immediately orders the attack.

Countryside

During the battle there is a fierce duel between Almonte and Milone.

The Saracen warrior splits the weapons of Milone one by one, denying him the right to get a new armor.

Before dying Milone bids his farewell to his wife Berta, trusting that his son Orlando will be able to avenge him one day. Almonte gives him the final blow.

Don Chiaro arrives, hits Almonte with a stick and carries away the body of Milone to the Christian encampment.

Christian Encampment

The Duke Namo from Bavaria is scolding Orlando who has run away from Paris and has arrived in Aspromonte, since he would like to fight next to his father Milone. Namo is very upset, does not have the courage to tell him what has happened, and sends him to look for his uncle Charlemagne in order to have news of his father.

Orlando has a sudden intuition of the tragedy and runs in order to look for Charlemagne.

Walls of a Castle

Orlando is looking for his father Milone and for his uncle Charlemagne. Here he is attacked by a wicked fairy who wants to force him to enter the castle. After a furious struggle Orlando succeeds in defeating her.

The castle vanishes and Orlando finds himself at a fork between two roads.

He is very confused and does not know which one to take.

At this point the angel appears and, while indicating to him the road on the right, he informs Orlando that his uncle Charlemagne is in danger. Orlando immediately runs to help him.

COUNTRYSIDE

Almonte has escaped from the battlefield because of the beatings he has received and he does not want to fight anymore. He is lying on the grass resting after having thrown his sword Durlindana away, vowing never to fight again against the Christians.

Charlemagne arrives, sees Almonte and tries to kill him. But this would be a cowardly action, and he decides to wake him up and challenge him for a duel.

During the fighting Charlemagne is about to be defeated. At this point Orlando arrives and he refuses to help his uncle.

But as soon as Charlemagne reveals to him that the Saracen has killed his father Milone, Orlando is so furious that he kills Almonte. Charlemagne thanks him for having saved his life and for having avenged his father at the same time.

Charlemagne nominates him General Captain of his army and Orlando puts on the weapons of Almonte.

The True Story of St. Geneviève from Brabante

This type of show was called *serata* (evening show) because it started and finished in one evening only. Especially in the Palermo area, it was part of the repertory of puppeteers that was active in Sicily in the 19th century. As a proof of this, there exist two posters that feature this story and, exactly in that period of time, they were painted by the famous poster painter Nicolò Rinaldi. One of them belongs to the Teatro Arte Cuticchio Company and it has been exhibited for a long time in the theaters the company has used for its shows.

When a puppeteer would put on stage this captivating episode, it marked a quite different event. Entrance to families was allowed; as already mentioned, typically only men would be present at puppet shows.

ROYAL PALACE IN GERMANY

Count Sigfrid is holding a meeting with his subjects and announces the good news that his wife Geneviève will soon give him an heir to the throne. He hears from a soldier that the Saracen army is about to put the city under siege, and he decides to face the enemy in the countryside, leaving to the faithful Golo the task of governing the city and taking care of his spouse.

Countryside in Germany

The Saracen King Branzardo and his subjects want to conquer Germany, but all of a sudden they hear the Christian army is approaching and they decide to attack it.

Bedroom

Countess Geneviève is worried because her husband has left the city to go fighting in the war. Golo enters her bedroom without asking for permission and he informs her that he will rule the city while the Count is away and will take care of her in his absence, revealing openly his love for her.

Geneviève, quite upset, hits and slaps him quite hard and threatens to tell her husband, Count Sigfrid, all about it.

Plane in the Countryside

The two armies have started to fight. Sigfrid is betrayed and badly wounded from his back. His general captain Tebaldo arrives and saves him.

Royal Palace in Germany

Golo knows that as soon as Count Sigfrid learns from Geneviève what has happened, he will put him to death. So he sets up a plot, organizing a meeting between the main cook of the castle and Geneviève.

Bedroom

Genevieve is worried. The chef enters the room asking why she summoned him into her bedroom. All of a sudden Golo arrives and accuses both of them to be lovers and kills the man. He orders to put Geneviève into a dark prison and writes a letter to Count Sigfrid to tell him all that happened.

Christian Encampment

Count Sigfrid is in bed badly wounded and he learns what has happened from the letter. He is furious and desperate and orders Tebaldo to write the death sentence for his wife in order to follow the custom of his lands, that is, the wife who is has betrayed her husband must be punished with death.

Prison

Geneviève has delivered her baby thanks to the wife of the prison keeper who has helped her. With her help she has also put a letter in Sigfrid's room that contains all the truth and where everything is explained. Golo enters the room informing her that her husband had signed her death sentence. Golo also tells her that if she had accepted his courtship, he would have turned the situation upside down. He also adds that in that case she and her baby would be safe.

Geneviève refuses in disdain. Golo then orders the executioner to take her and the baby to the wood. As a proof of her death, he is supposed to bring back her undergarment smeared with blood.

Wood

The executioner feels pity for Geneviève and does not have the courage to kill her. But he makes her promise she will never return to the city and suggests that she take refuge in a cave nearby. He needs proofs of her death though. At this point, through divine intervention, a dog appears and he orders Geneviève to hand him her undergarment which he will smear with the dog's blood.

Royal Palace in Germany

Golo is happy that the executioner has brought him the proof of Geneviève's death. He hears Count Sigfrid arriving. As soon as the Count learns about his wife's death, he does not want to celebrate the victory with his subjects and retires into his bedroom.

There he finds his wife's letter and as soon as he reads what has really happened, he orders the arrest of Golo.

Sigfrid, desperate for having condemned his wife, tries to kill himself. Tebaldo arrives and saves him.

Wood and Cave

Eight years have gone by following these events and Sigfrid every once in a while goes to the woods for hunting. All of a sudden he sees a deer entering a cave. As Sigfrid is about to enter it, a woman in rags stops him. Sigfrid wants to make her acquaintance and he throws his mantel to her in order to give her something to cover herself.

The woman reveals her identity, but Sigfrid does not believe her saying she could only be Geneviève's soul coming to torment him.

When the woman tells him that because of the executioner's pity she got her life saved, they hug each other and together with their son they go back to the city.

ROYAL PALACE IN GERMANY

Sigfrid is happy to have found his wife and son again. Since Golo is still alive in the castle's prison, he asks the Count's wife what she thinks he should do with him.

Geneviève forgives him for all the suffering in the years she lived in the grotto, but she faints, falls to the ground and dies.

The angel takes her soul away declaring that the extraordinary gesture of forgiving the person who ruined her life will bestow her glory in heaven and on this earth, making her a saint. Count Sigfrid decides to retire in a monastery.

Chapter Notes

Preface

1. Giuseppe Pitrè, *Biblioteca delle tradizioni popolari Siciliane* (Library of Sicilian folk traditions) (Palermo: Pedone Lauriel, 1871–1910). It originally appeared in 25 separate volumes. It has been completely and partially reprinted various times, one of the most recent in 1978 by Il Vespro publ. Palermo.

2. Giuseppe Pitrè, *Le tradizioni cavalleresche popolari in Sicilia* (Popular chivalric folk traditions in Sicily) (Romania, 1884), vol. 13, 315–98; later in *Usi e costumi, Cre denze e pregiudizi del popolo siciliano* (Uses and customs, beliefs and prejudices of the Sicilian people), vol. 1 (Bologna: Forni, 1969), 121–336. All quotations will refer to the Romania edition.

3. "Italy without Sicily, does not leave any image in the soul. In Sicily can be found the key to everything." Johann Wolfgang von Goethe, *Italienische reise* (Travels in Italy), 1816.

4. Giusto Lodico, *Storia dei Paladini di Francia cominciando da Milone conte d'Anglante sino alla morte di Rinaldo* (History of the Paladins of France starting from Milone, count of Anglante, until Rinaldo's death) (Palermo: Gaudiano, 1856–60). Reprinted by Felice Cammarata, editor, in 13 volumes (Trapani: Celebes, 1972).

5. Luigi Pulci, *Il Morgante maggiore* (The greater Morgante) (Milano: Sonzogno, 1876).

6. Marcella Croce, *Pupi carretti contastorie: L'epica cavalleresca nelle tradizioni popolari siciliane* (Puppet, carts, storytellers: Chivalric epic poems in Sicilian folk traditions) (Palermo: Dario Flaccovio, 1999).

7. Marcella Croce, *Pupari: Storia di Girolamo Cuticchio, dei pupi e di una tradizione Palermo* (Puppeteers: Story of Girolamo Cuticchio, of the Sicilian puppets and of a Palermo tradition) (Palermo: Dario Flaccovio, 2003).

Chapter One

1. Giuseppe Pitrè, *Le tradizioni*, 392.

2. Giuseppe Cocchiara, "I pupi" (The Sicilian puppets), *Sicilia* 25 (1960): 14.

3. Paolo Toschi, *Stampe popolari italiane dal XV al XX secolo* (Italian popular prints from the 15th to the 20th century) (Milano: Electa, 1964).
4. Luigi Natoli, "Le tradizioni cavalleresche in Sicilia" (Chivalric traditions in Sicily), *Folklore italiano* 2 (1927): 100.
5. Ettore Li Gotti, *Sopravvivenze delle legend carolingie in Sicilia* (Carolingian survivals in Sicily) (Firenze: Sansoni Antiquariato, 1956), 16.
6. Li Gotti, 10.
7. Li Gotti, 11.
8. Natoli, 101.
9. Antonino Uccello, *Risorgimento e società nei canti popolari siciliani* (Risorgimento and society in Sicilian folk songs) (Firenze: Parenti, 1961).
10. Virgilio Titone, *Storia, Mafia e Costume in Sicilia* (History, Mafia and customs in Sicily) (Milano: Il Milione, 1964), 193.
11. Natoli, 102.
12. Robert Folz, *Le souvenir et la légende de Charlemagne dans l'Empire germanique médiévale* (The memory and legend of Charlemagne in the German Medieval Empire) (Paris: Les belles lettres, 1950), 262.
13. Denis Mack Smith, *Storia della Sicilia Medievale e Moderna* (History of medieval and modern Sicily) (Bari: Laterza, 1970), 48.
14. Pitrè, *Le tradizioni,* 391–392.
15. Cecilia Wærn, *Mediaeval Sicily: Aspects of Life and Art in the Middle Ages* (London: Duckworth, 1910), 260.
16. Pitrè, *Le tradizioni,* 392.
17. Arturo Graf, *Artù in Sicilia: Miti e leggende* (King Arthur in Sicily: Myths and legends) (Roma: Atanor, 1980), 11–17.
18. Graf, 23.
19. Natoli, 109.
20. Natoli, 111.
21. Pio Rajna, "Intorno a due antiche coperte con figurazioni tratte dalla storia di Tristano e Isotta" (About two old bed covers with images taken from the stories of Tristan and Iseult), *Romania* 13 (1913): 517–579.
22. Ettore Gabrici and Ezio Levi, *Lo Steri di Palermo e le sue pitture, Atti della Reale Accademia di Scienze, Lettere ed Arti di Palermo,* suppl. al n. 1 (The Steri Palace in Palermo and its painting, Proceedings of the Royal Academy of Science, Humanities and Arts of Palermo) (Milano-Roma: Bestetti e Tumminelli, 1932), 97.
23. Natoli, 106.
24. Carmelina Naselli, *Figure e scene dell "Orlando Furioso" in un'antica pergamena catanese* (Images and scenes of the "Orlando Furioso" on an ancient parchment document from Catania), *La Rinascita* 4 (1941): 206–228.
25. Naselli, 228.
26. Pitrè, *Le tradizioni,* 395.
27. Cocchiara, 13.
28. Cocchiara, 14.

Chapter Two

1. Pio Rajna, "I Rinaldi o i cantastorie di Napoli" (The Rinaldi, or the storytellers from Naples), *Nuova Antologia,* December 1878, 55.
2. Paolo Toschi, *Fenomenologia del canto popolare* (Characteristics of popular songs) (Roma: Edizioni dell'Ateneo, 1947–49), 101.

3. Toschi, *Fenomenologia*, 116.

4. Arnold Hauser, *Storia sociale dell'Arte* (Social history of art) (Torino: Einaudi, 1955), Vol. 1, 186.

5. Antonino Buttitta, *Cantastorie di Sicilia: Premessa e Testi* (Storytellers of Sicily: Preface and texts), *Annali del museo Pitrè* 8–10 (1957–59): 149.

6. For an accurate description of storytellers and their techniques: Toschi, *Fenomenologia*, 53.

7. Buttitta, *Cantastorie*, 158.

8. Pitrè, *Le tradizioni*, 361.

9. Uccello, *Risorgimento*, 10.

10. Wærn, 329.

11. Ettore Li Gotti, *Il teatro dei pupi* (The puppet theater) (Firenze: Sansoni, 1959), 47.

12. Li Gotti, *Il teatro dei pupi*, 46.

13. Buttitta, *Cantastorie*, 150.

14. Buttitta, *Cantastorie*, 151.

15. Buttitta, *Cantastorie*, 163.

16. Elsa Guggino, "I cantastorie ciechi a Palermo," *I canti degli orbi vol. 1, Archivio delle tradizioni popolari siciliane* (Blind storytellers in Palermo, The songs of the blind storytellers, Archive of Sicilian folk traditions), 7.

17. Leonardo Vigo, *Raccolta amplissima di canti popolari siciliani* (Very ample selection of Sicilian popular songs) (Catania: Galatola, 1865).

18. Pitrè, "I cantastorie," in *Le tradizioni*, 349.

19. Pitrè, "I cantastorie," in *Le tradizioni*, 346–364.

20. Rosalia Perret, "U cuntu," *Annali del Museo Pitre* (Sicilian chivalric story telling, itrè Museum magazine) 5–7 (1956): 107.

21. Carlo Levi, *Le parole sono pietre: Impressioni di Sicilia* (Torino: Einaudi, 1955), 128. English translation: *Words are Stones: Impressions of Sicily* (New York: Farrar, Straus & Cudahay, 1958).

22. Rajna, "I Rinaldi," 573.

23. Rajna, "I Rinaldi," 569.

24. Rajna, "I Rinaldi," 566; Benedetto Croce, "I 'Rinaldi' o i cantastorie di Napoli" (The Rinaldi or the storytellers from Naples), *La Critica* 34, no. 1 (1936): 71.

25. Benedetto Croce, 70.

26. Armando Balduino (a cura di), ed., *Cantari del Trecento* (Cantari from the 14th century) (Milano: Marzorati, 1970), 13.

27. Lodico.

28. Pitrè, *Le tradizioni*, 359.

29. Pitrè, *Le tradizioni*, 381–82.

30. Felice Cammarata, *Pupi e carretti: Nell'arte popolare siciliana* (Puppets and carts in Sicilian folk art) (Palermo: i.l.a. Palma, 1969), 62.

31. Pitrè, *Le tradizioni*, 381.

32. Antonio Pasqualino, "Le orme di Orlando in Sicilia," *Sulle orme di Orlando—Leggende e luoghi carolingi in Italia* (On the footsteps of Roland in Sicily in Carolingian legends and places in Italy), ed. Anna Imelde Galletti and Roberto Roda, Ferrara Ethnographical Center, 294 (Padova: Interbooks, 1987).

33. Li Gotti, *Sopravvivenze*, 11–12.

34. Pitrè, *Le tradizioni*, 380.

35. Luigi Natoli, 105.

Chapter Three

1. Paolo Toschi, *Le origini del teatro italiano* (The origins of the Italian theatre) (Torino: Einaudi, 1955).
2. Toschi, *Le origini*, 438 and following.
3. Antonio Pasqualino, "La storia trasfigurata," in *Il Mastro di Campo a Mezzojuso* (History transfigured in The master in the field in Mezzojuso), Antonino Buttitta and Antonio Pasqualino, 48 (Palermo: Associazione per la conservazione delle tradizioni popolari, 1984).
4. Toschi, *Le origini*, 440.
5. Ignazio Gattuso, "Il Mastro di Campo," in *Il Mastro di Campo a Mezzojuso* (The master in the field in Mezzojuso), Antonino Buttitta and Antonio Pasqualino, 34 (Palermo: Associazione per la conservazione delle tradizioni popolari, 1984).
6. Pasqualino, "La storia trasfigurata," 47.
7. Serafino Amabile Guastella, *L'antico Carnevale nella contea di Modica* (Old Carnival in the Modica county) (Ragusa: Piccitto & Antoci, 1887).
8. Giovanni Matranga, *Lettera dal Giappone in Sapori, Incontri, Fragranze a cura di Richter Melita e Dugulin Lorenzo* (Letter from Japan in flavors, encounters, perfumes), ed. Melita Richter and Lorenzo Dugulin, (Trieste: Coordinamento delle Associazioni e delle Comunità degli Immigrati della Provincia di Trieste, 2006), 131.
9. Giancarlo Santi, *La Strada dei Santi, viaggio sentimentale per le feste religiose di Sicilia* (The road of Saints, sentimental journey across the religious celebrations of Sicily) (Sasso Marconi [Bologna]: Bolelli, 2001).

Chapter Four

1. Antonio Pasqualino, *L'opera dei pupi* (Palermo: Sellerio, 1977).
2. Albert B. Lord, *The Singer of Tales* (Cambridge: Harvard University Press, 1960).
3. Pitrè, *Le tradizioni*, 329–30.
4. Antonio Buttitta, *L'opera dei pupi* (Palermo: Sellerio Editore, 1978), 34.
5. Pitrè, *Le tradizioni*, 330.
6. Lodico. All subsequent quotations from this book refer to a more recent edition edited by Felice Cammarata (Trapani: Celebes, 1972), vol. 12.
7. Buttitta, *L'opera dei pupi*, 34.
8. Antonio Pasqualino, *Le vie del cavaliere* (The knight's roads) (Milano: Bompiani, 1992).
9. Pasqualino, *Le vie del cavaliere*, 141.
10. Pasqualino, *L'opera dei pupi*, 109.
11. Helen Brown and Jane Seitz, "With the Bread and Puppet Theater: Interview with Peter Schumann, "*Drama Review* 12, no. 2 (Winter 1968): 62–73.
12. René Bazin, *Sicile: Croquis Italien* (Paris: Calmann-Lévy, 1892).
13. Titone, 150.
14. Giuseppe Alongi, *La Maffia nei suoi fattori e nelle sue manifestazioni* (The Mafia in its aspects and manifestations) (Torino: Fratelli Brocca, 1886), 58.
15. Leopoldo Franchetti, *Condizioni politiche e amministrative della Sicilia* (Political and administrative conditions in Sicily), vol. 1, *La Sicilia*, Franchetti Leopoldo and Sidney Sonnino (Firenze: Vallecchi, 1876), 7.
16. Marino Salvatore-Salomone, *Costumi e usanze dei contadini di Sicilia* (Customs and traditions of peasants in Sicily) (Palermo: Sandron, 1897).

17. Salvatore F. Romano, *Storia della Mafia* (History of Mafia) (Milano: Mondadori, 1966), 101.
18. Romano, 135.
19. Romano, 45.
20. Romano, 48.
21. Li Gotti, *Il teatro dei pupi*, 31.
22. Romano, 65.
23. Francesco De Maria, "L'epopea francese nella tradizione popolare siciliana" (The French epic in Sicilian folk traditions), *La Giara* 3, no. 2 (1954): 39–44.
24. Giuseppe Alongi, "Spettacoli e coltellate in Sicilia," *Archivio di psichiatria* (Shows and knives in Sicily, Archives of psychiatry) 8 (1887): 246–252.
25. Pitrè, *Le tradizioni*, 395.
26. Giovanni Verga, *Tutte le novelle* (Complete collection of short stories), 6th ed., vol. 2 (Milano: Biblioteca Moderna Mondadori, 1964), 246–252.

Chapter Six

1. Paolo Toschi, *Arte popolare italiana* (Italian folk art) (Roma: Bestetti, 1960), 14.
2. Toschi, *Arte popolare*, 14.
3. Antonio Buttitta, *La pittura su vetro in Sicilia* (Glass painting in Sicily) (Palermo: Sellerio, 1972), 18.
4. Buttitta, *La pittura su vetro*, 16.
5. Toschi, *Arte popolare*, 14.
6. Hauser, 24–25.
7. Ettore Li Gotti, "Nicola Faraone, chi era costui?" (Nicola Faraone, who was he?), *Annali del Museo Pitrè* 5–7 (1956): 102–106.
8. Buttitta, *La pittura su vetro*, 17–18.
9. Antonino Buttitta, *Il carretto racconta* (The cart is telling) (Palermo: Giada, 1982), 14.
10. Janne Vibaek, "Le scene e le figure," in *I colori del sole* (The scenes and the colors, The colors of the sun) (Palermo: Flaccovio, 1984), 229.
11. Buttitta, *La pittura su vetro*, 22.
12. Buttitta, *La pittura su vetro*, 22.
13. Buttitta, *La pittura su vetro*, 25.
14. Janne Vibaek, "I cartelli dell'opra" (The playbills of the Sicilian puppet theater), *Quaderni di teatro* 4 (August 1981): 69.
15. Antonino Buttitta, *Cultura figurativa popolare in Sicilia* (Folk Art in Sicily) (Palermo: Flaccovio, 1971), 235.
16. Vibaek, "Le scene e le figure," 238.
17. Charlotte Christensen, *Catalogo della mostra dei cartelli dell'opra* (Catalogue of the exhibitions of playbills for the puppet theater) (Palermo: 5–17 Giugno, 1972), 5.
18. Aurelio Rigoli, *Eroi di Sicilia* (Heroes from Sicily) (Palermo: Gi due, 1983).
19. Antonio Pasqualino. "Una mostra di cartelli dell'opra dei pupi" (An exhibition of playbills for the puppet theater), *Uomo e Cultura* 2, no. 3–4 (1969): 281–82.
20. Antonio Pasqualino, "Gli eroi e le maschere," *I colori del sole* (Heroes and masks, The colors of the sun) (Palermo: Flaccovio, 1985), 222.

Chapter Seven

1. Stuart Piggott, *Wagon, Chariot and Carriage: Symbol and Status in the History of Transport* (New York: Thames and Hudson, 1992), 17, 18, 23.

2. Antonino Cusumano, "I carri nell'età antica" (Wagons in ancient ages), in *Il legno, il ferro, il colore* (Wood, iron, color), ed. Maria Carcasio, 45–46 (Palermo: Università degli studi di Palermo, 1991).

3. Carmelo Trasselli, "Les routes siciliennes" (Sicilian roads), *Revue Historique* (1974): 27.

4. Alexis de Tocqueville. *Oeuvres* (Works), Vol. I (1991): 10.

5. Frances Elliot, *The Diary of an Idle Woman in Sicily* (Leipzig: Bernhard Lauchnitz, 1882): 42.

6. Henry Tuckerman, *Isabel, or, Sicily: A Pilgrimage* (Philadelphia: Lee and Blanchard, 1839), 189.

7. Gonzalve Baron de Nervo, *Un Tour en Sicile: 1833* (Paris: Chez les marchands de nouveautés, 1835), 143–44.

8. Luigi Maria Majorca Mortillaro. *Lettighe e Portantine: Richerche Storico-Artistiche* (Litters and sedan chairs: Historical and artistic research) (Palermo: Alberto Reber, Editore, 1897), 16.

9. Majorca Mortillaro, 19, 21.

10. A translation by D. H. Lawrence of Giovanni Verga's "So Much for the King" (1883) is included in Verga's *Short Sicilian Novels* (London: Dedalus, 1984).

11. Giuseppe Pitrè, *Biblioteca delle tradizioni popolari Siciliane* (Palermo: Pedone Lauriel, 1871–1910), 351.

12. Gabriella D'Agostino, ed., *Arte Popolare in Sicilia: Le Tecniche, i Temi, i Simboli* (Folk art in Sicily: Techniques, themes, symbols; exhibition catalogue Palermo and Siracusa) (Palermo: Flaccovio, 1991), 310. The *ex voto* belongs to the Museo Pitrè (#3299).

13. Giuseppe Tomasi di Lampedusa, *The Leopard* (New York: Pantheon Books, 1961), 220.

14. Giuseppe Cesare Abba, *The Diary of One of Garibaldi's Thousand,* translated by E. R. Vincent (London: Oxford University Press, 1962), 27.

15. Antonino Buttitta, *Folk Art in Sicily* (Palermo: Flaccofio, 1961), 185.

16. Louis Golding, *Sicilian Noon* (New York: Alfred A. Knopf, 1926), 146.

17. William Agnew Paton, *Picturesque Sicily* (New York: Harper & Brothers, 1898), 17.

18. Giuseppe Capitò, *Il Carretto Siciliano* (Milano: Piantanida Valcaregni, 1923), 3. The book was reprinted with an introduction by Antonino Buttitta, published by Sellerio in 1978.

19. Capitò, 5.

20. Salvatore Lo Presti, *Il Carretto: Monografia sul Carretto Siciliano* (The cart: Monography on the Sicilian cart) (Palermo: Flaccovio, 1959).

21. Gaston Vuillier, *La Sicile: Impressions du Présent et du Passé* (Paris: Librairie Hachette, 1896), 39–41.

22. Wærn, 314.

23. Wærn, 315.

24. Capitò, 28.

25. Dorothy Leadbeater, "The Sicilian Cart: Origins of a Western European Folk Art," in *The Artist in the Tribal Society, Symposium Proceedings,* ed. Mariam W. Smith (London: Routledge Kegan Paul, 1961), 41–42.

26. Leadbeater, 39.
27. Giovanni Verga, *I Malavoglia* (Milano: Treves, 1881, first English edition, 1890); *The House by the Medlar Tree* (New York: Grove, 1953), 49.
28. Wærn, 287.
29. Lo Presti, 78.
30. Giuseppe Capitò, *The Sicilian Cart* (English edition, Palermo: [s.n.], 1943), 21.
31. Maria Carcasio, ed. *Il legno, il ferro, il colore*: Fig. 1, 5.
32. Buttitta, *Folk Art in Sicily,* 170, 171.
33. Levi, *Words Are Stones: Impressions of Sicily,* 64.
34. Guy de Maupassant, *La Sicile* (Paris: Séquences, 1998), 35.
35. Bazin, 169–170.
36. Antonio Daneu, "Pittura e sculture del carretto siciliano," *Le vie d'Italia* 57 (March 1951): 528.
37. Pitrè's annotated bibliography of books, magazines and newspaper articles written by foreigners about Sicilian folklore and folk life has been published in five volumes. See Giuseppe Pitrè, (Italian and foreign travellers in Sicily), ed. Aurelio Rigoli (Palermo: ILA Palma, 2000).
38. Daneu, 529.
39. Buttitta, *Folk Art,* 199.
40. Mrs. Alec-Tweedie, *Sunny Sicily: Its Rustics and Its Ruins* (New York: Macmillan, 1904), 122.
41. "From Palermo to Syracuse," *Scribner's Monthly Illustrated Magazine* XX, no. 3 (July 1880): 406.
42. Capitò, *Il Carretto Siciliano,* 107.
43. Pitrè, *Biblioteca delle Tradizioni Popolari Siciliani,* 416.
44. Paton, 178.
45. Examples of the original prints and *viline* were exhibited in 1991. See Carcasio, 96.
46. Daneu, 331–32.
47. Buttitta, 34.
48. Pitrè, *Biblioteca delle Tradizioni Popolari Siciliani,* 416.
49. Antonino Buttitta, *Il carretto racconta* (Palermo: Giada, 1982), 16.
50. Guiseppe Pitrè, *Studi di poesia popolare* (Studies in folk poetry), 42, quoted in Buttitta, *Sicilian Folk Art,* 189.
51. Emily Jackson, *A Student in Sicily* (London: John Lane the Bodley Head, Ltd., 1926), 8.
52. Jackson, 154.
53. Pitrè, *Biblioteca delle Tradizioni Popolari Siciliane,* 338; Capitò, 12.
54. Henri Bresc. *Un monde Méditerranéen: Economie et société en Sicile, 1300–1450.* Vol. II (Rome: Ecole française de Rome, 1986), 755.
55. Buttitta, *Folk Art in Sicily*, 17.
56. Pitrè, *Biblioteca*, 344.
57. Capitò, *Il carretto*, 5.
58. Elio Vittorini, "Questione Meridionale, Il Canto delle Ruote" (Southern Italy's problems, the singing of the wheels), *Diario in Pubblico* (Milano: Bompiani, 1976), 221–222. The column originally appeared in *Il Politecnico* in 1945 and was translated by Mary Taylor Simeti.
59. Gavin Maxwell, *The Ten Pains of Death* (London: Longmans, 1959), 87–88.
60. Jackson, 36.
61. Vuillier, 296–298.

62. Capitò, *Il carretto,* 5.
63. Alessandra Lavagnino, *I Daneu* (Milano: Rizzoli, 1981), 105.
64. *The Collected Letters of D. H. Lawrence*, ed. Harry T. Moore, Vol. II (New York: Viking, 1962): 695.
65. Howard La Fay, "Sicily Where All the Songs are Sad," *National Geographic Magazine* (March 1976): 426.
66. Salvatore Pappalardo, "Il Carretto Siciliano e la Lapa," *Lares* XLIII (1978): 364, 366–67.
67. Francesco La Cecla, *La Lapa e l'antropologia del quotidiano* (The Lapa and every day's anthropology), with photographs by Minnella Melo (Milan: Eleuthera, 2005).
68. Capitò, *Il Carretto Siciliano,* 34, 35.
69. The cart was first presented to Leon Dayton, director of the aid program for Italy, in Palermo. It was then sent to the United States where Marshall received it at the Pentagon, where he was then the secretary of defense. See *New York Times*, February 4, 1951: 16, and April 26, 1951: 11.
70. Marcella Croce, *Viaggio nella Sicilia Profonda* (Travels into Deep Sicily) (Palermo: Kalòs, 2012), 63–66.
71. Salomone-Marino Salvatore, 311.
72. Antonino Uccello, *La Civiltà del legno in Sicilia, Contadini e Pastori Iblei* (Catania e Caltanissetta: Cavallotto, 1973), 211.

Conclusion

1. Pier Paolo Pasolini, *Scritti corsari* (Milano: Garzanti, 1975), 164.
2. Pasolini, 168. The article "of the fireflies" was originally published with the title "The lack of power in Italy" by the newspaper *Corriere della sera* on February 1, 1975.

Bibliography

Abba, Giuseppe Cesare. *Noterelle d'uno dei Mille edite dopo vent'anni.* Bologna: Zanichelli, 1880. *The Diary of One of Garibaldi's Thousand.* Translated by E.R. Vincent. London: Oxford University Press, 1962.

Alberti, Carmelo. *Il teatro dei pupi e lo spettacolo popolare siciliano.* Milano: Mursia, 1977.

Alec-Tweedie, Mrs. *Sunny Sicily: Its Rustics and Its Ruins.* New York: Macmillan, 1904.

Alongi, Giuseppe. *La Maffia nei suoi fattori e nelle sue manifestazioni* (Mafia in its aspects and manifestations). Torino: Fratelli Brocca, 1886.

_____."Spettacoli e coltellate in Sicilia," *Archivio di psichiatria* (Shows and knives in Sicily, *Archives of psychiatry*) 8 (1887): 246–252.

Baird, Ed. *The Art of the Puppet.* New York: Macmillan, 1965. Italian edition *Le Marionette—Storia di uno spettacolo.* Milano: Mondadori, 1966.

Balduino, Armando, ed. *Cantari del Trecento* (Cantari from the 14th century). Milano: Marzorati, 1970.

Bazin, René. *Sicile, Croquis Italien* (Sicily, Italian sketch). Paris: Calmann-Lévy, 1892.

Boner, E. G. "La festa dell'antenna." *Fanfulla della domenica* 24 (1889).

Bonomo, Giuseppe. "Lettere di Pio Rajna e Giuseppe Pitrè" (Correspondence between Pio Rajna and Giuseppe Pitrè). *Annali del Museo Pitrè* 2–4 (1951–53) 13 and following, then in *Studi Demologici.* Palermo: Flaccovio, 1970.

Bragaglia, Anton Giulio. "I pupi." (The puppets). *Il Dramma* (1954): 195–196.

Bresc, Henri. *Un monde Méditerranéen. Economie et Société en Sicile 1300–1450* (A Mediterranean world, economy and society in Sicily), Vol. II. Rome: Ecole française de Rome, 1986.

Brown, Helen, and Jane Seitz. "With the Bread and Puppet Theater: Interview with Peter Schumann." *Drama Review* 12, no. 2 (Winter 1968).

Buttitta, Antonino. "Cantastorie di Sicilia—Premessa e Testi" (Storytellers of Sicily—Preface and texts). *Annali del museo Pitrè* 8–10 (1957–59): 144–236.

_____. "Caratteri, momenti e motivi della pittura del carro siciliano" (Characteristics, moments and motifs of the Sicilian cart). *Annali del Museo Pitrè* 5–7 (1954–56), 92–101.

_____. *Il carretto racconta* (The cart is telling stories). Palermo: Giada, 1982.

_____. *Cultura figurativa popolare in Sicilia* (English translation *Folk art in Sicily*). Palermo: Flaccovio, 1971.

_____. *La pittura su vetro in Sicilia* (Glass painting in Sicily). Palermo: Sellerio, 1972.

_____. "Rime e canti siciliani del Risorgimento" (Sicilian rhymes and songs from the Risorgimento). In *Ideologie e Folklore* (Palermo: Flaccovio, 1971), 63–134.

_____. "Le ruote del mito" (The wheels of myth). In *I colori del sole* (Palermo: Flaccovio, 1985): 251–270.

_____. "Strutture morfologiche e strutture ideologiche nelle storie dei cantastorie siciliani" (Morphological and ideological structures in the stories of Sicilian storytellers). *Uomo e Cultura* 5, no. 10 (July–December 1972): 159–78.

_____, and Pasqualino Antonio. *Il Mastro di Campo a Mezzojuso* (The master in the field in Mezzojuso). Palermo: Associazione per la conservazione delle tradizioni popolari, 1984.

Cammarata, Felice. *Pupi e carretti: Nell'arte popolare siciliana* (Puppets and carts in Sicilian folk art). Palermo: ILA Palma, 1969.

_____. *Pupi e mafia—L'eroe carolingio nella demopsicologia siciliana* (Puppets and mafia—The Carolingian hero in Sicilian traditions). Palermo: ILA Palma, 1969.

Capitò, Giuseppe. *Il Carretto Siciliano* (The Sicilian cart). Milano: Piantanida Valcaregni, 1923. Reprinted with an introduction by Antonino Buttitta (Palermo: Sellerio, 1978).

Chiesi, Gustavo. "I cantastorie in Sicilia." In *La Sicilia illustrata nella storia, nell'arte e nei paesi* (Storytellers in Sicily, in Illustrated Sicily in history, art and villages). Milano: Sonzogno, 1892.

Christensen, Charlotte. *Catalogo della Mostra dei cartelli dell'opra* (Catalogue of the Exhibition of Puppet Theatre Posters). Palermo: 5–17 Giugno, 1972.

Cocchiara, Giuseppe. "Il cartellone dell'opra dei pupi" (Posters of the Sicilian puppet shows). *Sicilia* 5 (1954): 18–22.

_____. *Il Folklore siciliano* (Sicilian folklore). Palermo: Flaccovio, 1957.

_____. *Le origini della poesia popolare* (The origins of folk poetry). Torino: Boringhieri, 1966.

_____. "I pupi" (The puppets). *Sicilia* 25 (1960): 13–31.

_____. *Le vastasate—Contributo alla storia del teatro popolare* (The farcical sketches—Contributions to the history of folk theatre). Palermo: Sandron, 1926.

_____. *La vita e l'arte del popolo siciliano nel museo Pitrè* (Life and art of the Sicilian people in the Pitrè Museum). Palermo: Ciuni, 1938.

Croce, Benedetto. *Poesia popolare e poesia d'arte* (Folk poetry and art poetry) Bari: Laterza, 1929, 3rd reprinting, 1952.

_____. "I 'Rinaldi' o i cantastorie di Napoli" (The Rinaldi or the storytellers from Naples). *La Critica* 34, no. 1 (1936) 70–74.

Croce, Marcella. *Pupari—Storia di Girolamo Cuticchio, dei pupi e di una tradizione Palermo* (Puppeteers—Story of Girolamo Cuticchio, of the Sicilian puppets and of a tradition). Palermo: Dario Flaccovio, 2003.

_____. *Pupi carretti contastorie—L'epica cavalleresca nelle tradizioni popolari siciliane* (Puppets, carts, storytellers—Chivalric epic poems in Sicilian folk traditions). Palermo: Dario Flaccovio, 1999.

_____. *Viaggio nella Sicilia Profonda* (Travels into deep Sicily). Palermo: Kalòs, 2012.

_____, and Moira F. Harris. *History on the Road: The painted carts of Sicily*. Preface by Mary Taylor Simeti. Minneapolis: Pogo Press, 2006.

Cusumano, Antonino. "I carri nell'età antica" (Wagons in ancient ages). In *Il legno, il ferro, il colore* (Wood, iron, color), edited by Carcasio Maria, 45–46. Palermo: Università degli studi di Palermo, Facoltà di lettere e filosofia, 1991.

D'Agostino, Gabriella, ed. *Arte Popolare in Sicilia—Le Tecniche, i Temi, i Simboli* (Folk art in Sicily—techniques, themes, symbols). Exhibition Catalogue Palermo and Siracusa. Palermo: Flaccovio, 1991.

Daneu, Antonio. "Pitture e sculture nel carretto siciliano" (Paintings and sculptures in the Sicilian cart). *Vie d'Italia* 57 (1951): 328–335.

De Felice, Francesco. *Storia del Teatro Siciliano* (History of the Sicilian theatre). Catania: Giannotti, 1956; 2nd ed., Catania: Elefante, 1979.

De Maria, Francesco. "L'epopea francese nella tradizione popolare siciliana" (The French epic in Sicilian folk traditions). *La Giara* 3, no. 2 (1954): 39–44.

Di Mino, Calogero. *Il teatro siciliano nella tradizione mediterranea* (Sicilian theatre in the Mediterranean tradition). Roma: La Navicella, 1962.

Di Palma, Guido. *La fascinazione della parola—Dalla narrazione orale al teatro—I cuntastorie* (The magic of the word—From oral narration to theatre—The storytellers). Roma: Bulzoni, 1991.

Elliot, Frances. *The Diary of an Idle Woman in Sicily.* Leipzig: Bernhard Lauchnitz, 1882.

Fiocco, A., ed. *Quaderni del Centro teatrale Italiano 2* (Notebooks of the Italian theater center). Roma, 1963.

Folz, Robert. *Le souvenir et la légende de Charlemagne dans l'Empire germanique médiévale* (The memory and legend of Charlemagne in the German medieval empire). Paris: Les belles lettres, 1950.

Franchetti, Leopoldo. *Condizioni politiche e amministrative della Sicilia* (Political and administrative conditions in Sicily). Vol. 1. In *La Sicilia*, edited by Franchetti Leopoldo and Sidney Sonnino. Firenze: Vallecchi, 1876.

Gabrici, Ettore, and Levi Ezio. *Lo Steri di Palermo e le sue pitture, Atti della Reale Accademia di Scienze, Lettere ed Arti di Palermo*, suppl. al n. 1 (The Steri Palace in Palermo and its paintings, Proceedings of the Royal Academy of Science, Humanities and Arts of Palermo). Milano-Roma: Bestetti e Tumminelli, 1932.

Gaspary, Adolfo. *Storia della letteratura italiana* (History of Italian Literature). Milano: Sonzogno, 1887.

Gattuso, Ignazio. "Il Mastro di Campo." In *Il Mastro di Campo a Mezzojuso* (The master in the field in Mezzojuso), Antonino Buttitta and Pasqualino Antonio. Palermo: Associazione per la conservazione delle tradizioni popolari, 1984.

von Goethe, Johann Wolfgang. *Italienische Reise* (Travels in Italy), 1816.

Gold, Donna Lauren. "Plucky Puppets are the Stars in One Family's Saga." *Smithsonian* 14 (August 5, 1983): 68–73.

Golding, Louis. *Sicilian Noon*. New York: Alfred A. Knopf, 1926.

Graf, Arturo. *Artù nell'Etna—Miti e leggende* (King Arthur in Sicily—Myths and legends). Roma: Atanor, 1980.

Guastella, Serafino Amabile. *L'antico carnevale nella contea di Modica* (Old Carnival in the Modica county). Ragusa: Piccitto & Antoci, 1887.

Guggino, Elsa. "I cantastorie ciechi a Palermo." In *I canti degli orbi* (Blind Storytellers in Palermo). Palermo: Archivio delle tradizioni popolari siciliane, 1981.

_____, ed. *I carrettieri* (Cartdrivers). Palermo: Archivio delle Tradizioni Popolari Siciliane, 1978.

Hauser, Arnold. *The Social History of Art.* New York: Vintage, 1955. Italian translation, *Storia sociale dell'arte.* Torino: Einaudi, 1955.

Jackson, Emily. *A Student in Sicily.* London: John Lane the Bodley Head, 1926.

La Cecla, Francesco. *La Lapa e l'antropologia del quotidiano* (The Lapa motorscooter and daily life's anthropology), with photographs by Minnella Melo. Milan: Eleuthera, 2005.

La Fay, Howard. "Sicily Where All the Songs Are Sad." *National Geographic Magazine,* March 1976.

Lavagnino, Alessandra. *I Daneu* (The Daneus). Milano: Rizzoli, 1981.

Leadbeater, Dorothy. "The Sicilian Cart: Origins of a Western European Folk Art." In *The Artist in the Tribal Society*, Symposium Proceedings, edited by Mariam W. Smith, 41–42. London: Routledge Kegan Paul, 1961.

Le Goff, Jacques. *Time, Work, & Culture in the Middle Ages.* Chicago: University of Chicago Press, 1980. Italian edition, *Il basso Medioevo.* Milano: Feltrinelli, 1967.

Levi, Carlo. *Le parole sono pietre.* Torino: Einaudi, 1955. English edition, *Words Are Stones.* New York: Farrar, Straus & Cudahy, 1958.

Li Gotti, Ettore. "Nicola Faraone, chi era costui?" (Nicola Faraone, who was he?). *Annali del Museo Pitrè* 5–7 (1956): 102–106.

_____. *Sopravvivenze carolingie in Sicilia* (Carolingian survivals in Sicily). Firenze: Sansoni Antiquariato, 1956.

_____. *Il teatro dei pupi* (The puppet theatre). Firenze: Sansoni 1959; 2nd ed., Palermo: Flaccovio, 1978.

Linares, Vincenzo. "Il cantastorie." In *Racconti popolari* (Folk tales). Palermo: Pedone Lauriel, 1840.

Lodico, Giusto. *Storia dei Paladini di Francia cominciando da Milone conte d'Anglante sino alla morte di Rinaldo* (History of the Paladins of France starting from Milone, count of Anglante, until Rinaldo's death). Palermo: Gaudiano, 1856–60. Reprinted in 13 vols., Felice Cammarata, ed. Trapani: Celebes, 1972.

Lo Piparo, Franco. "La Sicilia linguistica." In *Storia D'Italia—Le Regioni dall'unità ad oggi—La Sicilia* (Linguistic Sicily in History of Italy—The Regions from the Unification of Italy till today), edited by Aymard Maurice e Giarrizzo Giuseppe, 735–807. Torino: Einaudi 1987.

Lo Presti, Salvatore. *Il Carretto—Monografia sul Carretto Siciliano* (The cart—Monography on the Sicilian cart). Palermo: Flaccovio, 1959.

_____. *I pupi—vagabondaggi siciliani* (The puppets—Sicilian wonderings). Catania: Studio Editoriale Moderno, 1927.

Lord, Albert B. *The Singer of Tales.* Cambridge: Harvard University Press, 1960.

Mack Smith, Denis. *Storia della Sicilia Medievale e Moderna* (History of medieval and modern Sicily). Bari: Laterza, 1970.

Majorca Mortillaro, Luigi Maria. *Lettighe e Portantine. Richerche Storico-Artistiche* (Litters and sedan chairs, historical and artistic research). Palermo: Alberto Reber, 1897.

Matranga, Giovanni. "Lettera dal Giappone" (Letter from Japan in flavors, encounters, perfumes). In *Sapori, Incontri, Fragranze,* edited by Melita Richter and Lorenzo Dugulin. Trieste: Coordinamento delle Associazioni e delle Comunità degli Immigrati della Provincia di Trieste, 2006.

de Maupassant, Guy. *La Sicile.* 1885. Newer edition, Paris: Séquences, 1998.

Maxwell, Gavin. *The Ten Pains of Death.* London: Longman, 1959.

Mazzoleni, Achille. "Gli ultimi echi della leggenda cavalleresca in Sicilia" (The last echoes of the chivalric legend in Sicily). *Acireale: Atti e rendiconti dell'Accademia degli Zelanti* 3 (1891): 44–69.

Meier, John. "L'organizzazione degli studi sul canto popolare tedesco" (Organization of research on German folk songs). *Lares* (10 August–4–6 December 1939): 307–340.

Mondello, Fortunato. "Le pitture popolari nei carretti di Trapani" (Folk painting on the carts from Trapani). *Archivio per lo studio delle tradizioni popolari* 13, no. 4 (1894): 576–581.

Moore, Harry T., ed. *The Collected Letters of D. H. Lawrence*, Vol. II. New York: Viking, 1962.

Naselli, Carmelina. "Figure e scene dell'Orlando furioso in un'antica pergamena catanese" (Images and scenes of the Orlando Furioso on an ancient parchment document from Catania). *La Rinascita* 4 (1941): 206–228.

Natoli, Luigi. "Le tradizioni cavalleresche in Sicilia" (Chivalric traditions in Sicily). *Folklore italiano* 2 (1927): 99–120.

Pappalardo, Salvatore. "Il Carretto Siciliano e la Lapa." (The Sicilian cart and the Lapa motor scooter). *Lares* XLIII (1978): 364, 366–67.

Paris, Gaston. "La Sicile dans la littérature française du Moyen Age" (Sicily in French literature in the Middle Ages). *Romania* 5 (1877): 108–113.

Pasolini, Pier Paolo. *Canzoniere Italiano* (Italian folk songs). Milano: Guanda, 1955.

_____. *Scritti corsari* (Writings). Milano: Garzanti, 1975.

Pasqualino, Antonio. "Bibliografia delle edizioni cavalleresche popolari siciliane dell'Ottocento" (Bibliography of Sicilian chivalric popular editions in the 19th century). *Uomo e cultura* 23–24 (1979): 150–166.

_____. "Codici gestuali del teatro dei pupi." In *Intorno al codice, Atti del III Convegno dell'Associazione Italiana di Studi Semantici* (Gestual codes of the Sicilian puppet theatre in About codes, Proceedings of the meeting of the Italian Association of Semantic Studies), 77–89. Firenze: La Nuova Italia, 1970.

_____. "Come si costruisce un pupo." In *La cultura materiale in Sicilia* (How to build a puppet in Material Culture in Sicily). *Quaderni del Circolo Semiologico Siciliano* 12–13, Palermo, 1980, 533–53.

_____. "Gli eroi e le maschere" (Heroes and masks). In *I colori del sole*, 205–26. Palermo: Flaccovio, 1984.

_____. "Narrative structures of the Reali di Francia." In *Strutture e generi delle letterature etniche, 71–100.* Palermo: Flaccovio, 1978.

_____. *L'opera dei pupi* (The Sicilian puppet shows). Palermo: Sellerio, 1977.

_____. "Le orme di Orlando in Sicilia." In *Sulle orme di Orlando—Leggende e luoghi carolingi in Italia* (On the footsteps of Roland in Sicily—In the footsteps of Roland—Carolingian legends and places in Italy), edited by Anna Imelde Galletti and Roberto Roda. Centro Etnografico Ferrarese. Padova: Interbooks, 1987.

_____. "Per un'analisi morfologica della letteratura cavalleresca: I Reali di Francia" (For a morphological analysis of chivalric literature). *Uomo e cultura* 3, no. 5–6 (1970): 76–194.

_____. *I pupi siciliani* (The Sicilian Puppets). Palermo: Associazione per la conservazione delle Tradizioni popolari, 1975.

_____. "Il repertorio epico nell'opera dei pupi" (The epic repertory of the Sicilian puppet shows) *Uomo e cultura* 2, no. 3–4 (1969): 59–106.

_____. "La storia trasfigurata." In *Il Mastro di Campo a Mezzojuso* (History transfigured in The master in the field in Mezzojuso), Antonino Buttitta and Antonio Pasqualino, 48. Palermo: Associazione per la conservazione delle tradizioni popolari, 1984.

_____. "Tradizione e innovazione nell'opera dei pupi contemporanea" (Tradition and innovation in contemporary Sicilian puppets) *Quaderni di Teatro* 4, no. 13 (August 1981).

_____. "Transformations of chivalrous literature in the subject matter of the Sicilian marionette theatre." In *Varia Folklorica*, edited by Alan Dundes, 183–200. The Hague, Paris: Mouton, 1978.

_____. *Le Vie del Cavaliere* (The knight's roads). Milano: Bompiani, 1992.

_____, and Antonino Buttitta. "Una mostra di cartelli dell'opra dei pupi" (An exhibition of posters for the Sicilian puppet theatre). *Uomo e Cultura* 3–4 (1969): 282–283.

_____, and Janne Vibaek. "Magia rappresentata e magia vissuta: un problema di pertinenza." In *La magia: segno e conflitto* (Magic in performances and in real life in Magic: sign and conflict), 163–181. Palermo: Flaccovio, 1979.

Paton, William Agnew. *Picturesque Sicily.* New York: Harper, 1898.

Perret, Rosalia. "Due copioni dell'opra" (Two notebooks—copioni—for the Sicilian puppet theatre). *Bollettino del Centro Studi filologici e linguistici siciliani* 4 (1956): 405–421.

_____. "U cuntu" (Sicilian chivalric storytelling). *Annali del Museo Pitrè* 5–7 (1956): 107.

Piggott, Stuart. *Wagon, Chariot and Carriage: Symbol and Status in the History of Transport*. New York: Thames and Hudson, 1992.

Pitrè, Giuseppe. *La famiglia, la casa, la vita del popolo siciliano* (Family, house and life of the Sicilian people). Palermo: Reber, 1910. Reprinted in *Biblioteca delle tradizioni popolari siciliane* (Library of Sicilian folk traditions), edited by Aurelio Rigoli. Palermo: Il Vespro, 1978.

_____. *Le tradizioni cavalleresche popolari in Sicilia* (Chivalric folk traditions in Sicily), vol. 13. *Romania* (1884): 315–98; later in *Usi e costumi, Credenze e pregiudizi del popolo siciliano* (Uses and customs, beliefs and prejudices of the Sicilian people), vol. 1, 121–336. Bologna: Forni, 1969.

_____. *La vita in Palermo cento e più anni fa* (Life in Palermo one hundred or more years ago). Palermo: Pedone Lauriel, 1904–5; reprinted, Firenze: Barbera, 1950.

_____. *Viaggiatori italiani e stranieri in Sicilia* (Italian and foreign travellers in Sicily), edited by Rigoli Aurelio. Palermo: ILA Palma, 2000.

Pulci, Luigi. *Il Morgante Maggiore* (The greater Morgante). Milano: Sonzogno, 1876.

Rajna, Pio. "Intorno a due antiche coperte con figurazioni tratte dalla storia di Tristano e Isotta" (About two old bed covers with images taken from the stories of Tristan and Iseult). *Romania* 13 (1913): 517–579.

_____. "I Rinaldi o i cantastorie di Napoli" (The Rinaldi, or the storytellers from Naples). *Nuova Antologia* (December 1878): 557–579.

_____. "La Rotta di Roncisvalle nella letteratura cavalleresca italiana" (The rout of Roncevaux in Italian chivalric literature). *Il Propugnatore* 3, part 2, 1870: 384–409; 4, part 1: 52–94, 333–390; 4, part 2, 53–133.

Rigoli, Aurelio. *Eroi di Sicilia* (Heroes of Sicily). Palermo: Gidue, 1983.

_____, ed. *Figurazione e messaggio: Analisi del carretto siciliano* (Figures and messages: Analysis of the Sicilian cart). Palermo: Il Vespro, 1977.

Romano, Salvatore. *Storia della Mafia* (History of Mafia). Milano: Mondadori, 1966.

Salomone Marino, Salvatore. *Costumi e usanze dei contadini di Sicilia.* Palermo: Sandron, 1897. Edited by Aurelio Rigoli. Palermo: Andò, 1968. Translated by Rosalie N. Norris. *Customs and Habits of the Sicilian Peasants.* Toronto: Associated University Presses, 1981.

Singer, M. "Opera dei pupi." *New Yorker*, September 17, 1979, 154–164.

Tichenov, G. "Marionette Furioso." *Theatre Arts Monthly* (1939): 913–919.

Titone, Virgilio. *Storia, mafia e costume in Sicilia* (History, Mafia and customs in Sicily). Milano: Il Milione, 1964.

Tomasi di Lampedusa, Giuseppe. *Il gattopardo.* Milano: Feltrinelli, 1958. English translation, *The Leopard.* New York: Pantheon, 1961.

Toschi, Paolo. *Arte popolare italiana* (Italian folk art). Roma: Bestetti, 1960.

_____. *Fenomenologia del canto popolare* (Characteristics of popular songs). Roma: Edizioni dell'Ateneo, 1947–49.

_____. *Le origini del teatro italiano* (The origins of the Italian theatre). Torino: Einaudi, 1955.

_____. *Saggi sull'arte popolare* (Essays on folk art). Roma: Ed. Italiane, 1944; 2nd ed. Torino: Boringhieri, 1971.

_____. *Stampe popolari italiane dal XV al XX secolo* (Italian popular prints from the 15th to the 20th century). Milano: Electa, 1964.

Trasselli, Carmelo. "Les routes siciliennes" (Sicilian roads). *Revue historique* 251, no. 1 (1974): 27–44.

Tuckerman, Henry. *Isabel or, Sicily: A Pilgrimage.* Philadelphia: Lee and Blanchard, 1839.

Uccello, Antonino. *Carcere e mafia nei canti popolari siciliani* (Prison and mafia in Sicilian folk songs). Palermo: Libri siciliani, 1965; 2nd ed., Bari: De Donato, 1974.

_____. "I cartelloni dei pupi nella Sicilia orientale" (Posters of the puppet theater in Eastern Sicily). *Sicilia* (1958–59): 89–93.

_____. *La civiltà del legno in Sicilia. Contadini e pastori iblei* (The culture of wood in Sicily—Peasants and shepherds in the Hybleian region). Catania—Caltanissetta: Cavallotto, 1973.

_____. "Motivi d'arte popolare in Sicilia" (Sicilian folk art motifs). In *Libro siciliano.* Palermo: Flaccovio, 1970.

_____. "L'opra dei pupi nel Siracusano—Ricerche e contributi" (Puppet shows in the Syracuse province). *Archivio storico Siracusano* 8 (1962): 119–143.

_____. Pupi e cartelloni dell'opra (Puppets and posters for the puppet theater). Exhibition Catalogue Syracuse May 28–June 2, 1970, Ente Provinciale per il Turismo Siracusa.

_____. *Risorgimento e società nei canti popolari siciliani* (Risorgimento and society in Sicilian folk songs). Firenze: Parenti, 1961.

Verga, Giovanni. *I Malavoglia.* Milano: Treves, 1881. First English edition, *The House by the Medlar Tree* (1890).

_____. "So Much for the King" (1883). Translated by D. H. Lawrence and included in Verga's *Short Sicilian Novels.* London: Dedalus, 1984.

Vibaek, Janne. "I cartelli dell'opra" (The posters of the puppet theatre). *Quaderni di teatro* 4, no. 13 (August 1981): 69.

_____. *Orlando nei cartelli dell'opera dei pupi* (Roland in the posters of the puppet theatre). Exhibition Catalogue, May 5–19, 1977.

_____. "Le scene e le figure." In *I colori del sole* (The scenes and the colors in *The colors of the sun*), 229–248. Palermo: Flaccovio, 1984.

Vigo, Leonardo. *Raccolta amplissima di canti popolari siciliani* (Very ample selection of Sicilian popular songs). Catania: Galatola, 1865.

Vittorini, Elio. "Questione Meridionale, Il Canto delle Ruote" (Southern Italy's problems, the singing of the wheels). In *Diario in Pubblico,* 221–222. Milano: Bompiani, 1976. The column originally appeared in *Il Politecnico* in 1945 and was translated by Mary Taylor Simeti.

Vuillier Gaston. *La Sicile—Impressions du Présent et du Passé* (Sicily—Impressions of the present and of the past). Paris: Librairie Hachette, 1896.

Wærn, Cecilia. *Medieval Sicily: Aspects of Life and Art in the Middle Ages.* London: Duckworth, 1910.

Index

Page numbers in ***bold italics*** indicate pages with illustrations.